The Effective Teaching of Secondary Science

THE EFFECTIVE TEACHER SERIES

General editor: Elizabeth Perrott

For series list see pages v and vi

The Effective Teaching of Secondary Science

John Parkinson

LONGMAN
London and New York

Pearson Education Limited
Edinburgh Gate, Harlow
Essex CM20 2JE, England
and Associated Companies throughout the world.

*Published in the United States of America
by Addison Wesley Longman Inc., New York*

© Longman Group UK Limited 1994

First published 1994
Third impression 1999

ISBN 0 582 215102 PPR

British Library Cataloguing-in-Publication Data

A catalogue record for this book is
available from the British Library

Library of Congress Cataloging-in-Publication Data

Parkinson, John, 1947–
  The effective teaching of secondary science / John Parkinson.
    p. cm. -- (Effective teacher series)
  Includes bibliographical references and index.
  ISBN 0-582-21510-2 (pbk.)
  1. Science--Study and teaching (Secondary) I. Title.
  II. Series.
  Q181.P336   1994
  507'.2--dc20   93-41712
                                         CIP

Set by 7 in Times
Printed in Malaysia, VVP

CONTENTS

EDITOR'S PREFACE

This well-established series was inspired by my book on the practice of teaching (*Effective Teaching: a Practical Guide to Improving your Teaching*, Longman, 1982), written for trainee teachers wishing to improve their teaching skills as well as for in-service teachers, especially those engaged in the supervision of trainees. The books in this series have been written with the same readership in mind. However, busy classroom teachers will find that these books also serve their needs as changes in the nature and pattern of education make the in-service training of experienced teachers more essential than in the past.

The rationale behind the series is that professional courses for teachers require the coverage of a wide variety of subjects in a relatively short time so the aim of the series is the production of 'easy to read', practical guides to provide the necessary subject background, supported by references to guide and encourage further reading, together with questions and/or exercises devised to assist application and evaluation.

As specialists in their selected fields, the authors have been chosen for their ability to relate their subjects to the needs of teachers and to stimulate discussion of contemporary issues in education.

The series aims to cover subjects ranging from the theory of education to the teaching of mathematics and from primary school teaching and educational psychology to effective teaching with information technology. It looks at aspects of education as diverse as education and cultural diversity and pupil welfare and counselling. Although some subjects such as the legal context of teaching and the teaching of history are specific to England and Wales, the majority of the subjects such as assessment in education, the effective teaching of statistics and comparative education are international in scope.

Elizabeth Perrott

AUTHOR'S PREFACE

There is no quick and easy recipe for becoming a good science teacher. It is not just a matter of mastering a few survival skills such as the ability to discipline a class, but an on-going learning process where practice is constantly reviewed and new, more effective techniques used. A good teacher has many qualities, starting with his/her own personality and characteristics through to the hard work that is required in helping schools to be effective places of learning. HMI have outlined the absolute minimum requirements that we would expect of teachers. They should be:

- reliable
- punctual and cooperative
- willing to take on essential tasks that relate to the care and safety of those in their charge, and
- of such personality and character that they are able to command the respect of their pupils

As you work through this book you will develop a whole range of different skills and increase your expertise in helping pupils to learn. By having a sound knowledge of your subject and by making the work interesting through a variety of approaches and patterns of working, you will gain the respect of your pupils. Good teaching takes place through sound planning and skilful management of classes, requiring the teacher to be flexible and to adapt to situations as the lesson progresses.

Science teaching has undergone some major changes over the last ten years or so with the result that some teachers have felt disillusioned and left wondering as to when will it all stop. It is unlikely that the changes will ever stop as education attempts to meet the demands of educating young people for the ever-changing world. The modern science teacher must be prepared for syllabus reviews and changes in the assessment procedures as the curriculum developers try to match what is taught to what is required for life in the twenty-first century.

Reference

1. HMI 1985, *Education Observed 3: Good Teachers*, HMSO, London.

ACKNOWLEDGEMENTS

I wish to express my gratitude to my colleagues both in the Department of Education at University College of Swansea and in the many schools throughout South Wales who have been involved with me in training science teachers. I am indebted to all the PGCE students with whom I have been fortunate to be associated with over the years for their unending flow of helpful suggestions and comments.

And finally I should like to thank Linda, Christina and Andrew for their constant encouragement and for allowing me to go out running when the stress took over from the inspiration.

The publishers are grateful to the Controller of Her Majesty's Stationery Office for permission to reproduce an extract from *Science 5–16: A Statement of Policy* by DES and WO, an extract from *Aspects of Secondary Education in England* by DES and WO, extracts from *Science in the National Curriculum* by DES and WO (1991), an extract from *A Language for Life* by A. Bullock, an extract from *Technology in the National Curriculum* by DES and WO, an extract from *Technology for Ages 5 to 16* (1992) and an extract and figure from Assessing Investigations at Ages 13 and 15, all Crown Copyright.

To my Mum

Getting started

1.1 WHAT IS SCIENCE TEACHING ALL ABOUT?

Every reader of this book will have spent some time, and in many cases a great deal of time, attending science lessons of one sort or another and will have a mental picture of what is understood as science teaching. The purpose of this section is to get you to reflect on these thoughts and start to consider how you, as an individual, will approach the teaching of science. Many of the teaching techniques used in the past are valuable but there are many new ways of helping pupils to learn. As you are learning about science teaching, approach each technique with an open mind and make your judgements on its merits as you and your tutor or school mentor find them.

Why teach science?

Everyone would agree that there is a place for reading, writing and arithmetic in the school curriculum but can you, as a scientist, put forward the case for including science? Obviously somebody must have thought it was important as the writers of the Education Reform Act[1] (ERA) and the National Curriculum[2] (NC) have put it alongside English and mathematics as one of the core subjects for all pupils.

There appears to be two main reasons for teaching science to pupils in schools. First, it is reasonable to accept that in any society we would like the citizens to be able to look at situations from a variety of standpoints. There are occasions when individuals have to make decisions based on their feeling or their gut reaction to a problem. But there are also occasions where people need to think things out in a clear, logical fashion, weighing up the evidence before making a decision. Science education does a lot to help people to think in this sort of way. Secondly, we are living in a society where we come in contact with new developments in science on an everyday basis. The development of microelectronics has revolutionised the way we live, drugs have been produced that alleviate pain and prevent disease. There is no doubt that science has done a great deal in recent years to improve the quality of all our lives. But not all of this scientific growth has been to the benefit of mankind and in areas where human greed has outweighed reason we have been left with environmental problems on a massive scale. Pupils need to be aware of how rapidly science can progress and should be able to argue for positive scientific development, having learned a basic level of scientific literacy at school. It should be taken as every pupil's right to have some understanding of the world around him/her and the way things work.

It is surprising how many of today's adults find difficulty in explaining even the simplest of scientific ideas. Historically, science has been seen as a difficult subject on the school curriculum and because of this many pupils have shied away from it. As a world hanging on the verge of environmental disaster we need all the scientific brainpower we can muster to try to get us out of the mess. It is essential that, through good teaching, we encourage our pupils to study science.

Pupils should be able to see that the science taught them in schools is relevant to their world outside school and the adult world of work. There have been great strides forward in curriculum development to remove the more erudite aspects of secondary science and introduce topics that are of interest to young people.

Things to do

1. Why do you want to teach science? Write down a list of reasons. You will find it useful to talk through your thoughts with a friend.
2. Spend a few minutes listing the way a knowledge of science can be of use in our everyday lives.

What is science?

This may sound like a silly question to someone who has pursued a science degree course but sadly very few of us spend the time to reflect on the nature of our subject. You may go on to say that not only is it a silly question but what does it matter anyway, all that we have to do is tell the pupils what is written in the syllabus or textbooks. However, it is important that we have an understanding about the nature of science because it will affect our attitude towards science and thereby the approach we use to teach it. The answer to the question, 'What is science?' is not a simple one and is a topic that has kept the philosophers arguing for the last 400 years or so.[3]

In the past science has been depicted in schools as a list of statements, rules and laws to be copied down and learned by rote. Teachers have often ignored the personal side of science and the way in which individuals, with all their different strengths and weaknesses, have contributed to our present state of knowledge. It has also been customary to present a picture of science as a list of facts that have been 'proved' to be correct and will remain as the truth for ever. Science is not fixed or set in tablets of stone but is changing and expanding as we learn more about ourselves and the universe we live in. It is important that these aspects are reflected in today's approach to teaching. The humanistic side can be presented to pupils through a study of the contributions made by famous scientists, indicating their failures as well as their successes. In addition, pupils will experience both the frustration and the elation of the research scientist when they carry out investigative practical work as part of their NC studies.

Things to do

1. Reflect on your views about the nature of science by writing down a scientific law or principle that you are familiar with, such as Boyle's law, and consider how it was established and how it has changed, or might change, as further investigations are carried out.
2. Write down the meanings of the words: theory, hypothesis, principle and law as used in science.
3. Discuss with colleagues the way in which research scientists in the different science disciplines, chemistry, physics and biology operate.
4. Think about how you would teach: evolution, and the nature of light (wave properties and corpuscular nature).

Science teaching in school

Science teaching in schools has undergone many changes during the last century but perhaps none so significant as those that have taken place in recent years. The General Certificate of Education (GCE) O-level examinations of the 1950s and 1960s were criticised by some as being only suitable for those pupils who attended grammar schools. The large school population attending secondary modern schools were not catered for until the introduction of the Certificate of Secondary Education (CSE) in the late 1960s. The aim of this examination was to provide a different type of assessment to meet the needs of the less-academic pupil. In practice the CSE became a watered-down version of the GCE with the top grade being given equivalent status to the C pass of the GCE. Many employers did not recognise it as having sufficient academic status for employment, even at the top grade. There were also changes afoot in the way secondary education was organised. Comprehensive schools replaced the grammar and secondary modern schools in many Local Education Authorities (LEAs). The principle of educational equality brought with it new ideas about grouping pupils for teaching purposes. It was thought unsuitable to stream pupils on the basis of their ability into different classes for science. Rather it was thought that pupils would benefit from being taught in a mixed-ability situation. With the implementation of all these changes it seemed natural that the two examination systems should amalgamate into one and in 1985 the General

Certificate of Secondary Education (GCSE) was introduced. The main aims of the GCSE are as follows:[4]

- to improve the quality of education
- to raise standards of attainment by stretching and stimulating pupils throughout the ability range and to bring at least 80–90% of all pupils up to the current (in 1985) average level of GCE grade 4
- to produce a system that is fairer to candidates both in the award of grades and in access to examinations
- to motivate teachers and pupils by setting clear targets and by provision of stimulating and engaging courses
- to enhance the esteem in which examinations are held and make the results more intelligible to users
- to promote improvements in the secondary school curriculum and the ways subjects are taught, particularly in the fourth and fifth years
- to remove the need for schools to enter candidates for O-level and CSE* in the same subject or to prepare pupils in the same class for entirely different examinations.[5]

GCSE has remained the main examination for 16-year-olds in England and Wales but the types of GCSE science courses offered to pupils have changed. In the early days of the examination, syllabuses were available in chemistry, physics, biology and in science as a combined subject. The science examination may have gone under the heading of 'general science', 'applied science' or 'science at work' and was usually the examination taken by lower-ability pupils. Other, more specialised science areas, were offered by examination boards, such as electronics, human biology and science in society. At the end of the pupils' third year (year 9) in secondary schools they had to make the choice of science subjects they were going to study in the fourth (year 10) and fifth form (year 11) for their GCSE examination. While the more scientifically orientated pupils took all three science subjects other pupils took two, one or even no science course at all. This led to a general feeling of concern amongst many teachers that some pupils were leaving school with little or no science experience beyond the third year and in the majority of cases the science studied was not balanced in terms of chemistry, physics and biology. In particular, girls were opting out of studying physics at the end of the third form with the result that many career opportunities in later life were denied them.[6] In order to remove this problem the Department of Education and Science (DES) set up a body, the Secondary Science Curriculum

---

* Pupils were sometimes entered for both examinations when it was thought they were on the borderline of an O-level pass.

Review (SSCR), whose task was to examine ways of improving the science provision for all secondary pupils.

It is now widely accepted that science should have a place in the education of all young people of compulsory school age whether or not they go on to follow a career in science or technology. The Secondary Science Curriculum Review was established in 1981 to consider the implications of providing suitable science courses for all students aged 11–16 years, and to stimulate and support the developmental work that is required to enable schools to make the appropriate provision.[7]

The principle that all pupils, from the age of 5 to the age of 16, were entitled to a broad, balanced science course was firmly established by the introduction of a policy statement from the DES and the Welsh Office (WO).[8] The terms 'broad' and 'balanced' require a few words of explanation. In respect of science provision for young people the term 'broad' refers to a curriculum that incorporates the various traditional branches of science, chemistry, physics and biology and other aspects of science such as astronomy and Earth sciences. A balanced science course has a reasonable curriculum mix of the various branches of science and should have a balance between the acquisition of scientific knowledge and the practice of scientific method.

Towards the end of the 1980s many schools moved away from offering the separate sciences at GCSE level and began to offer GCSE courses given the general title 'balanced science'. These courses led to either a double award or a single award being given on successful completion of the examination. With the double award, pupils are given two GCSE grades which are the same, e.g. AA, BB, DD. The single award has a reduced syllabus content but is still balanced and leads to a single grade at GCSE.

Balanced science can be presented to pupils in a variety of different formats and it is up to the head of the science department as to which approach s/he favours and you will find that even neighbouring schools may have quite different methods of presenting the science curriculum. There are three main ways of organising the science curriculum:

- integrated science
- co-ordinated science
- modular science.

Integrated or combined science can be thought of as the opposite end of the scale to teaching the separate sciences. In integrated science the work is delivered under topic headings such as 'water', 'movement' and 'energy'. There have been many notable integrated science schemes in the past such as the Schools Council Integrated

Science Project (SCISP) and Scottish Integrated Science (SIS).[9] The more recently published schemes[10] are suitable resource material for teaching lower-school pupils and any of the integrated science GCSE courses. There are, however, some areas of science that are difficult to present in an integrated form and you may find that some so-called integrated science courses have units that are clearly identifiable as biology, physics and chemistry. In integrated science teaching one teacher generally teaches the whole course to one class. This is the approach most often used in the first three years of secondary education and in some schools it is used throughout.

With a co-ordinated approach each teacher teaches his/her own subject specialism to the class and the class attends lessons in chemistry, physics and biology. The three teachers teaching one class co-ordinate their work so that there are connecting links or common approaches in all the science lessons. Some schools may use an integrated approach in the first three years and then use a co-ordinated scheme[11] in the final two years leading up to the GCSE examination.

A modular approach is used by some schools where the class moves from one teacher to another, each one teaching a unit of work s/he has prepared. There are various types of modular courses with some being related to the separate sciences and others being integrated in nature. With some modular schemes all the pupils must do all the modules whereas in others all the pupils follow a core science programme and they opt to study certain other modules.

There is a fourth approach to science teaching but this is not used widely in the secondary sector. It is worthy of mention at this point as its popularity may increase as teachers become more familiar with NC requirements. It is the approach used in primary schools where science teaching is integrated with other areas of the curriculum as teachers present their work as part of a theme or topic. A theme, such as 'buildings' would involve some creative writing, measuring, work on materials and their strength, location of buildings and many more areas of the curriculum. In most secondary schools there is a tendency for separate subject teachers to go their own way with little co-ordination between departments. As the NC cross-curricular themes (see Chapter 10) become fully incorporated into school life there may be more thematic work carried out in secondary schools.

Table 1.1 lists the GCSE science courses currently available from the five examination boards in England and Wales. In addition to these the separate sciences are offered by each board but pupils who wish to follow these courses to GCSE must study all three sciences in the years 10 and 11.

Table 1.1 **Major GCSE science syllabuses and the examination boards that administer them**

Examination board	Syllabus
University of London Examinations and Assessment Council	Science: Double Award (Combined)(Balanced Science) Science: Single Award (Combined)(Balanced Science) Science: Double Award (Modular)(Science at Work) Science: Single Award (Modular)(Science at Work) Science: Double Award (Co-ordinated) Science: Single Award (Co-ordinated) Science: Double Award (Integrated) Graded Assessments in Science (GASP)
Southern Examining Group	Science: Double Award Science: Single Award (These syllabuses allow for combined, integrated or co-ordinated teaching approaches) Science: Double Award (Modular) Science: Single Award (Modular) (These syllabuses are based on Science at Work)
Midland Examination Group	Nuffield Co-ordinated Sciences: Double Award Nuffield Co-ordinated Sciences: Single Award Science: Double Award Science: Single Award Science (Salters): Double Award Science (Salters): Single Award
Northern Examinations and Assessment Board	Science: Double Award (Modular Approach) Science: Single Award (Modular Approach) Science: Double Award (Co-ordinated Approach) Science: Single Award (Co-ordinated Approach) Science: Double Award (Integrated Approach)
Welsh Joint Education Committee	Science: Double Award (Modular Approach) Science: Single Award (Modular Approach) Science: Double Award (Co-ordinated Approach) Science: Single Award (Co-ordinated Approach) Science: Double Award (Integrated Approach)

Things to do

This task will take some time but it will help you to familiarise yourself with some of the syllabuses and teaching schemes that are available. The materials you start to collect here will be used in other chapters in the book.

- Obtain copies of different science syllabuses from the examination boards. You will also find it useful to have a copy of the GCSE Key Stage 4 Examinations Criteria for Science.[12]
- For each board compare the content for each syllabus. Which approach do you prefer?

Things to do continued

- Look through a number of books written for pupils in their first three years of secondary school. Which approach do you think would be most suitable as a precursor to the GCSE syllabus you have chosen?

  You will need to bear in mind that syllabuses and schemes change periodically or are removed from circulation making it necessary to keep up to date with your notes.

Knowledge, skills and processes in science courses

There are two distinct types of science course, those that are essentially knowledge based and those that are process based. Traditionally science courses have laid the greatest emphasis on the recall of knowledge and the understanding of content. A number of courses developed during the last ten years have placed greater emphasis on the processes of science, arguing that for most pupils the scientific method is much more important than remembering scientific facts. Prominent amongst these courses are *Science in Process*[13] and *Warwick Process Science.*[14] But what are these skills and processes that we, as science teachers, should consider for inclusion in our work? Many lists of skills and processes are available and educators still argue over the inclusion of this term or that but the following list, developed by the SSCR,[15] is one that is well established.

A skill is a specific activity which a student can be trained to do. For example,

listening	non-verbal communication
talking	observing
writing	searching
drawing	measuring
reading	manipulating
numeracy	graphicacy
estimating	recording
small group skills	

A process is a rational activity involving the application of a range of skills. For example, communicating and discussing, which includes:

thinking	seeking help
questioning	negotiating.

processing of information, which includes:

selecting	designing, and
using relationships	drawing conclusions
controlling of interacting	
variables	

problem solving, experimentation and decision making, which includes:

predicting	evaluating
inferring	assessing
formulating hypotheses	classifying, and
interpreting	managing time
modelling	

Just as curriculum developers have difficulty deciding which items of content should be included in syllabuses they also need to consider which skills and processes should be included. All modern syllabuses have a balance between knowledge and skills and processes. It is, perhaps, the emphasis given by the syllabus writers to skills and processes that gives each syllabus its distinct flavour. After all the NC has clearly laid out the content that must be learnt, leaving the examination boards and teachers to add their own personal style to the way that it is presented.

There is no doubt about it, a science teacher requires a great deal of expertise and ability if s/he is to be good at his/her craft. One issue that concerns many new teachers to the profession is that of teaching outside his/her own subject specialism. Most new teachers start their careers as a specialist in one of the major science areas but they quickly have to adapt to teach other science disciplines. There is no need to worry as you will find plenty of help from teaching colleagues within your school and there are abundant resources available from publishers and other organisations. To a large extent the skills you have learned in your science specialism can be transferred to the other areas of science and it should not be long before you have a firm grasp of the other subjects. It is worth working on the basis that you can do anything in science that you would expect the pupils to be able to do.

Most school science departments work as a team, pooling ideas and perhaps producing common teaching materials. You will be invited to contribute to the work from your area of expertise and the conversations you have with colleagues will help you in your own professional development.

There is no getting away from it, you will have to look up any science that you are not familiar with and make notes so that you have sufficient background information to be comfortable standing in front of a class. However, you are not expected to be the fountain of all knowledge and you should be honest with pupils when there is some aspect of science that you are not familiar with. Encourage pupils to go and find out things for themselves by talking to other teachers, looking things up in books, pamphlets or databases, or by writing away to an expert person or organisation.

Things to do

Think back to a lesson that you have recently observed or one that you have taught yourself. Try to analyse it in terms of the time spent on activities that are concerned with the pupils learning subject content work and the time spent on learning the processes of science. This will only be a rough analysis as there will be quite a lot of overlap between content and process. (You cannot teach a process in isolation. It must be latched on to some science content.)

1.2   YOU AND YOUR SCHOOL

There are over 4500 secondary schools in England and Wales, all of them teaching the same National Curriculum and yet they are all different in their ethos, traditions and culture. When you enter a school as a member of staff or a student teacher you become part of that environment and have to take on the responsibilities that go with becoming a member of that community. In order to be successful in a school you must be happy working with both the pupils and your colleagues. Becoming a new teacher in a school can be a fairly traumatic time as you merge into the school life. It is a time for getting to know many new people and a time for getting to know yourself, your own personality, your capabilities and limitations.

When you first visit your new school you will be full of questions to ask about how things are organised and what you will be expected to do. You will need to remember that schools are complex systems and it will take some time for you to assimilate all the information. A good place to start learning about the school is to read the school prospectus or brochure to see how the school tries to market itself to parents. You should also read the staff handbook, which will give you information about the aims of the school, the management structure, the key information about the day-to-day running of the system and the discipline procedures. Table 1.2 highlights the information you should search for during your first few visits to the school.

Table 1.2 **A list of useful information to be obtained during your first visits to the school.**

Absences	• What do I do about absences at the start of the day (in the initial pastoral or registration period)?
	• What do I do about absences in my lessons?
	• Where is the register sent to and who co-ordinates pupil absence?
	• What is the procedure when I am ill and cannot get to school?
	• What is the procedure if I have to supervise a class for an absent member of staff?
Discipline	• What do I do if I see breaks of discipline outside my classroom?
	• What are the punishments for minor offences?
	• What are the punishments for major offences?
	• What type of detentions are given in the school and how much notice must I give the pupils?
	• Can I send pupils out of my lesson for misbehaviour? Where do they go and who do they report to?
Resources	• Where do I get my chalk, board rubber, overhead projector (ohp), pens, books and other resources from?
	• Who does my photocopying? If someone does it for me how much notice do I have to give?
	• What is the procedure for giving pupils new exercise books?
	• What do I do if a pupil has lost his/her exercise book?
Rooms	• Where are all the science laboratories (including mobiles)?
	• What facilities are available in the different laboratories?
	• Where is the school nurse situated?
	• Where are the staff rooms?
Staffing	• Who looks after new teachers in the school?
	• Who is my immediate boss for (i) academic work and (ii) pastoral duties?
Teaching	• What will be the make up of the classes I have to teach, e.g. age, ability, number of pupils, general behaviour of class?
	• What do I have to teach and what teaching methods are open to me?
	• How long do I have to teach the work?
	• How will the pupils be assessed?
Timing	• What are the lesson times?
	• Are there rooms in the school where the bell cannot be heard?
	• What do I do about children who ask to go to the toilet during lesson time?
Technicians	• How is technical assistance organised?
	• How much notice does the technician require to prepare materials for a lesson?
	• What is the procedure for clearing away apparatus at the end of a lesson?

The school

What should I wear on my first visit to the school? A common enough question and one that concerns many trainee teachers. It is best to wear something fairly smart and not too way-out. Some schools are quite happy with modern forms of dress and jewellery but the majority tend to keep to traditional standards for their staff. The best idea is to make a good impression on the first day and then to look round at other members of staff and get a feeling for what is acceptable. If in doubt ask, you do not want the ignominy of being sent home by the headteacher for wearing inappropriate dress.

The school is part of the community and you should find out how your school interacts with other key organisations within the community such as libraries, churches, industry and commerce, the social services and the police. You will find it helpful to become familiar with the local housing, amenities, facilities and other aspects of the neighbouring geography. There will be key indicators here that will help you in building up a picture of the environment in which your pupils live. Also there may be local facilities that you could incorporate into lessons later on, perhaps a piece of waste land for an environmental survey or a local manufacturer linked to one of the industrial processes you are covering.

It is important that you have a clear understanding of how your school is organised and run in terms of the management, the academic and the discipline structures. Try to talk to as many people as you can about the running of the school and slowly build up a profile of different people's responsibilities. Spend some time walking around the school getting to know where all the rooms are. You will find it very troublesome if you are suddenly asked to supervise a class in room B138 if you have no idea where it is. When you arrive late at the room you will probably find considerable disruption from the bored children, which may take a great deal of expertise to calm. As you journey around the school try to imagine yourself in various situations and consider what you would do in those circumstances. Discuss your plans with experienced teachers by asking them what would they do in the same situation. Although you are unlikely to cover every possible scenario, it is better to be prepared by having thought things through beforehand than having to make on-the-spot decisions.

The science department

The science department will probably be one of the largest in the school and it is essential that every member of the science team works together efficiently. You will need to know the responsibilities of each member of staff so that you know where to go to get help. A good science department will have plenty of resources from which you will be able to select teaching materials for your classes. Remember that in a lot of cases these will have taken a long time for a member of staff to prepare and s/he will be displeased if you take the last copy. You should check on the availability of any resources before you take it. You will also be expected to produce material of your own, which you should show to other teachers for comment before you try it out on children. You should be clear about what books, pamphlets and other resources you are allowed to borrow and when you need to return them. It can cause a great deal of bad feeling in a department if you have got the only copy of a resource that is required for the next lesson at home.

Good technicians can make your life much easier but they are very busy people and you must play fair with them and not expect them to drop what they are doing to attend to your needs. In order to be efficient, technicians often have to work to strict regimes and require teachers to get their requirements to them by a fixed time interval. They may not have time to completely tidy up between periods and so it is a good idea to get pupils to take things to unused side benches at the end of each session.

You need to be very clear about what you have to teach and the best document to consult for this information is the scheme of work for your class. This should not only tell you what information to cover lesson by lesson but also give the aims of the work, a list of experiments and resources and indicate how the work is to be assessed. Before you start on a topic you should have a look at the assessment package for the unit of work and pay particular attention to the content of the end-of-unit test. This is not a matter of 'teaching to the test' but to help you to understand where the emphasis should lie in your lessons in your early days of teaching.

The science staff will advise you on teaching methods and you will greatly benefit from talking to experienced teachers and committing to memory their useful ideas. As an eager new teacher you will also want to try out new approaches and different experiments. Tread carefully at first, some new teachers tend to think that they know it all and that they were born to teach. While not wishing to dampen this enthusiasm, it is worth having all new ideas checked out by an experienced teacher before trying it out in the classroom. Teaching is an exciting and interesting profession with plenty of variety and you will have the opportunity to experiment with different methods.

Teaching is very intensive work, for the whole of the lesson you are heavily involved with the pupils and when the bell rings they leave you and another batch comes into the laboratory. It can drain you of all your mental energy if you are not careful and you will go home thoroughly tired. You must make the most of the timetabled breaks during the day to recharge your batteries so that you can be fresh and full of enthusiasm for your next class. You will need to find out where people have their coffee and tea breaks and what people do for lunch. Although you will want to spend time with colleagues in the science department try not to restrict yourself to this group but go and find out what is happening elsewhere in the school. Science teachers have a reputation for never coming out of the preparation room and drinking their coffee from mugs that have not been properly cleaned for the last ten years. As a new teacher you need to know what is going on in the school at large and need to meet teachers from other subject areas. These meetings have more that just a social and recreational benefit, they will help you to develop your conception of the whole teaching process and to respect the contributions made by other subjects to the development of the individual child.

Things to do

When you go to your new school find out the following:

What will be your duties in addition to your teaching commitment?
Where will you find information related to the day-to-day running of the school?
What is the procedure in the case of fire?
Whom do you notify if you are going to be absent or late?
What are the arrangements for whole staff and departmental meetings and training sessions?
What syllabuses are used by the school?
Who will monitor your progress during your early days of teaching?

1.3 BEING ORGANISED

This section is made up of three distinct parts all connected with getting yourself organised as a teacher. It is important to try to clarify what you are doing right from the start of your career in teaching. You will find that an organised person will be able to save a tremendous amount of time and frustration over someone who is not sure what s/he is doing and cannot find things when they are needed.

The first part of this section is concerned with organising your teaching resources. You will be bombarded with all sorts of useful literature during your teaching career and, no doubt, you will produce some excellent resources yourself. All this needs to be carefully filed away if you wish to avoid having to re-invent the wheel each year.

The second part is about clarifying your goals in science teaching. We have already established that science is not a catalogue of facts that have to be fed to the pupils so that they can regurgitate it at the next examination. There is information to be learned, explanations to be understood, skills to be mastered and the procedures of science to be grasped. This section helps you to start organising your own thoughts about the aims of science teaching.

The final part of this unit is about using the correct scientific terms in science lessons. It is quite confusing to pupils if they come across different terms for the same substance or quantity in different science lessons. It may well be that you have entered teaching from industry or university where old names have been used and you have got into the habit of using terms such as ferric chloride or calories. However, in schools pupils must get used to using the standard scientific terms as these are the terms they will come across in examinations.

Resources

It is worth while spending some time and thought towards the start of your teaching career as to how you are going to store the vast amount of useful information you are going to come across in your years of teaching. Resource material is only of use to you if you can find it in time for the lesson. You should consider buying in a filing cabinet or, at least, having space in one at school. In addition you should have a quick reference filing system to remind you about useful teaching material. This could be on a card index system or on a computer database.

You should start collecting interesting articles from newspapers, colour supplements and magazines, such as reports on environmental disasters, new inventions and methods of saving energy. These often provide useful stimulus material for lessons and help pupils to consider how they should make judgements based on newspaper accounts. You may also wish to store information from journals such as *Scientific American* or *New Scientist* to give an up-to-date picture of developments in scientific research. There are always plenty of interesting ideas for teaching and reports of the latest developments in science education in the journals of the Association for Science Education (ASE), *Education in Science* (EiS), published five times a year and the *School Science Review* (SSR), published quarterly. Each of the separate science subjects has its own educational journal published through its own professional body:

the Royal Society of Chemistry publishes *Education in Chemistry*
the Institute of Physics publishes *Physics Education*
the Institute of Biology publishes *Journal of Biological Education*, and
the Biochemical Society publishes *The Biochemist*

In addition each Society publishes pamphlets, charts, books and other journals for both teachers and pupils.

Industry and commerce produce a vast array of useful teaching aids, many of which are free to teachers. These may take the form of information leaflets, such as you may find in a supermarket, or pupil workbooks that can be used directly with the class. Some companies also market software packages, educational games and resource packs of materials at very reasonable cost.

Government bodies, such as the the Centre for Research Education and Training in Energy (CREATE) and the Health Education Authority, publish teaching materials that are free to teachers. In most cases it is possible to obtain class sets of the documents.

Videos on science topics can be hired, free of charge, from some firms and there are plenty of good science programmes that are broadcast on television. Provided these programmes are shown to pupils rather than a paying audience it is permissible to record them off air and play them back to the pupils during lesson time.

Things to do

Start building up your portfolio of useful information by writing to organisations such as B.P., Shell, British Telecom and Friends of the Earth. When you receive the information work out a system for classifying and storing it.

Take one of the items you have received and plan how you would use it with a class. Wall charts should be more than just decoration for the laboratory walls. Consider how you would get pupils to extract information from wall charts, pamphlets and similar items of literature.

The aims of science teaching

We all have aims in our lives: wanting to be happy and healthy; wanting to mark year 8's books before tomorrow morning; wanting to have some money left over by the end of the month rather than be in debt. All these are goals that we wish to achieve, they are general statements of intent.

It is important that science courses have clear goals of what we wish to achieve as teachers and what we want our pupils to achieve as learners. A list of educational aims highlights the philosophy of a course or to put it in layman's terms 'they give you a flavour of what the course is trying to achieve'. Not all science courses have the same list of aims but there are a number of aims that are common to all courses, such as the acquisition of scientific knowledge.

Things to do

Think about those things that you think are important in science education for young people. Write these down and then compare them with the list of aims given below.

Through consultation with its members the ASE has produced a list of aims for science education.[16] The aims of science education are to enable the learner to:

1. Appreciate science as a human activity

Science is a human construction, a way of thinking and acting. It is dependent upon context: cultural, social, economic, technological and political. Scientific activity can introduce and influence change for individuals and for society. Therefore, science needs to be interpreted at an individual as well as at a collective level. As scientific knowledge changes so does society; such changes are ecological and not merely additional.

2. Understand how science operates

The nature, form and value base of science should be understood so that the learner can recognise and interact with scientific activities.

3. Know and understand scientific concepts and principles

Identify the basic parameters, principles and concepts; this is essential in developing a progressive intellectual grasp of science, and the application of knowledge, understanding and skills.

4. Be able to be scientific

Knowing about science is important, but being able 'to do science', to act scientifically, to apply scientific knowledge, understanding and skills in individual and collective situations is more important. Learners should acquire scientific competencies and know when and how to use science in a positive way. They should communicate with others in appropriate terminology, scientific and non-scientific. This involves exploring science in action through the acquisition and application of skills and knowledge of scientific enquiry, capability and testing of ideas.

5. Relate scientific enquiry and action to other modes of human behaviour

Scientific endeavour, acquisition and application of new knowledge and skills are of lesser value if viewed in isolation. Scientific worth and progress is only meaningful when considered in terms of learning and activity. The learner should recognise the need to relate scientific advance within the wider context of human development if society as a whole is to benefit.

These five broad statements cover the important facets of all science courses in general terms. You will find it useful to expand these aims for individual courses that you are asked to teach or to reformulate them into other statements that you find more meaningful.

Things to do

Look through a copy of a science GCSE examination syllabus, preferably one that you have been asked to teach. If you are unable to obtain one from your school or college then you should write to one of the examination boards who will send you one for a small charge. In Table 1.1 the main GCSE science courses are listed together with the examination boards that administer them.

Read through the aims of the course, which are normally found towards the front of the documentation and then select two or three of the aims for further study. Looking through the description of the syllabus try to identify teaching opportunities where your selected aims could be implemented.

The aims of a course give general guidance to the teacher as to where the teaching emphasis should lie. In Chapter 3 you will see how these aims can be used to guide the teacher in preparing more specific objectives for individual lessons.

You will have read earlier on in this chapter that science syllabuses do not remain static, indeed over the last ten years or so there has been considerable change. There is no reason to believe that our aims for science education will stay as they are. The new teachers of today will be the curriculum developers of tomorrow and it may be that you will be involved in fashioning out new and exciting science courses for the next generation of school pupils.

Using the correct scientific terms

This section is concerned with getting yourself organised in terms of the scientific words and symbols that you use.

It would be nice to think that teachers knew all there is know about science. Unfortunately, this can never be true and even the limited amount we need to understand in order to be able to teach NC science can cause some problems. There are many difficult concepts in a science course and in our learning of science we will have studied some in depth and now have a clear picture of the science involved but there will be other concepts that have passed us by and left us with only a superficial understanding. For example, it is not uncommon to come across science teachers who are not sure of the difference between mass and weight or temperature and heat. It is obviously important that science teachers are completely clear about the nature of the topic they are teaching and that there is a consistency across all areas of science. For example, pupils will find it a problem if after being taught that weight is a force and it is measured in newtons (N) they come across another teacher asking the pupils to write down weight of the watch glass = 2 g

rather than

mass of the watch glass = 2 g.

Things to do

Test your understanding of some concepts in science by answering the following questions. Get an 'expert' to check your answers:

- What is the difference between heat and temperature and what units are each measured in?
- Describe the process of respiration in plants.
- Explain how a solution of sodium chloride conducts electricity.

As scientists we have to come to terms with the fact that many words have one meaning in science and a different meaning in everyday use. Pupils on the other hand sometimes find this difficult and will need gentle coaxing to use the words in a scientific way. It is worth reminding them that this phenomena is not peculiar to science and that there are many words in the English language that have more than one meaning.

In addition to getting the science right it is important that teachers give due emphasis to the grammar and spelling of science. Language teachers are often highly critical of grammatical and linguistic mistakes by pupils but science teachers often ignore related errors in science. This can lead to slipshod work and pupils can become confused if standard conventions or names are incorrectly used by some teachers.

It is better to use:	rather than:
the recommended name for chemicals (e.g. use **ethanoic acid**	the traditional name not **acetic acid**)
the recommended units (e.g. use $\mathbf{cm^3}$	the traditional units not **ml**)
the correct size and number of letters for abbreviations (e.g. (i) use **k** for kilo, as in kilogram – kg ((ii) use **g** for gram and grams	be casual about the latter not **K** which is only used for the Kelvin scale of temperature) not **gms**)

You should ensure that you use the correct scientific nomenclature right form the start of your teaching career by referring to the ASE publication *Chemical Nomenclature, Symbols and Terminology for use in School Science.*[17] This text lists the definitions of common terms, converts traditional names to recommended names and vice versa, and gives all the standard abbreviations that you are likely to come across. It is the standard text used by all the examination boards for setting their examination papers.

Before leaving this section it is worth mentioning the problems that calculators have brought to the writing up of science reports by pupils. Most pupils use calculators to work out their results of practical work that involves taking measurements but, unfortunately, they appear to think that the experiment takes on some new level of accuracy when they carry out their calculations. It is not uncommon for pupils to quote an answer to seven or so significant figures when the most accurate measurement has only been to two significant figures. Pupils should be encouraged to use calculators sensibly and to quote their result to as many decimal places as the accuracy of the experiment allows. They should realise that all measurements have an order of error and that it is scientifically incorrect to record a mass of, say, 2.30 g for a measurement taken on a balance that only records to one place of decimals.

NOTES AND REFERENCES

1. Department of Education and Science and The Welsh Office, 1987, *Education Reform: The Government's Proposals for Schools*, HMSO, London.

2. Department of Education and Science and The Welsh Office, 1991, *Science in the National Curriculum*, HMSO, London.

3. There are many useful books and articles concerned with the perceived nature of science. The following two references are given as examples of this literature: Richardson, M. & Boyle, C., 1979, *What is Science?*, ASE, Hatfield. Donnelly, J., 'The work of Popper and Kuhn on the nature of Science', *School Science Review*, 1979, **60**, 212, 489–500.

4. Secondary Examinations and Assessment Council, 1992, *GCSE/Key Stage 4 Examinations Criteria for Science*, HMSO, London.

5. Department of Education and Science and The Welsh Office, 1985, *GCSE: a General Introduction*, HMSO, London.

6. Kelly, A. (ed.), 1987, *Science for Girls*, Open University Press, Milton Keynes.

7. Secondary Science Curriculum Review, 1983, *Science Education 11–16:*

Proposals for Action and Consultation, Secondary Science Curriculum Review, London.

8. Department of Education and Science and The Welsh Office, 1985, *Science 5–16: A Statement of Policy*, HMSO, London.

9. SCISP was a double award science scheme that was established in the 1970s. Information about the approach can be found in: Hall, W. & Mowl, B., 1973, *Patterns Teachers' Guide 1 Building Blocks*, Longman, London. SIS was devised for pupils in the first three years of their secondary school and for lower-ability pupils in the remaining years of compulsory schooling. Information about the scheme can be found in: Scottish Integrated Science, 1977, *Teachers' Guide Sections 1 to 8*, Heinemann, London.

10. Many of the modern books that use an integrated science approach do not use the word 'integrated' in their title. There are a number of such texts on the market and the following two serve as examples: Boyd, J. & Whitelaw, W., 1989, *Understanding Science 1: Teachers' Resource Book*, John Murray, London. Coles, M., Gott, R., & Thornley, T., 1988, *Active Science 1*, Collins, London.

11. Examples of published co-ordinated science schemes are: Dobson, K., 1988, *Co-ordinated Science – Teacher's Book – Teaching for Active Learning*, Collins, London. 1992, *Nuffield Co-ordinated Sciences: New Teachers' Guide*, Longman, London.

12. Secondary Examinations and Assessment Council, 1990, *GCSE Criteria for Science*, HMSO, London.

13. *Science in Process*, Parts 1 and 2, Heinemann, 1987 and 1988.

14. Screen, P., 1986, *Introduction to Process Science*, Ashford Press, Southampton.

15. Secondary Science Curriculum Review, 1984, *Towards a Specification of Minimum Entitlement: Brenda and Friends*, Secondary Science Curriculum Review, London.

16. Association for Science Education, 1992, *Change in our Future: A Challenge for Science Education* (ASE Policy), ASE, Hatfield.

17. Association for Science Education, 1985, *Chemical Nomenclature, Symbols and Terminology for Use in School Science* (3rd edition), ASE, Hatfield.

CHAPTER 2

The science curriculum

2.1 SCIENCE IN THE CURRICULUM

This section examines the role of science within the 11–16 curriculum and the contribution science can make to the development of the whole child. The final section in this chapter goes on to look at post-16 science courses and the changes that are taking place there.

In Chapter 1 mention was made of the curriculum change that has taken place over the last few years and the fact that much of this has arisen from a sense of dissatisfaction amongst science teachers about the nature of the science taught. However, it is not just in the area of science that there has been a transformation of the curriculum. All other subjects have had to consider which elements of their field should be taught. Questions have been raised by curriculum developers as to the contribution each subject can make to the development of the whole child. Not only have the developers got to consider which subjects should be included in the curriculum but also they have had to reckon how much time should be allocated to each subject. It is easy to argue for the place of mathematics and English on the timetable of every pupil but can you argue for the place of science? In order to do this we need to appreciate the special contribution that science can make to the development of each pupil. In Chapter 1 there was a list of important skills, that form part of all science courses, related to enabling the pupil to think and act scientifically. In addition there is a bank of knowledge that will help pupils to have a better understanding of the world around them. But what are the important items of knowledge and what about the time allocation for science in comparison with other subjects? All subject teachers consider that their course is important and there are many strong arguments for increasing the time allocation for all subjects, for example:

Surely it is important for pupils to learn at least one additional European language thoroughly so that they can communicate effectively with our European partners? It is essential that pupils have a grasp of the historical development of our country to give them a clearer understanding of modern day events. Personal and social development sessions are a vital part of school life to help pupils come to terms with the complex world in which we all live.

Things to do

Get together with some other teachers who are at the same stage of their professional development as yourself. Working as a group write down a list of skills, processes and attitudes that you think the school ought to try to teach their pupils. For example,

Attitudes such as honesty, tolerance and respect for other people's property.
Processes such as the ability to communicate or the ability to classify information.
Skills such as being able to draw graphs from data or being able to make accurate observations.

Ask each subject specialist which skills, processes and attitudes can be taught in his/her subject area. You may find that there is considerable overlap between the different groups. What mechanism is used in the school to ensure that all the important process areas are covered? How does the school ensure that the same message is being transmitted by different subject specialists?

A list of all the knowledge that a pupil should receive in the secondary school would be a very long one indeed but if such a list was produced you would find that there are also areas of commonality between subjects. See the section on cross-curricular themes in Chapter 10 for examples.

All subjects are fighting for the limited amount of time available in a school day. In general it is common to find about 20% of curriculum time allocated to science in years 10 and 11 and slightly less time in the earlier years of secondary education. It would seem logical then that teachers should work together to find common topics within their subject areas and look for opportunities for working together in a systematic way.

Towards broad and balanced science

If we were given a blank sheet of paper and asked to write down the science that we thought ought to be included in a programme for 11–16 year olds we would probably experience a little difficulty.[1] In the first case our programme would be strongly influenced by our subject specialism and we may find that our curriculum was strongly biased towards our favourite type of science. We would also be influenced by the type of science we had been taught at school and probably wish to continue with the same traditions on the basis that what was good for us must certainly be good for the next generation. Writing a course that ensures that all pupils will experience a good grounding in a broad range of science areas is not an easy task but it has been the goal of curriculum developers for some time. As long ago as 1979, science teachers were starting to plan for a balanced, science-for-all curriculum. In the late 1970s and early 1980s the Association for Science Education (ASE) asked teachers to think about the aims of science education and to help formulate a policy statement for the future. Two of the recommendations and proposals that came out of the consultations were:[2]

All pupils should have the opportunity to benefit from a full and effective programme of science education throughout their period of compulsory schooling.

The science curriculum should incorporate a reasonable balance between specialist science and generalist aspects of education through science and should reflect the range of contexts and aims specified.

In other words the ASE were recommending that all pupils in schools should follow a balanced science course, putting an end to the 'dropping' of one or more science subjects at the end of the third year.

The DES and the WO carried out a similar consultative process in 1982 and produced, what many believe to be a milestone in science education, *Science 5–16: A Statement of Policy*[3] setting out clear priorities for schools. As part of the document the DES and WO listed ten principles that they wished all those concerned with the education of children to focus on. These principles are:

(a) **Breadth**: all pupils should be introduced to the main concepts from the whole range of science; to the technological applications and social consequences of science; and to a range of scientific skills and processes;

(b) **Balance**: all pupils should be able to continue their study of each of the main areas of science throughout the compulsory age range; and all science courses should achieve a balance between acquisition of scientific knowledge and the practice of scientific method;

(c) **Relevance**: science education should draw extensively on the everyday experience of pupils, and should be aimed at preparing pupils as effectively as possible for adult and working life;

(d) **Differentiation**: the intellectual and practical demands made by science education should be suited to the abilities of the pupils, in ways which will allow the highest existing standards to be maintained for the most able while catering fully for pupils unable to reach those standards and providing for all pupils the essential experience of broad and balanced science;

(e) **Equal opportunities**: science education should give genuinely equal curricular opportunities to boys and girls and should in particular actively seek ways of exciting the interest of girls in those aspects of science which some girls at present find unappealing or intimidating;

(f) **Continuity**: as science education develops in primary and middle schools, it is increasingly important for the schools to which pupils subsequently transfer to give attention to building on the foundations already laid; and links between secondary and further and higher education institutions should be fostered so that those institutions are better equipped to build on newly developed courses in the schools;

(g) **Progression**: courses should be designed to give progressively deeper understanding and greater competence, not only within individual schools but also over the compulsory period as a whole, whatever the age of transfer between schools may be;

(h) **Links across the curriculum**: in primary schools teachers should link work in science with the development of the language and mathematical competence of their pupils, and with the practical component of the curriculum more generally; in secondary schools science teachers should work closely with their colleagues, not only in mathematics, CDT and home economics departments but also more widely, to ensure that the generally applicable aspects of science, not least its investigative approaches, are firmly established in the curriculum, and that the contribution that other subjects can make to the teaching of science and vice versa is fully exploited;

(i) **Teaching methods and approaches**: science is a practical subject, and should be taught at all stages in a way which emphasises practical, investigative and problem solving activity;

(j) **Assessment**: progress in science should be assessed, both within the schools and in public examinations, in ways which recognise the importance of the skills and processes of science as well as rewarding the ability to reproduce and apply scientific knowledge; and which allow all pupils to show what they can do rather than what they cannot do.

The introduction of this government policy statement and other related developments led schools to introduce new balanced science courses into their schools. Such courses could lead to a double award at GCSE level (see Table 1.1).

Things to do

Obtain a copy of the *Science 5–16: A Statement of Policy*[3] document and read it through thoroughly. This will help you to have a clearer understanding of the ten principles and the implications they have for teachers. Clarify in your own mind the meaning of terms such as: progression, continuity, differentiation and relevance.

Start off by looking at 'relevance' by carrying out some, or all, of the following activities:

1. Talk to individual pupils about what excites or interests them about science.

Things to do continued

2.   Organise a brainstorming session with a class asking pupils to write down as many things as they can think of where a knowledge of science would be useful in everyday life.
3.   Organise a brainstorming session with a class asking pupils to write down a list of jobs where a knowledge of science would be useful.
4.   Check through some science textbooks looking for material that you think would be relevant to pupils' everyday experiences.

Some schools were quick to implement the government policy statement into their curriculum and provide science courses for all 11–16 pupils. Others found it difficult to introduce straight away for a variety of reasons, such as lack of suitably qualified staff, insufficient equipment or laboratory space, unavailability of suitable teaching resources or because of a resistance to balanced science amongst members of the science staff. Help came from a number of different directions. The Secondary Science Curriculum Review (SSCR) instigated the formation of teacher groups to develop teaching ideas and share these with colleagues throughout the country. LEAs gave support to teachers through in-service training programmes. The Open University prepared distance-learning materials to help biology and chemistry teachers increase their competence in physics. More recently they have produced a pack to help teachers learn more about chemistry.[4] Publishers started to produce books that were specifically aimed at teaching the new balanced science GCSE syllabuses. But perhaps one of the most significant influences on the move to introduce balanced science into the schools was the role played by the technical and vocational initiative (TVEI). TVEI[5] was set up by the government through the Manpower Services Commission (MSC) rather than the DES. It was able to initiate change in schools by providing funds that could be used for:

Extra teachers to plan, write and teach new courses
In-service training for teachers
New equipment and premises
Extra technical and administrative staff

In order to receive the support funding, schools had to set in motion a policy whereby all pupils received a broad, balanced science course. Many schools took advantage of this opportunity to develop new science courses.

These endeavours paved the way for the implementation of the Education Reform Act (ERA)[6] and, hence the National Curriculum, in 1988. The Act, which governs the school curriculum in England and

Wales, states that all pupils must receive a curriculum that is balanced and broadly based. It is a legal requirement that all state-maintained schools should follow the NC. However, independent schools[7] are not required to do so and City Technology Colleges (CTCs) only have to follow the substance of the NC. In order to help schools to introduce the NC, the DES set up two curriculum councils, the National Curriculum Council (NCC)[8] to look after affairs in England and the Curriculum Council for Wales (CCW).[9] In addition to these two bodies, the Schools Examinations and Assessment Council (SEAC) continued to oversee examination affairs.

All pupils in state-maintained schools must study religious education and the foundation subjects of the NC.[10] The foundation subjects include three core subjects, English, mathematics and science, and seven others: technology (including design), history, geography, music, art, physical education and a modern foreign language. In addition pupils need to experience activities that will enable them to develop their personal and social skills and attitudes. In order to provide a framework for this the curriculum councils have provided a framework of themes, competencies and dimensions that should pervade all school work.[11] An outline of how this is carried out with relation to science education is described in Chapter 10.

A curriculum that is broad and balanced must cover a wide range of academic activities as well as the development of cultural, social and aesthetic perceptions of the world around them. The curriculum councils have suggested[12] that in planning a curriculum, schools should consider eight aspects of learning, which together describe the full range of experiences to which pupils are entitled. These aspects are the:

- expressive and aesthetic
- linguistic and literary
- mathematical
- physical and recreational
- social and environmental
- scientific
- spiritual and moral
- technological

A curriculum containing these elements will have a certain richness that will help the pupil to develop and mature in a positive way. Science can contribute to most, if not all, of these areas of learning through collaborative working with other subject specialists in the school.

2.2   NATIONAL CURRICULUM SCIENCE

The science National Curriculum 1987–1991

NC science has been shaped and re-shaped over a four-year period starting in 1987. Many organisations have played their part in the remodelling process, not least of which has been the government itself. Fundamentally the NC was a realisation of the ten principles of the 1985 policy statement.[3]

In July 1987 the Secretary of State for Education, the Rt. Hon. Kenneth Baker, set up a working party of nineteen teachers, inspectors and lecturers to draft out a science National Curriculum. Their initial brief was to produce an interim report by November 1987 outlining:[13]

- the contribution of science to the overall school curriculum . . .
- the group's provisional thinking about the knowledge, skills, understanding and aptitudes which pupils of different abilities and maturity should be expected to have attained and be able to demonstrate at or around the end of the academic year in which they reach the ages of 7, 11, 14 and 16 . . .
- their provisional thinking about the programme of study from 5–16 that would be consistent with the attainment targets provisionally identified

This was later expanded to include technology at the primary school level. Teachers were invited to comment on the Interim Report as were various organisations that had an interest in science education. By August 1988 the working party had prepared a set of proposals,[14] which were submitted for further consultation. This, more substantial document, not only described their suggested framework for the curriculum but also indicated how the work could be delivered. Its publication marked a major change in the way science is taught in schools and although its structure was not carried through to the final curriculum document its principles set the foundations for the existing course. The major differences between the 1988 document and the current NC are:

1988	twenty-two attainment targets	1991	four attainmenti targets*
	four profile components		one profile component†
	included technology for KS1 and 2‡		technology in a separate curriculum document

* Attainment targets (ATs) represent the knowledge, skills and understanding that pupils of different abilities and maturities are expected to have by the end of each key stage.
† Profile components (PCs) are the means by which a pupil's progress is reported at the end of each key stage. The NC science (1991) document only requires teachers to give an overall report for science.
‡ Key stages (KS) represent certain age ranges of pupils (see page 31). KS1 and 2 cover the age range of primary school pupils.

By December 1988 the NCC had prepared a consultation report[15] based on the responses to the proposals earlier on in the year. By this time the science programme was being described in terms of seventeen attainment targets and two profile components.

In March 1989 *The Education (National Curriculum) (Attainment Targets and Programmes of Study) Order 1989*[16] was published and the NC became law. However, it was not going to happen to all children all at once, it was to be phased in over a period of time. The principle of seventeen attainment targets and two profile components was maintained. These attainment targets were:

1. Exploration of science.
2. Variety of life.
3. Processes of life.
4. Genetics and evolution.
5. Human influences on the earth.
6. Types and uses of materials.
7. Making new materials.
8. Explaining how materials behave.
9. Earth and atmosphere
10. Forces.
11. Electricity and magnetism.
12. The scientific aspects of information technology including microelectronics.
13. Energy.
14. Sound and music.
15. Using light and electromagnetic radiation.
16. The Earth in space.
17. The nature of science.

There were two profile components: PC1 was the exploration of science and was the substance of AT1 (Sc1); PC2 represented the knowledge and understanding of science and was composed of ATs 2–17 (Sc2–17).

Each AT has associated with it ten levels of increasing difficulty from 1 to 10. With each level there are a series of statements describing the qualities that the teacher would expect of a pupil who had reached that level. These descriptors are called statements of attainment (SoAs) and there were a total of 409 statements to be assessed for each pupil during his/her school career. The generally accepted shorthand form for any statement is shown in the following example:

Sc2/3a means that the statement of attainment is from AT2 of NC science and it is at level 3. 'a' refers to the sub-paragraph of the statement at level 3.

By the end of 1990 there was considerable unease over certain aspects of NC science. In particular teachers were concerned over the large numbers of assessments that were required for any one pupil. In addition SEAC advised the Secretary of State for Education that the consistency and continuity of GCSE standards would be at risk unless the number of ATs were reduced. In May 1991, therefore, the DES and WO produced revised proposals for NC science with five attainment targets.[17] The report refers to these as new attainment targets or NATs. In line with this move for using acronyms in science you will find that some writers refer to the old attainment targets as OATs.

The five NATs were:

1. Scientific investigation.
2. Life and living processes.
3. Earth and environment.
4. Materials and their behaviour.
5. Energy and its effects.

After further consultation the DES and WO decided that the best way forward was to have a science National Curriculum with four attainment targets with a total of 176 SoAs, reducing the number to less than half those in the 1989 order. In addition to making the task of assessment and record keeping that much easier, this new NC[7] had other features which made it a more workable document. The major changes were:

1. *In content.* Examples were given to help the teacher judge the level of the SoA.

Although the programmes of study (PoS) were largely unchanged from the 1989 document, there were a few changes in order to improve the sequence of ideas presented to the pupils. There were corresponding changes in the SoAs.

AT1 was simplified and the levels adjusted to refine the progression from level 1 to level 10.

2. *In layout.* The PoS for each KS was written separately making it easier to pick out the work for each age group.

The work was presented in the landscape format making it easier to connect parts of the PoS, the SoAs and the examples. The terms 'model A' and 'model B' science were replaced by 'double science' and 'single science'.

Things to do

Examine a copy of *Science in the National Curriculum (The 1991 Orders)*[7] paying particular attention to:

- the layout
- the *Science Non-statutory Guidance* (1992),[18] pages 1 to 7
- the General Introductions to KS3 (page 13) and KS4 (double science) (page 22)
- the poster that accompanies the non-statutory guidance

Write down five ways in which this science course differs from the way in which you were taught science.

The science National Curriculum 1991 onwards

The four key stages

For administrative and testing purposes the time of compulsory education is broken down into four periods called key stages (KS). These cover the age ranges 5–7 (KS1), 7–11 (KS2), 11–14 (KS3) and 14–16 (KS4). At the end of each key stage the pupil's progress is reviewed by teachers and they make a judgement as to their overall attainment in science. In addition, at the end of KS1–3, pupils take nationally set tests to help to standardise the teachers' judgements. These national tests are still referred to by some teachers as 'standard assessment tasks' or SATs, although this term has been dropped by the DES. The results of these tests are used along with the information from the results of teacher assessment (TA) to determine an overall result for a pupil's work in science. At the end of KS4 pupils sit the GCSE examination.

As part of the process of implementing the NC into schools it was decided to introduce a system for numbering the classes that would be continuous through primary and secondary education. This reinforces the principle that there is a continuum of education from the age of 5 through to 16 and no break in progress when the child leaves the primary school to go to the secondary school. The first year of compulsory education in the primary school (previously called 'infants 1' or I1 was renamed year 1. The first year in the secondary school then starts at year 7 and goes through to year 11 (the old fifth form).

The four attainment targets

In the 1991 version of the NC science there are four attainment targets (ATs), i.e. four headings under which the teacher has to describe the progress of the pupils in his/her class. The four ATs are:

Sc1   Scientific investigation
Sc2   Life and living processes
Sc3   Materials and their properties
Sc4   Physical processes

When referring to each of the science ATs they are generally prefixed by the letters Sc. Similar abbreviations are use for the other NC subjects, e.g. English is En, mathematics is Ma, geography is Gg. On a simplistic level the four ATs of science represent: practical work, biology, chemistry and physics in that order. Each of the ATs is divided into a number of strands of progression that describe how the main scientific ideas develop through the NC levels. In ATs 2–4 the PoS is written in separate paragraphs corresponding to the strand headings and, in general, the sequence of SoAs is the same as the sequence of strands for that AT (see the paragraph below on matching the PoS with the SoAs). Table 2.1 lists the four ATs with their associated strands for KS3 and KS4 (double science).

Table 2.1 **The strands of the science National Curriculum for key stage 3 and key stage 4 (double science)**

Attainment target	Strands
1. Scientific investigation	The activities should encourage the ability to plan and carry out investigations in which pupils: i) ask questions, predict and hypothesise ii) observe, measure and manipulate variables iii) interpret their results and evaluate scientific evidence
2. Life and living processes	Pupils should develop knowledge and understanding of: i) life processes and the organisation of living things ii) variation and the mechanisms of inheritance and evolution iii) populations and human influences within ecosystems iv) energy flows and cycles of matter within ecosystems
3. Materials and their properties	Pupils should develop knowledge and understanding of: i) the properties, classification and structure of materials ii) explanations of the properties of materials iii) chemical changes iv) the Earth and its atmosphere
4. Physical processes	Pupils should develop knowledge and understanding of: i) electricity and magnetism ii) energy resources and energy transfer iii) forces and their effects iv) light and sound v) the Earth's place in the Universe

The ten levels

As with the 1989 version of the NC each attainment target was described in terms of a PoS and ten levels with the attainment at each level described by a series of SoAs. It is not always easy to understand the full meaning of these statements and there is the possibility that different teachers might interpret them in different ways. Three terms that are frequently used in the SoAs have special meanings:

1. *Understand* means that a pupil is able to apply and use knowledge in new, given situations.
2. *Know that* means that recall is expected.
3. *Know about* means that a generalised awareness of a subject is expected, without necessarily having recall. This more generalised knowledge can be focused through different contexts.

There are various ways of determining the meaning of the statements such as looking at the examples given in the NC, checking through past national test papers for KS3, looking at the way examination boards have interpreted the SoA and by discussing the statements with teacher colleagues.

Things to do

Write down what you would expect of a pupil who, in your opinion, had fulfilled the SoAs listed below. Start off with an area of science that you are familiar with and then attempt to do the others. You must look through the corresponding section in the PoS. Pupils should:

Sc2/6d   understand population changes in predator-prey relationships
Sc3/4b   know that materials from a variety of sources can be converted into new and useful products by chemical reactions
Sc4/7c   be able to evaluate methods of reducing wasteful transfers of energy by using a definition of energy efficiency

   If possible, ask a colleague to do the same and compare your interpretation with your colleague's. Agreement over what each statement means can be achieved through this process of discussion.

The SoA for each AT are intended to be expressed and ordered in ways that indicate the progression that is possible in pupils' knowledge, skills and understanding. Obviously not all pupils will progress at the same rate but one of the goals of the NC is to cater for pupils of all abilities. Using the PoS teachers are able to prepare schemes of work that are sufficiently flexible so that all pupils can make progress through the levels as they move through the education system. Figure 2.1 shows the range of levels that pupils are expected to obtain at the end of the key stages. At the start of each PoS you will see a note indicating the range of levels that the PoS supports.

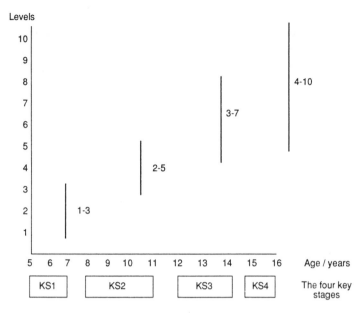

Figure 2.1   **The spread of levels at the end of the key stages**

The KS4 courses

Schools have made many changes as to the way they teach and assess 14–16 year-olds over the last few years. It is unlikely that the situation is now static but at present there are three possible routes for pupils at KS4:

- an extended course leading to three separate awards (biology, chemistry and physics) at GCSE level (first syllabuses were available in 1993)
- a full course leading to two GCSE awards (double science)
- a reduced course leading to one GCSE award (single science)

Details of both the single and double science courses are given in the NC science document. The separate sciences courses have been prepared by examination boards by building upon the PoS for KS4 double science using a set of criteria laid down by SEAC. The additional material required to give three separate syllabuses is shown in Table 2.2.

Table 2.2 **The framework for key stage 4 syllabuses in the separate sciences**

	Sc1	Subject core	Subject extension
Biology	25%	Sc2: 50%	New strands: 25%
Chemistry	25%	Sc3i, (Sc3ii), Sc3iii, (Sc3iv): about 40%	
			New strands: about 35%
Physics	25%	Sc4, (Sc3ii), (Sc3iv): about 60%	New strands: about 15%

The single science course has been constructed by omitting parts of the full course. These are:

- Sc2 strand iii   populations and human influences within ecosystems
- Sc2 strand iv   energy flows and cycles of matter within ecosystems
- Sc3 strand iii   chemical changes
- Sc3 strand iv   the Earth and its atmosphere
- Sc4 strand iv   light and sound
- Sc4 strand v   the Earth's place in the Universe

Matching the statements of attainment with the programme of study

Set out in the paragraph below is a section from the PoS for KS3 on the left and the corresponding sections from the SoAs on the right.

Programme of study for key stage 3	**Corresponding statements of attainment**
Attainment target 3: Materials and their properties	Pupils should:
Strand iii: Chemical changes	
Pupils should be made aware of the range of sources of raw materials, including those derived from the air, rocks, fossil fuels and living things. They should become aware of the role of oxygen in combustion. They should investigate examples of different types of reactions, such as combustion, thermal decomposition, salt formation, oxidation and reduction, neutralisation, electrolysis and fermentation, recognising that in chemical reactions energy changes may be evident. Pupils should construct word equations to describe chemical reactions. They should investigate factors such as temperature, concentration, particle	LEVEL 3a: be able to link the use of common materials to their simple properties. LEVEL 4b: know that materials from a variety of sources can be converted into new and useful products by chemical reactions. LEVEL 4c: know that the combustion of fuel releases energy and produces waste gases. LEVEL 5c: understand that rusting and burning involve a reaction with oxygen. LEVEL 6c: understand oxidation processes, including combustion, as reactions with oxygen to form oxides.

Table continued

Programme of study for key stage 3	Corresponding statements of attainment
size and catalysis, which influence the rate of a chemical reaction and, where possible attempt simple quantitative relationships and explanations. The work should illustrate ways in which chemical reactions lead to the formation of new materials and relate to everyday processes such as corrosion and food oxidation; they should relate reactions to information about manufacturing processes involved in metal extraction, the petroleum industry and fermentation.	LEVEL 6e: know that some chemical reactions are exothermic, while others are endothermic. LEVEL 6f: know about the readily observable effects of electrolysis. LEVEL 7a: be able to relate the properties of a variety of classes of materials to their everyday uses. LEVEL 7f: understand the factors that influence the rate of a chemical reaction. LEVEL 7g: be able to relate knowledge and understanding of chemical principles to manufacturing processes and everyday effects.

The PoS represents all the material that has to be taught and assessed. The SoAs give guidance as to the level of assessment. In some cases you may not find SoAs that are matched to the PoS but this does not mean that this particular part of the PoS is not to be assessed. Teachers will make judgements on a pupil's performance by examining related SoAs and by using their professional experience. It is not necessary to formally assess all the work that is taught. For example, in the example above, you will see that pupils will spend time studying a variety of different types of chemical reactions but they will not be asked questions on them all in one of the national tests.

Attainment target 1: scientific investigation

This attainment target is mainly about the type of practical work that pupils should be involved with during their NC course. The emphasis is on pupils finding things out for themselves through mini research exercises. Although the main emphasis is on experimental work, pupils are also required to search out relevant data in computer data banks and books. Investigations might also involve using computers to monitor or control experiments. Pupils may also carry out a survey or administer a questionnaire to help them find out the answer to their question. There is no intention that the pupils should be given the task of discovering the fundamental laws of science for themselves. This type of practical work is aimed at giving pupils the skills that they need to tackle scientific problems (see Chapter 5 for a fuller treatment of the various types of practical work used in schools).

Sc1 should not be taught in isolation but should be woven into the teaching programmes of the other attainment targets. There are examples in the NC science documents showing how this can be done.

Things to do

Using the NC science (1991) document, turn to an AT for KS3 where you are familiar with the subject matter and then focus in on the PoS for one of the strands. Locate the corresponding parts in the SoAs. Take a small section of the PoS where you can clearly link it to a SoA and then write down a list of teaching ideas that could be used to teach this area.

Write down ways that you could incorporate aspects of Sc1.

The nature of scientific ideas

Science should not be taught as an abstract list of concepts but as an activity carried out by humans with all the flaws that humans have. Our knowledge of science has been influenced by a whole array of factors, from the desire to grow more crops to the need to destroy our enemy. This area of the NC is concerned with the ways in which scientific ideas change with time and how the nature of these ideas and the uses to which they are put are affected by the social, moral, spiritual and cultural contexts in which they are developed. The general introduction to the PoS for each key stage reminds teachers about the importance of the nature of science and examples are given in the PoS for each AT. For example:

KS3, Sc1 PoS	Pupils should be encouraged to develop investigative skills and understanding of science through activities which offer opportunities to understand the limitations of scientific evidence and the provisional nature of proof
KS4, Sc4 PoS paragraph v	Pupils should examine ideas that have been used in the past and more recently, to explain the character and origin of the Earth, other planets, stars and the universe
KS4, Sc2 PoS paragraph ii	They (pupils) should consider the evidence for evolution and explore the ideas of variability and selective breeding. They should consider the social, economic and ethical aspects of cloning and selective breeding

Science in an everyday context

Pupils should be made aware that science is not just a process that is carried out in a laboratory but something that affects each one of us on a day-to-day basis. Most pupils quickly see the significance of the work they do on health and hygiene and see this as an important part of their work. An increasing number of young people are becoming 'environmentally aware' and find it easy to relate to this part of their studies. However, pupils find it difficult to come to terms with the very large impact that science has on our lives both in terms of the products produced and the financial and environmental considerations. The paragraph in the introduction to the PoS entitled 'the application of science' outlines the areas that teachers should include in their work. Teaching this aspect of the NC can involve working with other departments in the school. The cross-curricular guides give examples of interdepartmental co-operation.

Things to do

Two examples of the application of science are given below, showing how the area of study overlaps with other subject areas. Working with a trainee teacher from the appropriate subject specialism, devise plans for a joint approach to the teaching.

Example 1

Examine the links that could be made between the science department and the geography department over the teaching of iron and steel manufacture.

From NC science: Read through the PoS for KS4 Sc3 strand iii (page 27) and the corresponding SoA, Sc3/7g, and example given on page 28.

From NC geography:[19] In the PoS for KS4 it states, 'Pupils should be taught why economic activities may develop in particular locations . . .' (page 53). It also requires that pupils carry out a comparative study of a manufacturing industry (page 50). The corresponding section in the attainment targets is in Gg4/7c (page 21) where it states, 'Pupils should be able to explain the effects on selected economic activities of developments in communication and transport systems, and the issues that arise from these developments.'

Use the curriculum guidance documents on Environmental Education, Economic and Industrial Understanding, and Careers Education and Guidance to determine ways of linking the work in the two subjects. SATIS units 103 and 205[20] together with resources from British Steel are useful in teaching this topic.

Things to do continued

Example 2

Examine the links that could be made between the science department and the history department over the teaching of space exploration.

From NC science: Read through the PoS for KS4 Sc4 strand v (page 31).

From NC history:[21] One of the options at KS4 is a study of scientific and technological developments since 1945. The three topics in this option are: the nuclear age, space exploration and new technologies.

Communication

Scientists need to be able to communicate their ideas to other scientists and the world at large. NC science seeks to promote these skills in young people by encouraging them to seek out information for themselves using a variety of sources and to experiment with different ways of communicating their knowledge of science to others. They should recognise the teacher as only one of the many sources of information and should learn how to use reference material, databases, catalogues, articles in newspapers and magazines to increase their knowledge. It is also important that pupils use a variety of methods to report their work rather than just keeping to the traditional account in an exercise book. Pupils are now encouraged to give oral reports of some aspects of their work or you will find pupils presenting their findings from an experiment or survey on a poster. They will also use word-processing and desk-top publishing packages to give a really polished look to important aspects of their work. (See Chapters 6 and 7 for methods of improving pupils' communication skills.)

The use of microcomputers

Information technology (IT) is one of the cross-curricular competencies required of all pupils studying the NC. In each school an information technology coordinator will organise the use of microcomputers in all subjects areas. There are plenty of opportunities for using computers in science lessons, both as a learning aid and as a tool to help with experimental work. The NC science document makes several references to using computers, for example:

PoS for Sc1 KS4 (page 23)	give opportunities to use information technology to gather and display data from experiments, to access and organise data relevant to their study of science, and to use programmable systems to control external electronic, electrical or mechanical devices

Microcomputers, of various types, are now commonplace in schools. Some, hopefully, are situated in the laboratory while others are placed in a computer (or IT) room. Computer systems vary and, if you are not familiar with the type installed in your school, you will need to seek advice as to how to operate it and spend some time familiarising yourself with the science software available. (See Chapter 7 for a fuller treatment of using IT in science lessons.)

The assessment procedure

The assessment of pupils' learning of NC science is not very different from any other form of good assessment practice. It will take place throughout the pupils' career in school and will involve a variety of testing techniques. Through written tests, marking pupils' books and listening and watching pupils at work, the teacher will periodically make judgements on their capabilities. The criteria set out in the SoAs interpret their judgements into levels on a ten-point scale. These teacher assessments (TAs) of a pupil's performance are checked for consistency of standards within a school (internal moderation). Standards across schools (external moderation) are checked at KS3 by the national tests in Sc2–4. There are no national tests for Sc1. This is assessed by teachers and their reports of pupils' achievements are sent to the external moderating body. At KS4 pupils are assessed on Sc2–4 by the GCSE examination and Sc1 through their investigative work throughout the KS. (See Chapter 9 for further information on NC assessment.)

2.3 POST-16 SCIENCE COURSES

In the previous sections of this chapter we have seen how NC science has been devised by considering what skills and processes, knowledge and understanding all pupils need to possess in order to cope better with life. What then is the rationale behind A-level? How were these syllabuses devised? For the most part, A-level courses represent the skills and processes, knowledge and understanding that students need to know to go on to study the subject at a higher level, say at university. For years these A-level courses played a dominant role not just in the education of post-16 pupils but they also had an important influence in determining the content of O-level, and hence Certificate of Secondary Education (CSE), courses. The O-level courses were constructed in such a way that they prepared pupils for A-level courses even though the vast majority of students would not go on to study the subject at A-level, never mind go on to university. In other words the school curriculum was determined for the few who went on to higher education. This 'top-down' approach to curriculum design has fallen into disfavour. The NC would claim to be a 'bottom- up' approach catering for all pupils. This two pronged attack at writing science curricula has led to problems. At present there are areas of discontinuity between the pre-16 courses and the post-16 courses.

While the major upheaval in the 11–16 science curriculum has been taking place there has been a much quieter, and on-going, revolution taking place in post-16 education. As well as the problems highlighted above many teachers have come to realise that traditional A-level courses are inappropriate for the majority of students who now wish to remain in education post-16. Attention has been directed towards the vocational route to higher education in addition to the traditional academic one. Whereas the universities, the Civil Service and the professions have developed academic qualifications, the technical and vocational qualifications have been developed for trades and crafts, largely through the Business and Technician Education Council (BTEC), the Royal Society of Arts (RSA) and City and Guilds. There are a whole range of courses for the post-16 student.

Post-16 assessment and qualifications

At present there is no national policy on post-16 courses although the Secretary of State with the help of SEAC and the National Council for Vocational Qualifications (NCVQ) is attempting to develop one. The Secretary of State and SEAC are attempting to raise the status of vocational qualifications by the introduction of diplomas and certificates and the establishment by the NCVQ of standards criteria, in which academic and vocational courses are given a NVQ 'level' and more vocational courses are intended to lead to higher education.

Table 2.3 **Comparison of NVQ levels with more traditional qualifications**

Traditional qualification	NVQ level	General NVQ descriptor	Occupationally specific NVQ descriptor
	5	Vocationally related post-graduate qualifications	Professional qualifications (middle management)
Degree	4	Vocationally related degrees/ Higher National Diploma	Higher technician (junior management)
A/AS level	3	Vocationally related National Diploma. Advanced Craft Preparation	Technician, Advanced Craft Supervisor
GCSE	2	Broad-based Craftsmen Foundation	Basic Craft Certificate
Lower levels of the National Curriculum	1	Pre-vocational Certificate	Semi-skilled

Present post-16 qualifications

There is a range of post-16 qualifications which can be quite daunting to anyone coming to them for the first time. The following list give a brief outline of those currently available.

1. 'Academic' courses

The majority of 16-year-old students staying on full time in education are attempting A- or AS-levels. A fairly small percentage of pupils repeat GCSE examinations. Some part-time students may take further GCSE examinations.

2. Technological Baccalaureate (TechBac)

This scheme is being piloted in City Technology Colleges (CTCs), Further Education (FE) colleges and schools between 1991and 1993 and is accredited by City and Guilds. There are three levels of certification:

(a) TechBac for those wanting 'technological' employment (equivalent to GNVQ level 2).
(b) TechBac with credit for entry to technological, business or management diplomas (equivalent to GNVQ level 3, or two A-levels plus the NCC's six core skills, see later).
(c) TechBac with distinction meeting the entry requirements for undergraduate study (equivalent to three A-levels plus the NCC's six core skills, see later).

Science is a compulsory element for all students studying for the TechBac. The syllabus contains elements of physics, chemistry and biology under eighteen topic headings.

3. BTEC first

This is a vocational qualification, accredited by the Business and Technical Education Council (BTEC). Students start at 16 with no formal entry requirements and receive a certificate after one year of successful part-time study (after completing five units of study) or a diploma after one year full-time or two years part-time (after completing eight units of study). It is well established in further education and was introduced into schools in 1991. The BTEC first in science consists of a core studies component and option units from the separate science areas, information technology and specialist technologies.

Other courses include business and finance, distribution, construction, leisure, hotel and catering studies, engineering and caring.

4. BTEC National

This is a qualification for technicians and junior management. Students start at 16 with either a BTEC first or four GCSE's A–C, and receive a certificate after two years part-time or a diploma after two years full-time or three years part-time. It is equivalent to A-level and leads to higher education either following the vocational route to a BTEC Higher National or the academic route to a degree.

It is well established in further education and in 1991 started in schools. Courses include business, IT, agriculture, design, construction, catering and science. The courses cover the three main science disciplines and in addition allow students to study specialised options such as cell biology and biochemistry.

5. *Diploma of Vocational Education (DOVE)*

Until 1991 this was the CPVE, Certificate of Pre-vocational Education. It is accredited through City and Guilds and can now be taken by students aged from 14–19. The first level, Foundation level, can be taken alongside NC work at KS4. It gives students the opportunity to develop personal and social skills, and to acquire skills and knowledge within a broad vocational context, such as business studies, manufacturing and technical services or health and social care. The Intermediate and National levels are closely aligned with the nine occupational areas identified by the NCVQ, i.e.

Tending animals plants and land	Construction
Extracting and providing natural resources	Engineering
Providing goods and services	Manufacturing
Communication and entertaining	Providing business services
Providing health, social care and protective services	

6. *National Vocational Qualifications (NVQs)*

These are based on standards of competence set by industry and the actual awards are from such bodies as RSA, City and Guilds and BTEC. They are thus work qualifications. Each NVQ has a standard to be reached, a title and a level (there are five levels). All vocational qualifications will be awarded eventually within a NVQ framework and subject to control by the NCVQ. They are not intended for school pupils.

7. *General National Vocational Qualifications (GNVQs)*

These are intended for pupils or students at an FE institution who have not decided on a job. They are 'vocational qualifications of a general nature'. At level 3 they have the same standing as A-level and would thus facilitate entry into higher education. All GNVQs have an identical structure, which is analogous to NVQs. GNVQ science has eight mandatory units and a number of optional units from which the student has to choose four. The mandatory units are:

Unit 1: Data handling
Unit 2: Analysis and identification

Unit 3: Investigating materials and their use
Unit 4: Obtaining new substances
Unit 5: Obtaining products from living systems
Unit 6: Converting and using energy
Unit 7: Controlling reactions
Unit 8: Managing the human body and ecosystems

8. Certificate of Further Studies (CFS)

This is for post-16 and access students who want a pre-vocational or further year to improve their basic education. It was introduced in June 1991 and is intended for students who obtained grades D and E at GCSE. It could form part of an A- or AS-level programme – the standard being half-way to A level. There is one science syllabus, called *Science Health and Safety*. It is accredited by the Associated Examining Board (an A-level Examining Board).

The future of post-16 qualifications

The future of post-16 courses is not clear. There have been many reports and discussion documents published trying to rationalise the present picture. Notable amongst all these has been the Higginson report[22] which, besides other things, sought to broaden the education received by post-16 students. As the NC becomes established in schools it is likely that there will be changes in the curriculum for older children. Some educators are talking in terms of a key stage 5[23] continuation of the NC with a radical rethink of the present post-16 provision.

The National Curriculum has identified six core skill areas which should be incorporated into the study programmes of all 16–19 year-olds.[24] These are:

- communication
- problem solving
- personal skills
- numeracy
- information technology, and
- modern language competence

It is likely that SEAC will take on board this skill list and use it as a framework for future examination syllabuses. The NCC has recommended that the first three should be embedded, and wherever possible be an aspect of syllabus design, in all A- and AS-level syllabuses. The remaining three skills should be incorporated into total curricular provision for all students. TVEI funding is supporting the introduction of the core skills. The TVEI extension programme was introduced into schools over a period of four years starting in 1988. As a prerequisite to receiving the financial support, schools must ensure that post-16 courses contain a 'core entitlement' framework[24] consisting of the following common learning outcomes:

- communicate effectively (where possible in more than one language)
- compile and use numerical information
- use science and technology appropriately
- understand the world of work
- develop effective personal and interpersonal skills
- work independently and in teams
- solve problems
- cope positively with change

New courses are attempting to come to terms with the diverse needs of students, and curriculum developers are investigating mechanisms that give post-16 students more flexibility. Some students may wish to change the direction of their studies half-way through their course. How can they get credit for the work they have done? Some students may find that they have chosen the wrong type of course and should be aiming for a more vocationally based study rather than an academic one. How can they change from one type of course to another without losing too much ground? The modularisation of courses is one attempt at answering these questions.

A modular approach to post-16 courses

Modularisation is not peculiar to post-16 courses, in fact it is more common lower down in the school. A module is a free standing unit of learning, which usually lasts between six weeks and half a year. Each module is usually accompanied by an assessment package, which may be continuous throughout the time of the module or may be an end-of-module test. In any case the student gains feedback as to the relative success of his/her study in a relatively short timespan rather than waiting until the end of the whole course.

There has been increasing dissatisfaction with linear courses requiring students to remember large amounts of information in preparation for a terminal examination after two years of study. Breaking down the work into modules not only helps the pupils to plan out their study more effectively but also gives the teacher the opportunity to use different teaching and learning styles.

Advantages of post-16 modular courses

- They are more student-centred than traditional courses. (Students can choose the modules they wish to study. They can learn by supported self-study materials.)
- There is more choice and a wider range of opportunity. (There is a

large range of modules to choose from and some may be studied in different branches of science.)

- The modules provide short-term goals and regular feedback. (Students can sit end-of-module tests as part of their post-16 award. There may be the opportunity to re-sit module tests to improve their grade.)
- There is a reduction of examination stress as the emphasis on a final examination is diminished.
- Some modules may be common to both A- and AS-level, thus allowing students who have found the AS-course interesting, the opportunity to continue their studies to a full A-level. The opposite could also happen, where students who find the course difficult can 'cash in' their end of module tests for an AS-level.
- AS- and A-level students can be taught together as can lower and upper sixth groups.
- Some modules may bridge the academic–vocational divide.
- Courses may allow students to build up a bank of credits over a period of years, thus making them particularly attractive to part-time students.

Disadvantages of post-16 modular courses

- Students will be sitting important examinations that will contribute to their overall grade for the subject at an early stage in the course. Some may not have the necessary maturity to deal with the subject matter. Their work may be compared with other students who have studied the science subject for a longer period of time.
- The modules may be different in terms of their degree of difficulty. The end-of-module tests may vary in educational demand.
- Is a modular A-level of equal standing to a traditional A-level as far as higher education and employers are concerned?
- There may be increased pressure on teachers to complete the work in a small, fixed period of time.

A modular science course that is currently being developed is the University of Cambridge Local Examinations Syndicate Module Bank System.[25] With this system there are four A-level syllabuses available: biology, chemistry, physics, science (single award) and science (double award). Each module represents about one sixth of an A-level course and normally represents about forty-five hours teaching time. For each of the three separate science syllabuses students must study the appropriate subject foundation module and five other modules. Alternatively a set of three successfully completed modules would lead to an AS-level. One of the additional modules must be the Extended Study. This is a special feature of this course and it consists of written accounts of two, three or four investigations, one of which must be based on a work-related assignment.

Each module, with the exception of the Extended Study, is assessed by means of a written paper. The Extended Study is marked by the teacher, using criteria supplied by the board. Each of the modules is separately certificated. The student who is unable to continue with his or her studies may 'cash in' the modules for an AS-level or may store them in a 'bank' for up to five years. This gives students the flexibility of accumulating modules over a period of time.

Things to do

You will find it useful to examine a variety of syllabuses for post-16 courses. Write off to the examination boards if the selection available to you is limited.

- What type of course is going to best meet the needs of your pupils?
- Does the syllabus have options?
- How is practical work assessed?
- What support material does the examination board provide?
- What additional features are available that makes the course attractive?

NOTES AND REFERENCES

1. For an interesting discussion on what constitutes a balanced science course see: Kirkham, J., 'Balanced science: equilibrium between context, process and content,' in Wellington, J. (ed.), 1989, *Skills and Processes in Science Education: A Critical Analysis*, Routledge, London.

2. Association for Science Education, 1981, *Education through Science – Policy Statement*, ASE, Hatfield.

3. Department of Education and Science and The Welsh Office, 1985, *Science 5–16: A Statement of Policy*, HMSO, London.

4. Details about the two packs on INSET materials, *Physics for Teachers* and *Chemistry for Teachers*, are available from the Open University, Walton Hall, Milton Keynes, MK7 6YZ.

5. The focus of TVEI has now moved from 11–16 education to 16–19 education.

6. Department of Education and Science and The Welsh Office, *Education Reform Act 1988: Information Requirements Relating to the School Curriculum, and its Assessment*, HMSO, London.

7. Department of Education and Science and The Welsh Office, 1991, *Science in the National Curriculum, (The 1991 Orders)*, HMSO, London.

8. NCC and SEAC have been combined to form one body, the Schools Curriculum and Assessment Authority (SCAA).

9. CCW has become the Curriculum and Assessment Authority for Wales (CAAW).

10. National Curriculum Council, 1992, *Starting out with the National Curriculum: An Introduction to the National Curriculum and Religious Education*, NCC, York.

11. The following curriculum guides are available:

   (i) from the National Curriculum Council, York

   No. 3   The Whole Curriculum
   No. 4   Education for Economic and Industrial Understanding
   No. 5   Health Education
   No. 6   Careers Education and Guidance
   No. 7   Environmental Education

   (ii) from the Curriculum Council for Wales

   The Whole Curriculum: 5–16 in Wales
   CCW Advisory paper 7: Economic and Industrial Understanding
   CCW Advisory paper 11: Community Understanding

12. Curriculum Council for Wales, 1991, *The Whole Curriculum: 5–16 in Wales*, CCW, Cardiff.

13. Department of Education and Science and The Welsh Office, 1987, *National Curriculum: Science Working Group Interim Report*, HMSO, London.

14. Department of Education and Science and The Welsh Office, 1988, *National Curriculum Sciences for Ages 5 to 16 – Proposals*, HMSO, London.

15. Department of Education and Science and The Welsh Office, 1988, *National Curriculum Sciences: Consultation Report*, HMSO, London.

16. Department of Education and Science and The Welsh Office, 1989, *Science in the National Curriculum (The Orders)*, HMSO, London.

17. Department of Education and Science and The Welsh Office, 1991, *Science for Ages 5 to 16 (1991): Consultation Report*, HMSO, London.

18. There are two examples of non-statutory guidance (NSG) for the 1991 version of the Science NC, one for England and one for Wales. There is considerable overlap in the type of advice given in each document: National Curriculum Council, 1992, *Science: Non-statutory Guidance*, NCC, York. Curriculum Council for Wales, 1992, *Science in the National Curriculum: Non-statutory Guidance for Teachers*, CCW, Cardiff. In

addition there are the two versions of NSG for the 1989 version of the Science NC: Curriculum Council for Wales, 1989, *Science in the National Curriculum: Non-statutory Guidance for Teachers*, CCW, Cardiff. National Curriculum Council, 1989, *Science: Non-statutory Guidance*, NCC, York.

19. Department of Education and Science and The Welsh Office, 1991, *Geography in the National Curriculum*, HMSO, London.

20. Association for Science Education, *SATIS Units 103 and 205*, ASE, Hatfield.

21. Department of Education and Science and The Welsh Office, 1991, *History in the National Curriculum*, HMSO, London.

22. The following sample of reports on the future of post-16 education illustrate the nature of this important debate: Higginson Report, 1988, *Advancing A-Levels*, HMSO, London. Royal Society, 1988, *The 16–19 Science Curriculum and its Assessment: A Statement of Policy*, Royal Society, London. Schools Examinations and Assessment Council, 1989, *Consultation on the Secretaries of State's Remit to the School Examinations and Assessment Council on the Promotion of AS Examinations and the Rationalisation of A-level Syllabuses*, SEAC, London.

23. West, D. & Wilson, C., 'Key Stage 5: Science and post-16 education', in Watts, M. (ed.) 1991, *Science in the National Curriculum*, Cassell, London.

24. National Curriculum Council, 1990, *Core Skills 16–19: A Response to the Secretary of State*, NCC, York.

25. Details of the University of Cambridge Local Examinations Syndicate, Module Bank System (MBS) can be obtained from: UCLES, 1 Hills Road, Cambridge, CB1 2EU.

CHAPTER 3

Planning your work

Some people enjoy planning their days right down to the last minute, whereas others just coast through the day, doing things as they arise. The 'planners' tend to get more done but they can come up against problems and then 'the best laid schemes o' mice an' men' go awry. Most of us have some sort of semi-structured plan to our day based around key events such as times of buses and appointments. We all know that our plans may have to be changed as new circumstances arise and life teaches us to cope with these changes. In the classroom, we need to have careful planning to ensure that we achieve our teaching goals in the limited amount of time available to us. As teachers, we need to have clear plans about what we are doing and when we are doing it but, as with life in general, we need to be flexible and prepared to alter our plans. In many ways planning a one-hour science lesson is much more difficult than planning your own itinerary for the day because in your lesson you are concerned with the learning needs of each and every individual in your charge. It is, therefore, imperative that all your work is carefully thought out so that you can make the best use of the time available.

This part of the chapter is mainly about the mechanism of the planning process. It introduces you to ideas about collecting suggestions for lesson plans and how to set out your activities in a clear, logical way, which can be easily referred to in a lesson. You will need to revisit this chapter once you have a fuller picture of the teaching techniques that are available to you. It is worth while bearing in mind that you will not know everything there is know about teaching strategies in a short period of time. It is a long process based on reading and practising in the classroom. You will get more information about teaching methods in Chapter 4.

3.1 LESSON PLANNING

The planning process

Planning is a process that requires careful thought and a sound knowledge of the pupils you are going to teach. Good plans will often take a long time to prepare, especially in the initial stages of teaching. You should value them because of the time and effort you have put into them and it is worth while storing them in an appropriate place (see the section in this chapter on 'keeping a lesson note file'). There are three key questions that need to be asked in order to help you organise your plan:

What do the pupils know before they come to the lesson?
What do I want the pupils to know when they leave the lesson?
What teaching techniques and resources can I use?

To many student teachers who are starting off their career in the classroom, the task of preparing a lesson is a daunting one. 'Where do I start? The amount of information I am supposed to process is too much. I am suffering from brain overload.' Well if 'brain overload' is your problem why not start off the planning exercise with a brainstorming session. This is best done with a fellow science teacher but, if one is not available, try writing down on a piece of paper all the ideas you can think of associated with the topic of the day. You are unlikely to be able to use all of them in your lesson but it is quite likely that you will generate some useful ideas for this or even future lessons.

Things to do

Write down your good ideas on a computer or file index cards. You will need to categorise them so that they can be easily recalled, perhaps under topic headings. After a while you are likely to have a large number of ideas and may need some system of cross-referencing.

There are many other ways of gathering together suggestions for lesson plans. You will find it helpful to try some or all of the following:

- talk to pupils about the work they have been doing and any ideas they may have on the topic that you are going to teach them
- read through pupils' notes in their exercise books
- read through the workbooks or worksheets that the pupils use
- read through the scheme of work for the topic being taught
- talk to teachers who have taught the class before and other teachers who are teaching the same year group
- observe experienced teachers working with similar classes to those that you will be asked to teach
- talk to your tutor/mentor in your teacher-training department, and
- talk to the science technician who looks after your class

Objectives for science lessons

All science courses will have a series of broad aims (see Chapter 1) giving an indication of what the course is trying to achieve. The aims give general guidance to the teacher as to where the teaching emphasis should lie. However, they are not specific enough for the teacher to prepare individual lessons. More precise educational goals, called *objectives*, are derived from the aims and clearly define what the pupils should learn. Objectives are specific learning goals for your science lessons. They are a list of what you would like the pupils to be able to achieve in any one lesson or a series of related lessons. They play an important role in planning your work. As a teacher you will design the various learning activities for the lesson in order that the pupils achieve the objectives. There are two types of objectives: those that specify what a pupil should be able to do at the end of a lesson (a behavioural objective) and those that indicate the type of material being covered in the lesson (non-behavioural objectives).

Non-behavioural objectives are just one step down from the aims of a course. They indicate what the teacher intends to do during the lesson. Such objectives may begin with terms such as:

To introduce the class to –
To develop the classes understanding of the principle of –
A review of the factors involved in the –
To develop an appreciation for –
To develop a critical approach to –
To develop a positive attitude towards –

Behavioural objectives are much more specific and indicate the precise behaviour of the learner that the teacher desires. It must be possible for the pupil to demonstrate that s/he has achieved that objective through some oral, written or practical activity. This type of objective is then the basis for the assessment of pupils and by designing suitable questions or assessment exercises it is possible for the teacher to monitor whether or not the objectives have been achieved. It is important to be very specific when writing this type of objective so that they can act as an accurate checkpoint for assessment purposes. A vague behavioural objective would be, 'pupils should be familiar with the main groups of living things', as there is no precision with the word 'familiar' and the reader is left with uncertainty as to what the writer means by the 'main groups' of living things. The objective would be better written as 'pupils should be able to list the five categories of vertebrates and nine categories of invertebrates (listed in the lesson plan)'. Well-written behavioural objectives start with a phrase such as: 'At the end of the lesson pupils should be able' and continue with one of the following infinitives:

to write	to list	to demonstrate
to name	to identify	to distinguish
to describe	to select	to sequence

Things to do

- Examine a GCSE science syllabus that you are familiar with and look at the list of objectives given for the course. These may be listed under the heading 'Assessment Objectives'. Study the language used and compare it with the language used for writing the aims of the course. Examine the way in which the aims are reflected in the assessment objectives.
- You will find lesson objectives given in some teaching schemes such as the Nuffield or Salters' projects and of course in the schemes of work in your school. Examine these with reference to the teaching activities that have been designed to meet the aims.
- Ask an experienced teacher to tell you about how s/he plans teaching activities to ensure that his/her objectives are met by the pupils.
- Take one of the following paragraphs from the PoS for KS3 of the science National Curriculum and write down a corresponding list of objectives that could be used in your teaching. Do not attempt to write down a complete list as each paragraph will cover several lessons' work. You will find it helpful to look at textbooks for KS3 and to look at the appropriate sections of the NC where you will find the linked SoAs and examples.

Sc2: Life and living processes
Strand (iii): pupils should study a variety of habitats at first hand and make use of secondary sources, to investigate the range of seasonal and daily variation in physical factors, and the features of the organisms which enable them to survive these changes.

Sc3: Materials and their properties
Strand (iv): pupils should investigate practically, and by use of secondary sources, the properties of water, the water cycle, conservation of water resources and the effect of water on the Earth's surface.

Sc4: Physical processes
Strand (i): pupils should investigate qualitatively the properties of magnets, electromagnets and the nature of magnetic fields.

Check through your objectives with your tutor or an experienced science teacher.

Observing other teachers

You will learn a great deal about the planning and organisation of teaching by watching experienced teachers handle a class of pupils. Some trainee teachers regard this as the most informative way of learning about teaching. In order to make the most of these valuable occasions you should spend some time planning your observation strategy before the lesson. Lessons are a complex mixture of teacher and pupil activity and it would be impossible for you to focus on all the processes taking place in the classroom. It is, therefore, advisable that you key in on a small number of areas that you are going to pay particular attention to in any one lesson. The best way of deciding your targets for the lesson is to talk to the teacher well in advance of session and ask for some background information regarding the activities that are going to take place. Remember that most of us are sensitive to being watched and the first thing you ought to do is to ask the teacher's permission to observe the lesson. Explain to the teacher what you would like to do during the lesson and offer to help in any way you can. Table 3.1 lists a number of different techniques that a science teacher might use during the course of a lesson and linked to these are suggestions of areas for you to focus attention on.

Table 3.1 **Suggestions for observing science lessons**

Observation of	Pay particular attention to
Movement of pupils and equipment	• How the pupils are settled down at the start of the lesson • How the teacher sets out the equipment in the laboratory • How the pupils obtain equipment for practical activities • How the teacher gathers the pupils round a bench for a demonstration or class discussion • How the teacher organises the pupils for group work, role play, debate or discussion
Control and discipline	• The use of body language to control the class • How the teacher is able to calm potentially disruptive situations • The type of punishment used for different misdemeanours • How the teacher deals with particularly bad cases of disruption
Teacher talking and questioning	• The time spent on teacher talk • How the teacher involves pupils during teacher led sessions • How the teacher distributes questions around the class • Where the teacher stands during teacher led sessions • What types of questions are asked • How the teacher deals with incorrect responses
Use of audiovisual aids	• The amount of writing on the blackboard or ohp • The positioning of computers or TVs so that they can be seen by all the pupils

Table 3.1 **continued**

Observation of	Pay particular attention to
	• How the teacher presents a video or set of slides to the class
Methods of motivating the pupils	• How the teacher generates enthusiasm for the topic at the outset of the lesson • How the teacher maintains pupil interest in the subject • The way in which the teacher used the pupils' own interests and knowledge to generate enthusiasm • The teacher's attitude to the class and his/her expectations of pupils' performance
How the teacher uses the workbooks and textbooks	• How the teacher presents the topic to be completed by the pupils in their workbooks • How long the pupils spend working at their workbooks • The type of work the pupils do in their workbooks and whether any supplementary work is given • What the teacher does while the pupils are working • How the teacher directs the pupils to work from textbooks
How the teacher caters for the different abilities of the pupils in the class	• The use of differentiated work for pupils of different abilities • The way the teacher presents work to pupils with special educational needs (both gifted pupils and less-able pupils) • How the teacher rewards the pupils for good work within their own ability range • How the teacher organises the pupils for group activities within the class (e.g. mixed groups or friendship groups, single sex or mixed)
What the teacher does while the pupils are engaged in practical work	• How the teacher ensures that all the pupils are actively involved in purposeful work • How the teacher ensures that the pupils are working safely • How the teacher enables the pupils to improve their practical skills • The level of instructions given to the pupils and the ability of the pupils to carry out the practical activity • The questions the teacher asks the pupils about the practical work • How much written work is required and the style of the written work
How the teacher draws the lesson to an end	• How much the teacher uses the pupils' ideas in the summing up process at the end of the lesson • How the teacher sets the scene for the next lesson

Table 3.1 **continued**

Observation of	Pay particular attention to
	• What homework is set for the pupils • How the teacher checks that all the materials that have been used have been returned • How the teacher dismisses the pupils
How the teacher assesses pupils' progress	• How the teacher uses praise for correct answers given for oral questions • How the teacher assesses pupils' oral contributions • How the teacher assesses pupils' practical work • The frequency, composition and administration of written tests • How the teacher marks pupils' exercise books or workbooks and how these are returned to the pupils • The method of keeping records

What to include in the lesson plan

It is obviously silly to write down everything you intend to do in a lesson but it is also foolish to think that you will get away with a few comments written down on the back of an old envelope. The purpose of a lesson plan is to give you a clear picture of what you are going to teach and how you are going to teach it. It should not be cluttered with information as you will want to refer to the plan quickly during a lesson. You will probably find it useful to use different coloured pens or highlighter pens to indicate different aspects of the lesson. Try to avoid clutter on the page by spacing the work out, perhaps by writing on every other line. The list that follows indicates some of the items that should be included in a lesson plan.

A lesson plan should contain:

1. Basic information about the class, for example

*   the title of the work being covered
*   the date of the lesson
*   the time of the lesson
*   the name of the class being taught
*   a list of the equipment and resources required

2. Information about teaching the topic, for example

*   the objectives for the lesson
*   how you are going to introduce the work

- teacher and pupil activities during the lesson including questions you may wish to ask, memory joggers about snags with the equipment and how you are going to use visual aids
- how you intend to draw the lesson to a close

You may also wish to include other things in your plan such as when you are going to call the register or what you are going to write on the board. In addition to your plan you may also need to have some lesson notes. It may be that you have been asked to teach a topic that is unfamiliar to you and you have had to go away and research it prior to your lesson. In this case you will have made some notes and may want to keep them close by you during the lesson to boost your confidence. However, you should avoid reading from them in the class if at all possible, unless you can make a joke of it or it is a particularly unusual area of science and you want to emphasise to the pupils that you cannot possibly know everything.

You should consider what exactly the pupils are going to do at various times during the lesson. Think about ways of involving all the pupils actively in the learning process. If there are occasions when the pupils might be idle spectators then you should attempt to devise a method for getting them involved. Being a bystander in science lessons is not uncommon, particularly in certain types of practical activity when one pupil gets on with the experiment while the others talk about who is going out with who. You will find some ideas to overcome this type of problem in Chapter 5.

A double period of science can be a long time for some individuals and you should consider in your planning how you are going to keep up the impetus of work as the pupils get tired or just bored with a long task. Think about giving them a variety of shorter tasks or encourage them to work their way through a difficult procedure.

You will find it useful to include a brief lesson criticism when the lesson is over, pointing out to yourself where things went well and which activities went badly. If you are to improve the quality of your teaching you must be able to carry out self appraisal exercises (e.g. using a schedule such as the one shown in Figure 10.3) and be able to discuss your strengths and weaknesses with colleagues. Figure 3.1 summarises the main points in lesson preparation.

Layout of a lesson plan

Although you will find lesson plan outlines in a number of books about teaching, there is no set method for producing a 'correct' plan. You should construct a lesson plan that:

- contains all the information you require for the lesson, and
- is quick and easy to read

Things to consider   Worth consulting

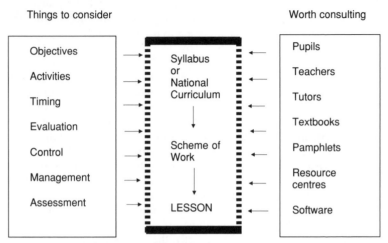

Figure 3.1 **An approach to planning**

After a few attempts at designing a suitable layout you will find a pattern that is workable for you. You may find it helpful to start off with the structure given in Figure 3.2.

Planning in detail

There are certain parts of your lesson plan that benefit from more attention to detail. In particular you should consider what is going to happen during the first five to ten minutes of the lesson. How are you going to interest the class in the topic and motivate them into doing some work? Many lesson introductions will involve some recapitulation of the previous work intermingled with questions aimed to check on the pupils' understanding. Plan in detail how you are going to introduce the new work. How can you 'sell' it to the class? Can you relate it to their interests or something topical? How can you structure it so that it is in an understandable form and not too academic? Introductions are often effective when you have all the pupils comfortably gathered round you at the front of the laboratory. They need to be sitting, preferably on stools, in a semicircle so that you can clearly see all of them and they can see you. One useful way of getting the pupils interested is through a short length of video, which may pose questions that can be answered by the work carried out in the lesson. Other methods include presenting a demonstration, reading from a newspaper article, talking about a scientific artefact that you are able to show the pupils, presenting a scenario that the pupils are going to investigate.

As well as planning the start of a lesson in detail, you need to pay

Topic[1]:   Date:

Teaching group[2]:   Room:

Number of pupils: Lesson number:

Time[3]:   Time:

Equipment list[4]:

Aims:

Objectives:

Reference[5]:

Time[6]   Introduction[7]

               Main section[8]

               Finishing off the lesson[9]

Lesson notes[10]:

Lesson criticism:

---

1 Giving a title to the lesson can be the first step in trying to give the lesson a
   focus.

2 This indicated the form/class or set that you are teaching.

3 Reminds you of when the lesson starts and finishes.

4 This may refer to the list you have given the technician. You will find it helpful to
   retain a copy.

5 A quick reference to books, articles, etc., that you have found useful in preparing
   the lesson.

6 A breakdown of roughly how long you plan to spend on each activity.

7 Details of how you are going to interest the pupils in the topic and set the scene
   for the lesson.

8 The main activities for the lesson in the order that they will be presented to the
   pupils.

9 Drawing together the main points of the lesson.

10 Additional notes that you may wish to refer to or key points that you intend to
   put up on the board.

To make important points stand out try using different coloured pens and/or highlighter
pen but be careful not to overdo it.

Figure 3.2 **The main areas of a typical lesson plan**

attention to how you are going to finish off. You may wish to draw together some key points from the work done. If the pupils have been working in groups, it may be valuable to have a short report from one or two groups about their work. It may be the case that you wish to prepare them for the next piece of work and want to send them away with something to think about. Whatever your plans are for the end of the lesson it is important that the lesson does have a definite end rather than just fading away. One problem that sometimes faces science teachers occurs when the practical work goes on until five to ten minutes before the end of the lesson. Once children have packed away their equipment they feel that the lesson has ended. It is advisable to make it clear to the class that they should not pack away their books and put on their coats until after they have tidied away their apparatus. You may find that you have to mention it several times over several weeks to 'condition' the pupils into behaving in this way.

Variation in lesson plans

There may well be times when you feel that the type of lesson plan described is inappropriate. This may be because the pupils' work on a topic spans over several lessons or because they are working in groups on different pieces of work. This should not mean that lesson planning has to be abandoned, indeed it is only with tight planning that there can be any guarantee that educational objectives can be met. In cases like these you may find it more beneficial to have plans for each task rather than a plan for the whole lesson. For each task you would consider the learning strategies to be employed and the nature of the final product from the pupils' activities. You should think about the questions you are going to ask the pupils as you move from one group to another. It is inadvisable to have too many tasks running at the same time. You may find that you have difficulty in keeping on top of the situation and may not even have a clear idea about what work individuals are involved in.

The proof of the pudding

Good planning takes a long time but you will be rewarded by having good lessons with plenty of valuable learning experiences for the pupils. As you gain in experience you will develop your planning approach so that you write down less information but in the early stages you will have to write down almost every move. If you find that you are standing around with nothing to do in your lesson, like a lemon at a lively party, then there is something wrong with your planning and the next time you prepare a lesson you ought to consider in more detail how you can relate to the needs of your pupils.

Things to do

Plan a lesson for a class that you are to teach. Make sure that you have the appropriate background information about the group and their work before you start. Use the checklist below to make sure that you have included all the relevant information.

Ensure that you have

- given the technician a clear, unambiguous list of your requirements for the lesson
- tried out the experimental work to make sure everything will run smoothly when the pupils carry out the practical
- worked out how you are going to distribute the apparatus and chemicals and how you are going to collect them in at the end of the lesson
- carried out a risk assessment for the chemicals you are going to use
- printed enough worksheets for the class
- planned what you are going to be doing in each part of the lesson and worked out approximate timings for these activities
- planned out the pupils' activities and approximate timings
- cross-checked the activities with the lesson objectives
- checked the suitability of the activities for the age and ability range of the pupils
- made a detailed plan of the start and end of your lesson
- decided on some key questions you are going to ask the pupils
- worked out how you are going to assess pupils during the lesson
- decided on how and when you are going to carry out any administration
- decided on how you are going to bring the pupils into the classroom and how you are going to settle them down
- decided on how you are going to get the pupils to change from one activity to the next

Keeping a lesson file

You will find it useful to have two levels of information: that which is in current use and that which has been used but is being retained for future reference. Your current lesson plans should be kept in a well-organised Teaching Practice file. The file should be divided into sections equating to the classes taught, with file dividers. You will find it helpful to have a title page listing the following information for quick reference:

1. Your name and present address (in case it gets lost).
2. The school's name, address and telephone number.
3. The names of the Headteacher and Deputy Headteacher(s).
4. The names of the Head (or Heads) of Department.
5. The names of class teachers.

6.   The names, addresses and telephone numbers of tutors/mentors or other individuals who are responsible for your progress as a trainee teacher.

You will also find it beneficial to collect some background information about the school and its environment. This may be obtained from the school brochure or you may need to collect it from different sources.

The information you should have may contain:

1.   Notes given to you by the school about its structure, organisation, discipline procedures and administration.
2.   A simple plan of the school, together with notes about its various facilities, etc.
3.   A neighbourhood study: a descriptive account of the physical and social background of the school and its pupils; a list of the neighbourhood facilities that may be of use during your periods of teaching (e.g. museum, library, natural environment, etc.).

In addition you will need to compile some lesson notes. These should contain:

1.   Any syllabuses, schemes of work, etc., provided by the head of department or class teacher.
2.   For each class:
     (a)   the title of the class, e.g. Y8P, Y10A, Y7Z;
     (b)   the ability group (set, stream, band, mixed);
     (c)   lists of names in each group;
     (d)   seating plans for each group;
     (e)   records: of attendance, achievements, marks, etc., and an outline sequence of work for each topic (possibly as an annotated flow diagram).

3.2   SAFETY IN THE LABORATORY

Keeping the laboratory tidy

School science laboratories are generally safe places but accidents do happen and it is the job of the science teacher to ensure that the pupils are working in the safest possible conditions. The teacher needs to be on the look out for potential hazards. The first step to take in accident prevention is to see that the pupils are working in a tidy, clutter free environment. Old worksheets, newspaper cuttings, disused yoghurt containers, all take up space where pupils may work, and can start a chain reaction for rubbish accumulation. You will need to be organised about putting materials away once they are finished with and also ruthless about throwing things away. Teachers tend to be hoarders by nature thinking that 'it will come useful one day' but if you do not file it away in some organised fashion you will never find it when you want to use it.

In most schools, coats and bags are a major problem. The pupils want to keep them nearby at all times in case they are stolen or vandalised in some way. Bags, in particular, are a major hazard in the laboratory when they are placed in the aisles between laboratory benches. There is always the possibility that someone may fall over them while carrying some glassware or even a dangerous chemical. Coats should ideally be placed on hooks at the rear of the laboratory and the bags deposited on or under a bench that is not being used for anything else. Obviously they should not be placed next to any dangerous chemicals such as acid or organic solvent. Make sure that the coats do not obscure any important signs, e.g. Fire Exit, or that they are not hung over objects such as the fire extinguisher.

The pupils' work area should be tidy and contain only those materials that are necessary for the lesson. This, of course, applies equally to teachers who should make sure that their desk is free from piles of books and papers. It is worth while setting a good example. If possible, the pupils should have an area for carrying out practical activities and another area, close at hand, for writing up the work. Pupils need to be told to inform the teacher of all chemical spills immediately. Pupils can wipe up spills of harmless materials but it is advisable for the teachers to deal with hazardous substances such as acids, alkalis and poisons.

Pupils should not be allowed to dispose of broken glass. The teacher should brush it up and place it in the special container kept in the laboratory for broken glass.

Teachers sometimes wear white laboratory coats for protection. These are a good idea as they do help to keep your clothes reasonably clean but they can be a hazard if they are not fastened up correctly. An unfastened coat can get caught on apparatus as you walk by and bring it crashing to the ground.

Safety rules for the pupils

A set of safety rules is an essential component of every pupil's notes but there is nothing more off-putting than being told that science is a dangerous subject and having the list of rules dictated to you during your first science lesson in the secondary school. A list of rules stuck in the back of a pupil's science notebook can, in some cases, be virtually useless. The pupil has to learn about safety and behaviour in the laboratory and, as in other aspects of learning about science, this cannot be done by taking down dictated notes.

An introduction to safety might involve asking the pupils about what dangers they are likely to come across in the laboratory. Eager year 7 pupils are likely to come up with lots of answers including 'explosions', 'rotting in acid', and other violent incidents. The teacher can allay their fears by telling them that laboratories are safe places to work in and that most accidents that occur are minor and are generally caused by pupils not doing what they are supposed to do. The pupils, with teacher guidance, could then be asked to compile a set of rules that everyone must obey. They could also prepare a set of posters to display around the room to remind others of safety procedures. This process will result in a set of safety rules that will be identical in content to the one that the teacher might have dictated in lesson one at the secondary school but the major difference will be in ownership. The pupil-generated rules will be more meaningful to the class than the ones handed down from on high. You should ensure that the rules cover the points listed below:

1. Never enter a laboratory without permission of a teacher.
2. Always place your bags and coats in the place provided.
3. Always walk in the laboratory, never rush or push anyone.
4. Never interfere with equipment or chemicals.
5. Never put anything in your mouth in the laboratory. In particular do not eat or drink anything. If you get something in your mouth accidently, you must spit it out at once, wash your mouth out with lots of water, and tell your teacher.
6. Never throw things in the laboratory.
7. Always wear eye protection when told to do so by your teacher.
8. Always wear disposable gloves when told to do so by your teacher.
9. Long hair must be tied back. Loose clothing (e.g. ties, long-sleeved blouses and shirts, cardigans) should not be allowed to hang freely.
10. Never take things from the laboratory without permission.
11. When heating things you must watch carefully what you are doing and:
    (a) wear safety glasses;
    (b) use only small amounts of materials; and
    (c) point the test tube into a clear space (i.e. not towards yourself or any other pupil);
    (d) never look down into a heated test tube.
12. If you get burned, or have a splash of chemical on your skin, wash it off immediately with lots of water.
13. Report all accidents and breakages to your teacher at once.

As teacher, you are in charge of the class and are responsible for the safety of the pupils. You must check that the safety rules are being implemented.

Preparing for safety

You should, wherever possible, carry out the experiments that you expect the pupils to do, well beforehand checking for possible hazards. This is particularly important for teachers who are teaching outside their subject specialism. In the case of investigations, this may not be possible but you will need to consider the various alternative strategies that you are likely to come across during the lesson and evaluate their safety. Pupils should be asked to check their own plans for possible safety problems which should be discussed with the teacher before the plan is implemented. The Control of Substances Hazardous to Health (COSHH) Regulations[1] requires teachers by law to make a risk assessment of the use of substances that are hazardous to health. You should not only consider the materials you use initially but should also consider the dangers of the products of your work. The COSHH guidance states:

Assessment Each substance must be carefully considered for the chance of it causing harm in the actual or likely circumstances of its use or storage. In the light of this assessment, any precautions to be taken should be decided upon and written down.

All science departments should keep a safety file, which will contain, amongst other safety information: DES *Safety in Education*[2] bulletins; DES *Safety in Science Laboratories* (3rd edition)[3]; Health and Safety Commission, *COSHH: Guidance for schools*; ASE *Safety in the School Laboratory,*[4] and ASE *Topics in Safety.*[5] If you are using chemicals, you must consult Chapter 8 in *Topics in Safety* where you will find a comprehensive list of school chemicals and their restriction in schools. You should also look up the chemical in the CLEAPSS School Science Service *Hazcards.*[6] This will give you detailed information about its toxicity and what to do in the event of an accident. It is your job as teacher to consult the safety literature and make decisions as to how to carry out the practical activity as safely as possible. Tawney[7] has suggested that teachers work through the following sequence of questions in order to carry out a risk assessment:

• Is it advisable to do the experiment at this level?	Guidance is given in Chapters 5, 7 and 8 in *Topics in Safety*, on the backs of *Hazcards* and elsewhere.
• If the substances to be used are toxic or corrosive, can substitutes be found or changes made?	Substitutes are suggested on *Hazcards* and in CLEAPSS Guide L195.[6] Dilutions or the use of smaller quantities can also be effective.
• Can procedures be made safer for pupils?	For example, by the teacher or technician pouring out hazardous substances into the appropriate apparatus prior to the lesson.

The information about the risks involved in an experiment should be written into all the relevant documents: the lesson plan, the scheme of work and pupils' worksheets. In addition to writing down the hazards they should be repeated orally to the pupils.

A danger can arise when substances are transferred from the stock bottle to another container, such as a beaker, for easier distribution to the class. In this situation the new container must be clearly labelled as to:

- the name of the substance
- the concentration of the substance if it is in solution
- the hazard involved, preferably with a hazard warning symbol

Under no circumstances should substances go unlabelled.

Terrible accidents have happened when teachers have carried out explosive reactions in an attempt to motivate pupils or to end the term with a bang. Teachers carrying out this type of activity could seriously injure themselves or pupils and could face legal action and subsequent dismissal from the profession. In a recent case a teacher was experimenting with gunpowder and the mortar held by one of the pupils exploded in his hand, causing extensive damage and perforating his eardrums. The teacher was fined and later dismissed from his post.[8]

Things to do

Safety situations

Using the books at your disposal on safety, write down what you would do under the following circumstances:

1. A pupil has prepared some copper(II) sulphate crystals and she has decided to take a particularly good specimen home to show her parents.
2. You are doing a topic about cells and you want the pupils to see some animal cells under a microscope.
3. You want the pupils to investigate the stretching of a wire by hanging a range of masses from the free end of the wire.
4. A mercury-in-glass thermometer has been broken by a pupil.
5. The technician has forgotten how to dilute concentrated sulphuric acid and asks you for help.

Comments on these five situations are given in the Notes at the end of this chapter.[9]

Wearing eye protection

Most pupils are quite co-operative about wearing eye protection either because they know it makes sense or because they think it makes the work look more scientific. It is a good idea to introduce pupils to using eye protection as soon as they start secondary science. Some pupils may have used it already in their primary school. Some pupils do not take to wearing eye protection either because it affects their hair style, it isn't trendy or they just want to be awkward. The worst group of pupils are those that want to hold the safety glasses over their eyes for a while as though they were an enlarged monocle and then put them down for an interval. It can be during this interval that disaster happens. For example, it has been known for chemicals to be accidently spilled into the upturned glasses while on the bench; when the owner goes to put the glasses on again after the interlude the chemical gets into his/her eye.

Whenever the eye is likely to be at risk the eye protection should be worn. This includes all experiments involving chemicals, heating experiments and those involving liquids (with the possible exception of cold water). Eye protection should be worn all the time the experiment is in progress, including during the collection of chemicals and it should be worn by all members of the experimenting group and, of course, by the teacher. It should even be worn when pupils are clearing away and washing up their apparatus. When the teacher is demonstrating a hazardous experiment s/he should protect the pupils, using a safety shield, but in addition, everybody in the class should wear eye protection.

There are three basic types of eye protection: safety spectacles, goggles and a face shield. Face shields give the most protection but they can be relatively expensive to buy and bulky to store. Goggles provide good protection for the eyes but they tend to mist up after a while and can become uncomfortable to wear. Goggles also affect certain types of hair style. Spectacles are probably the cheapest of the three to buy, they are comfortable to wear, they do not affect hair styles and they appeal to the more fashion conscious pupils who do not like to look too 'way out'. A full treatment of the relative merits of the different types of eye protection is given in *Topics in Safety*, page 6, and you should look out for the *Which?* type reports published by CLEAPSS School Science Service that are published periodically. The August 1991 report (Eye Protection L135)[10] comments on the current models available and lists their prices.

If a pupil is unfortunate enough to get some material in his/her eye then the best way of treating it is to wash the eye with a steady flow of water from the tap. The best way of doing this is to have a piece of wide-bore rubber tubing attached to the tap and gently play the stream of water on to the pupil's eye while his/her head is over the sink. If there is glass in the eye, or if the pupil continues to show discomfort, you should get immediate medical help.

The principle about wearing special safety goggles when working with lasers in schools is not fully established. The DES circular on this subject states that teachers and pupils should wear the appropriate eye protection. However, if these goggles are worn, it is impossible to see the laser beam. This could result in the beam being misdirected into a person's eye. Teachers should carefully consider the layout of the apparatus when setting it up so that any possibility of a stray beam is eliminated.

Keeping clean

In the first paragraph of this chapter it was mentioned that laboratories should be tidy places with things put back in their correct location and surfaces clear from clutter. They should also be clean places to work, where all spills are quickly wiped up and mess disposed of. The most likely place for pupils to pick up contamination is on their hands. Disposable gloves are available but they can be relatively expensive and teachers generally reserve these for dealing with the most harmful chemicals. It is generally quite sufficient for pupils and staff to wash their hands with warm soapy water (hot water could increase the likelihood of the chemical being absorbed into the skin) after dealing with chemicals, animals or animal material, plant material, or soil.

There are occasions when pupils need to share the use of mouthpieces and other objects that go in their mouths such as dental mirrors. These need to be washed in a disinfectant solution between use. It is advisable to clean the microscope eyepieces with disinfectant after pupil use to prevent the cross-infection of certain eye disorders.

Problems with electricity

Check that you know where the master switch is for each laboratory that you work in. You may need to switch the electricity off quickly if an emergency arises. You will always have the destructive element in the school who are hell bent on giving themselves electric shocks, short-circuiting your batteries, ruining your best voltmeter and trying to reproduce the 'Frankenstein' experiment. As a teacher your job is to direct pupils' energies into more productive tasks. It will require a clear explanation of what they are to do and what they are not allowed to do, together with the consequences for misbehaviour. It is worth checking all plugs on a regular basis to look for loose connections and to see if the correct fuse is fitted. Most items in a school laboratory require only a 3 A fuse. The fuse rating is sometimes given on the electrical item. Alternatively the power rating (in watts) is given and a simple calculation (see most GCSE physics textbooks) gives you the value of the fuse to be used. If you are in any doubt you should consult an electrician or a reputable electrical repair shop.

You should check that none of the thin electric cables appears outside the plug. The thicker cable containing the three types of wiring should be firmly anchored to the plug so that it would not easily come adrift if subjected to a sharp pull.

There have been cases reported of teachers suffering a severe shock from a demonstration of power lines. In this experiment 12 V is transformed up to about 200 V, passed along model power lines and then transformed down again. The Health and Safety Executive have issued the following advice on this experiment:[11]

The experiments may continue if one of the following precautions, or any other equally effective precautions are taken:

(a) the voltage of the transmission line is limited to 50 volt ac rms or 120 volt dc;
(b) the demonstration as a whole is located within an enclosure constructed, for example, in clear polycarbonate so that live conductors operating above 50 volt ac rms or 120 volt dc cannot be touched, or,
(c) all conductors and terminations, etc., operating above 50 volt ac rms are fully insulated so that live conductors cannot be touched.

If you are not familiar with the terms 'ac rms' and 'dc' you should check these out in a GCSE physics textbook.

Care must be taken that water is not spilled on to electric wire. If a spillage occurs the electrical device must be switched off immediately and the water mopped up.

Radioactivity

A qualified science teacher is allowed to use the standard sealed sources employed in schools together with the thoron generators and the uranium compounds required to prepare the protactinium source. No source should be handled or pointed at anyone. You should only use the tongs provided with the radioactivity kit.

Fire precautions

Most laboratory fires are small and can be extinguished within a matter of minutes. A common problem occurs when a pupil disobeys instructions and attempts to light his/her Bunsen burner from a friend's burner using a piece of scrap paper. The burning paper gets out of control and falls on to an exercise book. Another problem occurs when pupils forget to tie back long hair or when they have long baggy sleeves that they accidently put in the Bunsen flame. Parents are particularly displeased when expensive items of clothing are damaged in this way. Hair that has been treated with lacquer is a particular hazard as it can burn very rapidly.

You should check that:

- Bunsen burner flames are turned to yellow when they are not in use
- flammable materials are removed from the area around the Bunsen flame
- you know the location of the main gas tap and are able to switch it off in an emergency
- flammable solvents (e.g. alcohol, petroleum spirit, propanone) should not be heated directly with a Bunsen flame, instead a water bath should be used
- you are fully aware of the dangers of the materials you are dealing with and have carried out a formal risk assessment
- you know where the fire extinguishers are and how to use them
- both you and your pupils know the school fire drill

The various types of fire extinguishers have different uses in the laboratory. Table 3.2 summarises the purpose of each of the common types.

Table 3.2   **Fire extinguishers and their uses**

Extinguisher	Suitable for	Not suitable for
Carbon dioxide	Most laboratory fires	Fires in animal rooms and burning metals
Dry powders	All laboratory fires	
Expelled water	A few laboratory fires	Electrical fires and certain chemical fires
Foam	Useful for flammable liquid fires	
Halogenated hydrocarbons	Many laboratory fires	Burning metals (NB the vapour evolved is dangerous)
Sand	Burning metals	
Fire blanket (glass fibre)	Wrapping up pupils if their clothes have caught fire	

Things to do

Check that you know where all the fire extinguishers are in all the laboratories you teach in and that you know how to use them. Be clear about the fire safety drill used in the school. There should be two exits in each laboratory. Make sure that the doors are unlocked each time you use the room and that the exits are clear from clutter, stools, etc.

Practise putting out a small alcohol fire in a boiling tube by covering the top of the tube with a heat-proof mat and removing the source of ignition.

First Aid

You must be aware of those pupils who have been known to have had epileptic fits or bouts of unconsciousness. You should take advice from a medically qualified person as to what to do with these pupils if such a fit were to occur in your lesson.

Most of the first aid you will have to do will be limited to minor cuts and burns. In both cases the affected area should first be treated with lots of cold water. The burn should be left unbandaged but an open wound should be protected with a plaster.

You will find it useful to go on a first aid course such as those offered by the Red Cross and St John's Ambulance Brigade or at the very least become familiar with the principles of first aid by reading a suitable book.[12]

3.3 PREPARING WORKSHEETS

The word 'worksheet' covers many different types of documents given to pupils but they generally fall into the following broad headings:

Information sheets	These take the place of pupils' notes and require little work from them. They ensure that the pupils have a correct account of the work but do little to encourage them to learn. Pupils are pleased to accept them but often find the lessons boring because they are only passive receivers of knowledge.
Instruction sheets	These are often used with practical exercises. They give the pupils a step-by-step approach to carrying out an experiment. In some cases these can be little more than a recipe for pupils to follow mindlessly. The instructions need to be interspersed with questions asking the pupils about the stages of the practical.
A learning guide	This sheet will direct the pupil to other resources, such as textbooks or computer programs. It will contain exercises for the pupil to carry out. The pupil will be actively involved in the learning process.

| A text study | This may ask the pupil to fill in gaps in a piece of prose (a cloze procedure exercise) or it may involve pupils studying a piece of text to find the key points and subsequently producing their own notes from the text. |

Not all worksheets fall neatly into these headings and some are a mixture of two or more categories. The key question to ask yourself before proceeding to produce a worksheet is: 'Are there better ways of presenting the pupils with this information?'

Worksheets can act as a crutch for the teacher. In the quiet of your own workroom you can think clearly about the various steps you want the pupils to go through during the lesson and set these out in a logical fashion on the sheet, and because this information is there on paper in front of the pupils your confidence is improved. They can also act as a crutch for the pupils, where they may forget instructions given orally and have a second chance of finding out what to do by reading the worksheet.

Construction of worksheets

Pupils are used to high-quality printed materials being presented to them from many quarters outside school and they are quickly put off by poorly prepared, shoddy worksheets that are unattractive and difficult to read. Although a teacher may never be able to reproduce the same quality as some of the glossy brochures circulated by commercial organisations, they should nevertheless not be content with second-class handouts. Layout is very important in motivating the pupils to read the work. There is nothing so off-putting for a pupil than a page full of writing. It is essential that you consider the pupils' ability to read. In preparing sheets for pupils with low reading ability you should aim to keep the length of the sentences short and introduce only a few 'difficult' words. You may find it helpful to look at the layout in the tabloid newspapers with their narrow columns of print and produce worksheets that have distinct areas on the page as shown in Figure 3.3.

Use both upper and lower case letters in their correct places in sentences. Important instructions and comments on safety precautions should stand out in some way.

You may wish to cut out an article from a magazine and include this in the worksheet or even include a photocopied section from a textbook. If you are doing this you should first check that you are not infringing copyright regulations. Incorporate the material into the

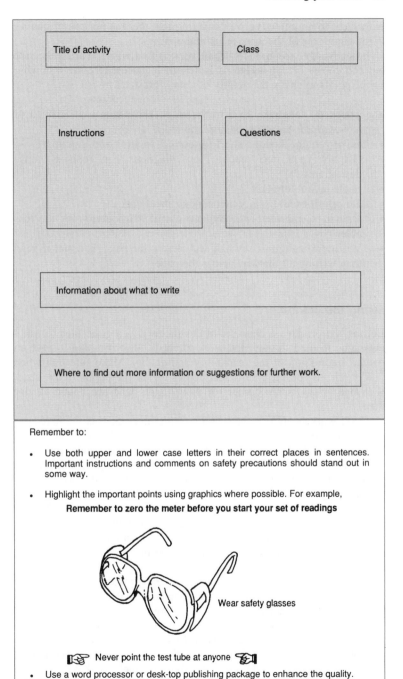

*Figure 3.3 **Example of worksheet with page divided into distinct areas***

worksheet in an attractive way ensuring that there is no loss of quality in the sharpness of the print or photograph.

It is advisable to produce a draft version first with the areas mapped out and copies of any additions laid in their places. Use the following list of points to check the quality of your worksheet.

- Check the language level of the sheet. Have you used difficult or new words? Are the sentences too long?
- Have you checked the sheet for correct spelling and grammar?
- Do not write too much. Flow diagrams can replace wordy descriptions.
- Is the layout attractive?
- Do priorities and safety precautions stand out?
- Drawings (pin-men will do) are useful, particularly for the less able.
- Writing in columns, say half-way across the page, is easier to read than writing all the way across the page.

Using the worksheet

Before you produce a class set of the sheets it is a good idea to ask a colleague to read through the work to check for errors and to give an overall impression of the readability and quality. Make sure that when you duplicate you have sufficient copies for all the pupils in the class, with one or two spare copies for those pupils who are bound to lose them.

Good worksheets may take hours to produce but it is the half hour or so in the lesson that is the most important time. All worksheets will need some initial explanation to the class and sheets involving information about practical work will probably require explanation while the pupils have the apparatus in front of them. It is not enough to tell the pupils to get on with working through the sheet on their own. You will need to ask the pupils additional questions and circulate around the class to check that they understand the information you have given them and that they are working through the exercises. Make notes of any difficulties the pupils are having so that they can be corrected in your revised version.

It is worth bearing in mind some of the problems that can arise from using worksheets, such as the boredom that can emanate from pupils who are constantly exposed to the same sort of printed material. If pupils are presented with individual sheets there can be the problem of how they are going to keep them. Lost sheets will mean that pupils do not have a full set of notes to revise from. Worksheets combined together to form a workbook have the advantage of having all the information together but they can lead to a very rigid course and a heavy diet of printed notes.

Things to do

Prepare a worksheet for pupils following KS3 of the NC either for a lesson that you are about to teach or from one of the following examples:

1. About the digestive system.
Sc2/4a   · Be able to name and locate the major organs of the human body (and the flowering plant).

2. About elements, mixtures and compounds.
Sc3/6a   · Be able to distinguish between metallic and non-metallic elements, mixtures and compounds using simple chemical and physical properties.

3. How we see objects.
Sc4/5e   · Understand how the reflection of light enables objects to be seen.

3.4 PREPARING A SCHEME OF WORK

The terms 'scheme of work (SoW)', 'learning programme' and 'teaching scheme' are different ways of saying the same thing. A scheme of work sets out the teaching sequence for a topic together with other key details such as resources, assessment opportunities and outline practical details together with their risk assessment. The starting point for the development of a SoW will be a syllabus or the PoS of the NC science document. It should take into account the school's policy on curriculum and assessment. It will generally be the job of the head of department or the head of a key stage to prepare the SoW. Trainee teachers will find it useful to talk to staff involved with preparing the document and in examining the logic behind the sequence of lessons. The scheme will probably be built up by an examination of the syllabus, a series of appropriate textbooks and the assessment requirements of the course. Teachers frequently work together in planning the SoW, considering such things as the most appropriate sequence of lessons, the inclusion of practical activities and the quantity of learning activity that can be accomplished in any one lesson.

As a trainee teacher you should find the SoW to be a very useful document to work from as it contains a lot of information in a compact form. At a glance you can see the sequence of lessons and check that the pupils are receiving a variety of learning activities. It will give you an overall picture of the assessment opportunities thus helping you to plan ahead. When you have completed the teaching of the topic you can again turn to the SoW and use it as a first step in reviewing the effectiveness of your work. Headteachers and inspectors also find these schemes useful as it enables them to see at a glance how the NC is being implemented in science.

Content of a SoW

Not unnaturally you will find that different teachers interpret the production of a SoW in different ways. On the most simplistic level you will have a list of topics in the order that they are to be taught. The more sophisticated the SoW, the longer it takes to prepare. It can be very disheartening for teachers who have prepared very thorough SoWs only to find that the syllabus is about to change the following year. As we seem to be living in an era of constant curriculum change it is advisable to prepare the scheme on a word processor so that it can be easily revised.

HMI[13] have suggested that a good SoW should:

- specify the skills, ideas and attitudes that are expected to arise as a result of the science teaching in the course
- give details of what is to be taught, and the order in which it is to be tackled
- suggest ways of teaching the material, related to the aims and objectives of the course
- give notes on the apparatus available
- indicate the depth of treatment required

In addition you should include cross-references to the syllabus or NC and information about safety or a risk assessment reference. Guidance for the production of SoWs can be found in publications from the ASE[14] and the non-statutory guidance for NC science.[15]

Just as with the preparation of lesson plans, there is no one set method but you may find the following guide useful.

A SoW should include the information below.

1. A sequenced and approximately timed set of lessons. In constructing this you will need to take into account:

- The degree of difficulty of the science concepts involved.
- What previous knowledge are the pupils likely to bring to these lessons?
- How can the work be sequenced so that each lesson builds on the work learned in the previous lessons?

2. A list of appropriate teaching activities.

- What are the learning objectives and what teaching strategies do I need to adopt in order to achieve those objectives? This will help to determine the time allocation required in (1).
- Practical activities must refer to a risk assessment.

	Topic NC ref.	Content	Homework	Opportunities for assessment	Resources
4	Burning and fuels Sc3/4c strand 1	1. Newspaper report on recent house fire 2. Group discussion on combustible materials 3. Fire triangle 4. Demo. of flash point 5. Fire extinguishers	Write a report on fire prevention in your home	Look for understanding of the role of oxygen in combustion	Recent newspaper articles on fires in homes. Briefing sheets for class discussion **Risk** Use small quantity of paraffin floating on water
5	Fossil fuels and the environment General intro. to KS3	1. Demo. of combustion of natural gas (testing for H_2O and CO_2) 2. Table completion exercise from article on air pollution 3. Teacher-led class discussion on methods of preventing pollution	Prepare a poster to encourage people to be more environmentally friendly	Has the pupil grasped the main principles of air pollution?	Science Scene Book 1 (pages 128–131) **Risk** No major risk
6	Combustion of metals Sc3/6c	1. Class discussion based around metal artefacts – some of which are corroded 2. Demo. of combustion of Mg, Zn and Fe in O_2 3. Discussion of reactions leading to general equation 4. Exercise on using the unreactive metals	Carry out a home survey of metals and their uses and examine which metals have corroded. Prepare a table of results	Show an understanding that metals burn in O_2 to form oxides	Starting Science Book 2 (page 20 extension work page 21) **Risk** Danger of hot metal coming into contact with skin or combustible material + very bright flame of burning Mg – use small quantities and heatproof mat – pupils should not look directly at burning Mg

Figure 3.4 Part of a SoW for KS3 showing lessons 4 to 6 on the topic of combustion

3. Guidance regarding differentiation within each learning activity. This should include indications of:

- Strategies for managing learning in mixed-ability classes.
- Learning difficulties that many pupils experience with particular topics.
- Suggestions for extension work.

4. Assessment opportunities. This should include:

- Cross-referencing to the SoAs of the National Curriculum or other science syllabus.
- Methods of assessment.
- Criteria for assessment, i.e. transposing the SoAs to the particular situation being studied during the lesson.

5. Suggestions for homework.

6. Resources required. This should include:

- Textbooks to be used with the page references.
- Other written materials, e.g. worksheets, pamphlets, posters (reference to the location of these documents).
- Apparatus and equipment including audiovisual (reference to the company supplying the video, etc.).

Figure 3.4 shows how a SoW might be set out.

Things to do

Locate the scheme of work for a topic taught to pupils at KS3 in your school. Analyse the teaching of the topic under the following headings:
1. Coverage of Sc1.
2. Use of information technology.
3. How the work is differentiated for pupils of different abilities.
4. Assessment strategies.

NOTES AND REFERENCES

1. Health and Safety Commission, 1989, *COSHH: Guidance for Schools*, HMSO, London.

2. Department of Education and Science, *Safety in Education* bulletins published occasionally: Bulletin No. 1 (November 1981); No. 2 (July 1982); No. 3 (June 1984); No. 4 (March 1986).

3. Department of Education and Science, 1978, *Safety in Science Laboratories* (3rd edition), HMSO, London.

4. Association for Science Education (Laboratory Safeguards Committee), 1988, *Safety in the School Laboratory* (9th edition), ASE, Hatfield.

5. Association for Science Education, 1988, *Topics in Safety* (2nd edition), ASE, Hatfield.

6. CLEAPSS School Science Service/SSSERC, *HAZCARDS* (1981) (most Local Education Authorities subscribe to CLEAPSS and thereby obtain all their literature, copies of which should be in the school. Ask the head of science for help in locating the CLEAPSS publications. If you are still unable to find them write to CLEAPSS at CLEAPSS School Science Service, Brunel University, Uxbridge UB8 3PH.

7. Tawney, D.A., 'Assessment of risk and school science,' *School Science Review*, 1992, **74** (267), 7–14.

8. 'Teacher fined after explosion,' *Education in Chemistry*, 1993, **30** (4), 89.

9. Comments on the safety situations:

(i) There are two points to note about this situation. Firstly copper(II) sulphate is poisonous and if pupils handle the chemical they should wash their hands thoroughly afterwards. This is good practice, of course, after handling all chemicals. The second point is that pupils should not be allowed to take substances out of the laboratory. You have no control over what happens to it when it goes out of the laboratory door. While on the subject of copper(II) sulphate, look out for it in 'disguised forms' such as in Fehling's solution and be aware of its poisonous nature.

(ii) The DES has strongly recommended that teachers should not use human blood and cheek cells, as a precaution against the spread of AIDS. For alternatives, see page 25 of *Topics in Safety*.

(iii) Stretched wire can be very dangerous if it snaps and whiplashes back. The pupil needs to wear safety glasses for this experiment. The apparatus should be secure and there should be a safe place for the masses to drop should the wire break. The pupil needs plenty of space so that s/he can move away quickly from the experiment should anything go wrong. It is advisable that pupils stand for all experiments so that they can withdraw quickly in the event of an accident.

(iv) After you have calmed down having had an expensive piece of equipment broken you should spread powdered sulphur on the area where the mercury has spilled. Place the large pieces of glass in the laboratory broken-glass container and brush up the rest and place in the bin.

(v) Concentrated acids are particularly unpleasant to deal with. First of all if you are not used to dealing with concentrated sulphuric acid you may be surprised at the weight of a Winchester bottle full of the material. It is very dense and you need to hold the bottle firmly. You should wear a laboratory coat, rubber gloves and a face shield. Pour the acid from the stock bottle into a beaker in a fume cupboard, making every effort to avoid spills. Measure out the amount of water you need into a large beaker and measure the volume of concentrated sulphuric acid. Slowly add the acid to the water with constant stirring. The protective clothing must be worn throughout the whole operation.

10. There are a number of CLEAPSS guides on safety matters which are periodically updated. You will find the following useful:

    Precautions with Mercury L144 (revised October 1984)
    Eye Protection L135 (revised August 1991)
    Chemical Storage L148 (revised August 1983)
    Chemical Spills L149 (revised September 1981)
    Electrical Safety L86 (revised November 1984)
    Substitute chemicals and alternative procedures L195 (January 1992)

11. See *Topics in Safety* (reference 5) page 9.

12. The British Red Cross, 1984, *Practical First Aid: The Basic Guide to Emergency Aid for Home, School and Work*, Dorling Kindersley, London. In addition you will find it useful to look out for safety posters that are published periodically from chemical companies and school suppliers.

13. HMI, 1979, *Aspects of Secondary Education in England*, HMSO, London.

14. Association for Science Education, 1985, *Planning for Science in the Curriculum*, ASE, Hatfield, p. 26. Hull, R. and Adams, H., 1981, *Decisions in the Science Department: Organisation and Curriculum*, ASE, Hatfield.

15. See reference 15 in Chapter 2.

CHAPTER 4

Working with pupils

4.1 THE CLASSROOM ENVIRONMENT

Images play an important part in our everyday lives. Pupils are very concerned about their image. Are they wearing the correct brand of jeans? Does their hair style comply with the latest fashion? Manufacturers entice us to buy products, not necessarily on the basis of quality, but on the image the product portrays. We tend to like things and be interested in them because of the image they depict. What then about the science laboratory? What type of an image is conveyed to pupils by the laboratories in your school? Pupils can come to science lessons with some very negative ideas such as science is difficult to understand, it is smelly, it is a boy's subject and it is dangerous. In order to get the best out of your pupils you need to establish a happy, encouraging working environment that portrays a positive image of science. You can start preparing better working surroundings by making sure that the laboratory is tidy and has attractive and interesting posters on the wall. These should be a mixture of pupil-prepared work together with some of the commercially produced posters. Pupils will be producing posters for many topics at different stages of their school career and you should have no problem in preparing attractive displays. Why not set the pupils the task of 'marketing' science through a poster display as an end-of-term task. The display will need to be changed on a regular basis and any damaged posters should be disposed of.

You, as a teacher, are part of the image that pupils have of science and scientists and your role is important in determining whether or not pupils like science and would wish to continue studying it. We do not want to present a picture of the 'mad scientist' or the 'bumbling professor' captured in many cartoons and children's films. Perhaps you would want to present an image of a scientist who is caring, interested in others, is concerned about the environment, considers things in a logical way and makes decisions based on evidence. Whatever your view is of science, you should attempt to illustrate your work with the benefits the study of the subject has brought to mankind.

Table 4.1 lists various methods that can be used to enhance learning by slight changes in our approach to dealing with pupils.

Table 4.1 **Creating an atmosphere for learning**

Indicators	Highest quality	Lowest quality
Room	Prepared, attractive room with posters creating a positive atmosphere towards the subject. Use of colour and 3-D effect on posters. Seats directed towards the front	Unprepared and untidy room. Scattered chairs or seating arranged so that some pupils cannot face the teacher. Blank walls
Visuals	Simple, clear ohp transparencies	Cluttered blackboard or no visual aids at all
Teacher talk	Consistent, positive, uplifting, inspiring, helpful	Critical, negative, sarcastic, cynical, apologetic, embarrassed, aggravated, angry
Intonation	Purposeful, varied, effective	Monotone
Authority	Authoritative, expert, master	Authoritarian, biased, hypercritical, unread and uninformed
Tone/mood	Fun, relaxed, pleasant, engaging	Hostile, punitive, fearful
Clarifications	Natural, extended, questions encouraged	Questions discouraged, hostile
Imagery	Vivid images, analogies	Negative examples, abstractions
Activities	Varied, flexible to meet the needs on the day, encouraging co-operation	Teacher–student interaction only, few activities

Things to do

Review the layout of your laboratory and consider ways of making it a more attractive learning environment. Talk to teachers in the art department or from one of your partner primary schools about presentation of pupils' work.

Consider the image you portray to different classes by using the following checklist at the end of the lesson:

Things to do continued

- How organised were you?
- Were your visual aids clear and well prepared?
- How much interest did you show in individuals by talking to them about their work and their hobbies?
- How clear were your explanations of science concepts?
- Did you involve girls and boys equally in the activities?
- Were you firm but fair in your discipline?

4.2 CLASSROOM CONTROL

Discipline is something that concerns all trainee teachers. Am I going to be able to control the class or will they eat me alive? For most of us, disciplining a large group of people does not come naturally and needs to be learned as do other aspects of teaching. You must be firm right from the word go. Some trainee teachers believe that they can relax with pupils, perhaps feeling that because of the small difference in age they will be able to get along with the pupils as friends. In order to attain the respect of pupils you must be able to control them and have a position of authority. You must work out a strategy of being firm and yet fair. Most misdemeanours that you will have to deal with will be fairly minor ones. You will probably find that the most common 'crime' is pupils talking out of turn. Whatever the type of misbehaviour, it is essential that you tackle it straight away. It is no use saying to yourself, *'I'll ignore it this time but if he does it again I'll tell him off'*. Pupils will be watching you to see how you respond in different situations. They are constantly 'trying you out' and you must show that you have complete command of the situation by responding immediately to any breach of discipline.

You will find it easier to discipline pupils if you know their names. It is far more effective to call out, *'John, stop talking while I am talking'* rather than, *'Will the boy third in from the right on the back row please shut up'*. Learning names is not an easy task, particularly if you have a large number of different classes or if you have a two-week timetable and only see your class once a fortnight. There are various strategies that can be used to help you learn names such as:

- Read through the class list several times before your first lesson, select several names and then identify them during the lesson. Carry on doing this until you have covered everyone. You may find that some schools have class lists with photographs of all the pupils.
- Prepare a seating plan for the laboratory and insist that all the pupils remain in their positions until you have learned their names.

- Ask the pupils to put their names on a folded piece of paper, which is then displayed in front of them. (You need to be aware that some pupils will be silly and write down incorrect names or swap their paper with a friend.)
- As the pupils are working on a task, go round and look at their books, make a mental note of their names while looking at their faces.
- When you are calling out the register, ask pupils to raise their hands so that you can put a face to the name. When you feel that you know the majority of the pupils, try marking the register in pencil by just looking round the class to see who is present and then check your knowledge by calling the register in the usual way.

There are as many causes of disruption as there are types. You may not have any influence over the cause of poor behaviour as it may involve an event that has taken place outside your classroom. However, pupils may show a lack of interest in your lesson, and therefore be disruptive, because:

- the content of the lesson is inappropriate for the pupils
- the teaching style you have chosen is inappropriate
- your manner of presentation is inappropriate

Misbehaviour can also occur when pupils start or change activities such as:

- entering or leaving the room
- getting books or writing equipment ready
- starting or stopping practical work

Ways of avoiding discipline problems:

- Prepare your lessons well so that the whole event can run smoothly.
- Plan your activities and the movement of pupils (try to avoid situations where pupils can bump into one another).
- Stand where you can be seen.
- Give the impression that nothing can happen in the classroom of which you will not be aware; keep your eyes roving round the room and pick up any incident of misbehaviour no matter how small. Do not devote all your attentions to one group for a long period of time during group work activities.
- Show at a glance by a facial expression that you have noted a sign of misbehaviour.
- Act on the first incident of misbehaviour, don't wait for the

second event to happen. As soon as the child misbehaves tell him/her off, by name if possible.

* Keep the pupils busy and involved with learning.
* Be consistent about your rules and discipline procedures.
* Sound confident.

Two mistakes made by some teachers are (a) to over-react to children's misdemeanours and (b) to become emotionally involved. Education should seek to develop rationality in pupils and an emotional reaction from a teacher may be counter-productive. A realistic comment made calmly and briefly can produce a satisfactory result by making the pupil aware of the consequences of his/her behaviour. You need to develop a sensitivity to pupils' reactions. Watch out for occasions when the class is fidgety, or when pupils start to daydream or otherwise show signs of uninterest. If the lesson is deteriorating it is better to alter the pace or change what you are doing rather than pursue your plans to the bitter end.

Each breach of discipline will be dealt with differently but there are a number of general points that need to be borne in mind. It has already been mentioned that responding to the first transgression is important. You must get the message across to the pupil, somehow or other, that you have noted the 'crime' and that it must not happen again. As a teacher you must be prepared to listen to the pupil but do not let this take up valuable teaching time. Find time after the lesson to hear the pupil's side of the story, with the understanding that some pupils are very good at telling lies. You should be polite and calm, asking questions that will help you to gain a clearer picture of the situation. Avoid being drawn into lengthy or complex arguments as they are unlikely to get you anywhere. Whatever you do, do not get into a heated argument with a pupil or worse still end up hitting the individual.

Each school has its own system of support for teachers and types of punishments. A good school will have a clear, documented system where all staff co-operate and apply the rules in a regular fashion. You should find details of these in the handbook for parents or the school brochure. You need to familiarise yourself with the discipline procedures of the school. For example, in some schools it is acceptable to send disruptive pupils out of your class to stand in the corridor, in others they have to go to a specific room, the 'sin bin'. An alternative approach is to reward positive actions, perhaps by allocating points to individuals or classes. When a target number of points has been achieved some sort of reward or privilege can be given. The 'report card' system is particularly effective, especially if parents are involved both at the start and the end of the time the pupil is placed on report. Detentions can take a variety of forms, from the 'being kept in at break time' to a school detention run by a senior member of staff. There are, of course, the extreme forms of punishment: suspension and finally expulsion from the school altogether. These are, for the most part, rare occurrences and require the authority of the headteacher and governors of the school.

The Elton Report[1] is the most comprehensive document produced on discipline in schools in recent years. It contains some 160 recommendations for teachers, governors, parents, LEAs and the government. It makes the point that trainee teachers and those in the early years of the profession should receive training in classroom management and control and that schools should provide a supportive structure for new teachers.

Whatever you do, you must not assume that you are the only person in the whole school with discipline problems. You should talk to experienced members of staff about the situations that concern you and obtain their help and guidance.

Things to do

You will find it helpful when you first start teaching to plan out what you would do in certain situations. Consider what your actions would be if you were faced with the following scenarios:

Two pupils start chatting to one another while you are talking to the class.
A pupil is eating in the laboratory.
A number of pupils have not handed in their homework.
A pupil thumps his neighbour.
A pupil is rude to you.

It is worth while reflecting on your actions. Consider your discipline in a series of lessons. Do you think that your strategies worked? Were you consistent from one lesson to the next? Did you praise or reward good behaviour?

4.3   SOME IDEAS ABOUT LEARNING

Things to do

How do you think pupils learn? In order to help you answer the question you might think about a learning experience that you have been through recently. It might also help to look at the statements made below:

- All pupils want to learn. As long as you make it interesting they will concentrate on learning the information.
- Pupils learn by copying. If you get them to copy down their notes from the blackboard or worksheet they will remember it far better than if you just give them the printed notes.

Things to do continued

- So long as you keep the pressure up they will learn. If you give them a test once a week they will learn their stuff.
- I tell them the key facts. I write them on the board. I tell them again and then you can be sure that they have understood.

Write down how you think pupils learn, then read through the rest of this section and compare your ideas with those of the researchers.

The ideas about learning that teachers hold have implications for the teaching strategies they choose to use in their lessons. You will find it worth while to spend some time reading through the literature on learning and to compare your ideas with those obtained through research into education.[2] Piaget has played a major role in developing our understanding of how pupils learn. His ideas are based around a model of pupils going through various stages of cognitive development as they get older. As they age, their ability to use more abstract ideas increases. Piaget's work generally describes pupils as being at a particular stage of development. There are two main stages, concrete operations and formal operations, and these are often subdivided into more specific categories. Concrete operations refers to the simple processes of science, such as classifying, manipulating single variables, recognising simple cause-and-effect relationships. Formal operations involve using science concepts to develop or understand further work in science. Followers of Piaget would argue that a pupil needs to have developed to a particular stage before s/he can understand the work in hand. Shayer and Adey[3] have used this model of learning in their analysis of GCE O-level Nuffield Science syllabuses.

Gagne[4] is another person who has made a major contribution to our understanding to how pupils learn. He belongs to what is sometimes called the behaviourist school of thought and his ideas are based around learning taking place through a series of responses to certain stimuli. Gagne also argued that knowledge is hierarchical and that it is essential to teach certain prerequisite skills and concepts before others. Each learner will start his/her learning from a different standpoint depending on his internal capabilities. S/he is also likely to demand a different external situation in order that learning can take place effectively.

Bruner[5] developed a theory of learning based on three almost simultaneous processes which he describes as:

1. Acquisition of new knowledge.
2. Transformation of knowledge.
3. Checking the adequacy of knowledge.

Bruner summarised the learning process thus:

Mental growth is not a gradual accretion of stimulus–response connections. It is much more like a staircase, with sharp risers, more a matter of spurts and rests. The spurts seem to be touched off when certain capacities begin to develop. Some experiences can slow the spurts down, some speed them up.

The Ausubelian[6] school of thought argues that there is no optimum age for learning and that the strategy for science teaching should be to look for the idea frameworks that children already hold when they come to a lesson and build the curriculum accordingly. Driver has built on the work of Ausubel, in particular, but argues that pupils often come to science lessons with ideas that are scientifically incorrect.

In the past many school science teachers have adopted the principle that the pupils come to lessons with no knowledge at all of science. They have ignored the fact that even as babies everyone starts to investigate the world in which s/he lives and start to build up a picture of why things happen in the way that they do. Some teachers have even ignored the formal science that pupils have studied in the primary schools and have adopted the approach, '*Assume that they know nowt, you've got to tell 'em everything*'. This sort of lesson would generally consist of the teacher, as the fount of all knowledge, talking to the whole class for long periods of time while the empty vessels of the pupils are slowly filed up with information. As this is often the approach to teaching (through lectures) that takes place in most universities and colleges, some trainee teachers believe that it is the correct one to use with young people in schools. Most teachers nowadays would agree that this is not the best way of enabling pupils to learn. They are certainly not empty vessels, in fact they come to science lessons with a whole range of ideas about how things work and what things are made of. Some of these ideas agree with the generally accepted scientific explanations but in other cases pupils have developed misconceptions of how things work. These misconceptions can often be deep rooted and can be the basis for the misunderstanding of whole areas of science. It is the teacher's job to try to unravel pupils' original ideas and guide them on the path to understanding the accepted view on science.

Things to do

You will find it valuable to read through some of the literature associated with children's learning in science and gather information about the types of misconceptions pupils have. In addition you should investigate for yourself, what ideas pupils have about the science topic you are about to teach them. No matter how hard you try, how many times you repeat things or how loud you talk, you will find it difficult to change some pupils' views. Pupils need evidence arising from personal experience or logical argument in their own language in order to help them to reconstruct their understanding.

Things to do continued

When you next start a new topic find out what ideas and theories the pupils already hold about the topic. There are a number of ways you could do this, for example

1. For homework prior to starting the work, set the class a few simple questions to elicit their prior understanding of it.
2. Start the topic with a group brainstorming session and ask each group to produce a poster with the title 'What we know about . . .' (Take up points of disagreement between group members and use those as a focus for later discussion.)

Research carried out recently by Shayer and his co-workers[7] has shown that it is possible to improve pupils' ability to learn. It requires a different, and for most teachers a new, approach to what happens in the classroom. Their work, called the Cognitive Acceleration through Science Education (CASE) project, is based on four principles:

- *Cognitive conflict*: Pupils are presented with problems that make them think. The CASE materials examine the setting up of the problem, its execution and the follow up activities.
- *Reflection*: Pupils are encouraged to think about their own thinking. They are asked to consider how they reached a solution to a problem and asked to explain their work to others.
- *Bridging*: A principle or idea is taken from the context where it was developed and applied to a new situation.
- *Reasoning patterns*: Certain types of reasoning have been identified as characteristic of higher level thinking. These include control of variables, proportionality, equilibria, ascribing cause-and-effect relationships, and comprehending a correlation between variables. These cannot be taught directly, but the teacher who is aware of them will be better equipped to help pupils develop the reasoning patterns for themselves.

In order to turn these principles into practice, teachers must be trained in the appropriate teaching techniques. Printed materials for use with pupils are available. The results of the research so far indicates that pupils who have followed a CASE programme, even at an early stage of their secondary schooling, achieve higher grades at GCSE than other pupils.

4.4 PUPIL GROUPINGS AND TEACHING STRATEGIES

An introduction to different teaching techniques

Once a teacher has decided on what s/he would like the pupils to achieve during a lesson the next step in the planning process is to consider what are the best teaching and learning strategies that can be employed to realise those objectives. There are a number of factors that need consideration in this part of the planning process.

First, there is the need to consider the composition of the class in terms of the abilities of the individual pupils. Certain activities are more effective with groups of pupils of similar ability whereas others work well with mixed-ability classes.

Second, you will find it necessary to consider the size of the group. For example, you may only be able to carry out certain practicals on an individual basis with small groups, whereas, some role-play activities may only be successful with large groups.

Third, there is the layout of the room to consider. Old laboratories are sometimes long, narrow rooms with fixed benches, making it difficult to carry out group discussion work.

The final factor to consider is concerned with motivation. The pupils will rapidly become bored if they are presented with the same menu lesson after lesson. As teachers we would like our pupils to come along to the lesson with a sense of excitement and a knowledge that they are going to do something interesting. Obviously, some topics tend to be intrinsically more interesting than others but, with a little imagination and careful planning, even those science topics that are generally regarded as dull can be given a new lease of life.

Many modern textbooks give suggestions for different types of teaching activities and are attractive and stimulating for pupils to use. They are designed to cater for pupils of different abilities by having a range of tasks, including extra work for those that finish early.

Teaching activities can be divided into two fundamental types:

1. Those where the student is actively involved in the learning process, i.e. where the pupil actually has to physically and mentally do something in order to increase his/her knowledge.
2. Those where the student 'absorbs' information by listening, reading or watching.

The first type is generally referred to as active learning and the second as passive learning. Learning is more effective if the pupil is actively involved in obtaining the information. Table 4.2 lists some teaching and learning activities used in science lessons and categorises them as either active or passive. These labels are dependent on the presentation by the teacher and could easily be reversed. You should aim to deliver lessons where the pupils are actively involved in the learning process. Chapters 5, 6 and 7 describe such teaching methods.

Table 4.2 **Pupil activities**

	Activity	Passive (P) or Active (A)
1.	Listening to the teacher	P
2.	Answering oral questions	A
3.	Working together in groups	A
4.	Role play	A
5.	Class discussion	A
6.	Class debate	A
7.	Watching a science video	P
8.	Working on a computer program	A
9.	Watching a demonstration	P
10.	Taking down notes (from dictation, copying from the board or ohp, copying from a worksheet)	P
11.	Writing own notes	A
12.	Preparing a poster or other item for display	A
13.	Answering written questions	A
14.	Reading about science	A
15.	Planning how to carry out experiments	A
16.	Carrying out experiments	A
17.	Drawing conclusions from experimental results	A
18.	Looking up data	A
19.	Peer group teaching	A
20.	Project work	A
21.	A circus of activities	A
22.	Quizzes, science games and crosswords	A

Teaching the whole class

Whole class teaching is widely used in science lessons. It is an opportunity for the teacher to pass on his/her enthusiasm for the subject and motivate the pupils to learn it. There are two major occasions when the teacher is likely to address the class: at the start of the lesson to set the scene and at the end to draw together the key points. A good introduction to a lesson helps to get the pupils organised for the task in hand. They should know what they have to do and be keen to do the tasks. The exposition should involve questioning the pupils and allowing time for pupil contribution. Pupils must be involved actively in this part of the lesson rather than just be passive recipients of knowledge. You should consider how you are going to involve pupils of different abilities in the lesson. If low-ability pupils are asked questions that are too difficult for them, or if they are ignored, they will soon become disillusioned with your science teaching and will switch off altogether.

The time spent in whole class discussion should be limited, giving time for individuals to work on their own. It is quite common for the structure of whole class lessons to be governed by the organisation of a workbook specially prepared for the topic. All teachers rejoice in the fact that somebody else has prepared this resource for them but such a situation can have its problems. Trainee teachers, in particular, sometimes fall into the trap of believing that because they have been presented with this resource, there is little or even no lesson preparation to do. If you follow this approach your lessons are likely to be of little value to the pupils. As a teacher you need to take ownership of the resource material you have been presented with. This will initially involve becoming fully conversant with the aims and objectives of the teaching unit by examining the associated teachers' notes and/or scheme of work. You will need to read around the topic and collect other resources so that you can present the work in a confident, lively and interesting manner. But perhaps the most important part of your preparation will be concerned with what the pupils are going to do during the lesson. There are many worksheets that just require the pupils to fill in blanks in a page of notes and, while this may be fine for the first few occasions that the pupils come across the technique, it tends to pall when used time after time.

4.5 PUPILS WORKING IN SMALL GROUPS OR INDIVIDUALLY

Types of group work

Group work is used extensively in primary schools to help to develop pupils' social skills and to allow teachers to set differentiated tasks to children of different abilities. Each group might contain pupils of similar ability working on similar or even identical tasks. Group work is an excellent approach to mixed-ability teaching and many secondary science teachers use it to help pupils progress at a rate determined by their ability. While a low-ability group might struggle to get through the tasks set for them, a high-ability group might race through the original set of work and then go on to do extension material. Alternatively pupils may be grouped in a mixed-ability arrangement so that the individuals can learn from one another.

Pupils working in pairs on a practical task can be described as a type of group work. Teachers often fail to take full advantage of this common activity in a science laboratory and are prepared to let pupils either stand and watch while the experiment is in progress, or to let them gossip. Valuable learning time can be lost while the pupils are waiting for something to happen such as for a beaker of water to boil. The pupils need to be directed to do something constructive during practical 'dead time'. It may be that there are key observations that have to be made periodically or it may be that the teacher requires the pupils to think about what is happening on a molecular scale during a particular process. Whatever the task, it is important that there is an additional outcome from the group discussion, which will feature in the presentation of the laboratory report.

Group work is also used in situations where there are likely to be differences of opinion. In this type of activity it is important that group members are properly briefed on the key points of both arguments. This type of activity forces pupils to challenge their own opinions and beliefs.

Alternatively, the group task could involve a discussion as to why a particular phenomenon occurs. This is an excellent way of finding out what pupils know. As mentioned earlier in this chapter, it can be used at the start of a topic to ascertain pupils' preconceived notions of the subject matter, or it could be used towards the end of a topic by presenting pupils with a new situation and asking them to explain it in terms of what they have just learned.

Pupils can also work together on a common task, where each member of the group brings his/her own area of expertise. A good example of this is where pupils are working together on an investigation. The group would come together with the plans for carrying out the investigation from the individual members. Working together they would look at the feasibility of each plan and come to some agreement as to which procedure would be the best one to use. It may be that the final method used would incorporate the best ideas from a number of different plans. Table 4.3 gives some examples of occasions where pupils could profitably work together in groups.

Table 4.3 **Opportunities for group discussion**

Task type	Example
During practical work	In a filtration experiment where pupils are investigating the porosity of different soils they will measure the volume of water eluted for each sample in a specific time interval. While waiting for the water to drain through they could be asked to decide in their groups what words describe the appearance of the wet soils and how this differed from the dry soil. They could be asked to think about the nature of the soil particles and try to explain what they observed
In planning practical work	Pupils involved in planning an investigation on how quickly lumps of limestone dissolve in acid. Each pupil may have a different idea as to the best way of carrying out the practical work. By discussing the ideas in groups pupils can eliminate unsuitable plans

Table 4.3 continued

Task type	Example
At the start of a topic to determine pupils' preconceptions	At the start of work on gravitational force, pupils could be asked to discuss the explanation for an object falling on to the Earth and then predict what would happen if the same object was to be dropped on the Moon
During a topic to determine the level of understanding	After a series of lessons on weather pupils could be given some data from country X and asked to interpret the information by discussing it in groups
During a topic to exchange views and opinions	Discuss how you would persuade someone to stop smoking

Setting the scene

Unfortunately many old school laboratories with their fixed benches, large sinks and uncomfortable stools do not readily lend themselves to providing an agreeable environment for group work. It is unsatisfactory to have pupils discussing while ranged in lines along the bench and it can result in an unacceptable level of noise. The quality of the discussion is improved when pupils are arranged in a circle, facing one another. This helps members of the group to interpret meaning from facial expressions, eye contact and gestures as well as the spoken word. The pupils are likely to respond better to the activity if they are sitting comfortably with each member having a reasonable space within the circle rather than having to jostle for position.

Composition of the group

As intimated earlier, the different types of group work may require different types of groups. Bentley and Watts[8] have prepared the following list of questions that teachers should ask themselves when considering the composition of a group:

- What is the purpose in mind?
- What gender and ethnic groupings would best fulfil that purpose?
- What balance of skills do youngsters need in each group – a variety of skills or similar skills?
- What level of concept development do youngsters need in a group, a variety of levels or a similar level?
- What activities will fulfil the purpose?

- What roles will individuals need to play to carry out the activities?
- What specific difficulties lie ahead because of the individuals put together?
- What action might need to be taken?

You should think carefully about your objectives for the group task and arrange the composition of the group accordingly.

Roles for group members

Group work gives pupils the opportunity to express their own ideas and have these challenged by their peers. Pupils quickly realise the power of positive argument and come to appreciate that others can have different, but equally valid, points of view from theirs.

For group work to be successful it is important that every member gets the opportunity to express his/her opinion. There may be reluctant members of the group who wish to be sleeping partners in the group process but the rules of the group should be such that everyone must make a contribution. To a large extent this relies on the skills of the chairperson whose job it is to make sure that everyone has an opportunity to talk. In setting up the group, you as teacher may find it useful to write out a mini job description for the key personnel in the group – the chairperson and the secretary.

Managing group work

It is essential that the teacher makes a good job of setting the scene for the discussion through an interesting introduction to the lesson. This could appear to arise quite naturally from an 'off-the-cuff' controversial remark or through copies of newspaper reports, or by relating it to previous lessons. Having predetermined the group size and composition it is necessary to get the pupils to move, in an orderly fashion, to their group locations. You will find it useful to have a specific target in mind for each group together with a time limit for achieving the target. Each group may have a different task to carry out or they may all be working on the same problem. It is a good idea to have some product from each group. This may be:

- an oral report to the whole class
- a report to another group
- a written report to the teacher
- a list of points based on the consensus of the group in preparation for a class discussion or role play, or
- a poster

You will have to consider the frequency and extent of your interactions with the groups during the time that the pupils are working on their task. There may be times when you have to keep pupils on the right track as their discussion wanders off into other areas of interest. Some groups may want assistance in getting organised and others are sure to have difficulties in understanding what they have to do. There will always be those groups who finish early either because they have treated the work superficially or because they have been able to solve the problem with speed. These groups will need additional encouragement or perhaps an additional task to work on. Once the pupils have finished their tasks you need to consider how they are going to report back and how you are going to draw the key points of the lesson together.

Flexible learning

Some teachers will argue that there is a need to create an environment where the learner can take some responsibility for her/his own learning.[9] The learner can be involved in setting personal targets of possible educational achievement and then evaluating his/her success in achieving those targets. This type of approach often goes under the general heading of 'flexible learning' and involves the pupils working in either small groups or as individuals.

Flexible learning is a term used to cover a whole range of methods of delivering the curriculum, which involves the flexible use and management of resources to meet the needs of the learner as an individual. The approach reduces the pupils' reliance on the teacher as the fount of all knowledge and encourages the pupil to seek out information from a whole variety of sources, which may or may not include the teacher.

The traditional teacher's role is, therefore, inappropriate for this method of teaching. With a flexible learning approach the teacher takes on the job of guide, helping the pupil to work through the topic and to advise on further work to be studied. Without proper teacher direction the system will crumble and pupils will revert to idle chatter. With good support from the teacher, pupils work well and progress through the work at a rate that reflects their ability. Different groups of pupils in any one class could be working on different tasks according to their ability.

There are two main ways of organising flexible learning in secondary schools, resource-based learning and supported self-study.

1. Resource-based learning

The individual needs of pupils are catered for by directing them to suitable resources, which may be situated in the laboratory and adjacent rooms or may be elsewhere in the school, such as the library.[10] The teacher has the complex task of managing the system so that the learning programme for each individual matches his/her ability, aptitude and interest. Not all lessons involve pupils working on their own or in groups, some time is given over to whole class teaching. In these sessions the teacher will either provide some extra stimulus material to create or maintain interest in the topic or explain a common misunderstanding.

2. Supported self-study

Supported self-study encompasses the ideals of resource-based learning but gives greater emphasis on the importance of the tutorial support of the independent learner helping the pupil to discover the personal meaning of new information and ideas.

Most of the resources for these approaches to teaching have been developed by individual schools[11] and there is little commercially available material. Amongst the publications available are three packages written for students following post-16 science courses: the Advanced Physics Project for Independent Learning (APPIL); the Independent Learning Project for Advanced Chemistry (ILPAC), and the Advanced Biology Alternative Learning Project (ABAL).[12]

There are other flexible approaches used in further and higher education such as open access workshops where students 'drop in' to a session on, say, solving organic problems. Tutorial support is usually available. The Open University was one of the pioneers of the flexible learning approach, called distance learning, where the student does all of the reading at home using specially designed materials often containing tasks and self-assessment questions. Tutorial support is often available by phone and by occasional meetings at an educational institution.

Advantages of a flexible learning approach over traditional methods:

- Pupils are always actively involved in their work.
- Pupils are trained to work on their own or in small groups. They develop their study skills and an independence that should help them to continue their learning beyond school.
- An opportunity arises for treating pupils in a more adult fashion. The teacher can be seen in a less threatening light and as a person who is there to help the pupils achieve their best.
- Individuals are presented with work that matches their ability. All children, even the less able, experience success with their work. For the less able the problem of generally being told that you are wrong can be very demotivating.
- The teacher is able to give more attention to individuals during the lesson time.

Disadvantages of a flexible learning approach:

- It is difficult to anticipate problems and, therefore, plan in detail.
- The teacher is extremely busy during the lesson time.
- A number of different experiments may be in progress at any one time. This may cause problems from a safety viewpoint.
- The materials can take a long time to prepare and put together in a suitable form.
- Good management of the system is required, otherwise papers get misplaced and the system becomes unworkable.

Homework

The status given to homework will vary from school to school and you should have a clear understanding of its position in your school. In some schools it is compulsory for all pupils and homework diaries have to be kept and signed by parents to ensure that the work is done. In others there may be little pressure to do homework, possibly because the home backgrounds of the pupils are such that they are likely to get little support for working at home. The vast majority of schools see homework as a valuable part of pupils' learning experiences and encourage them to carry out tasks outside normal school hours. Some of the reasons for setting homework are given below.

- It provides pupils with the opportunity to work on their own, without interference from their friends, and produce something that they can value.
- It gives pupils the chance to practise techniques and learn information at their own rate.
- It helps pupils to develop the skills necessary to become effective independent learners.
- It gives pupils the opportunity to reflect on work they have done in class and to identify areas of work that they do not fully understand.
- It creates an opening for parents to become more involved with their children's work.
- It creates the opportunity for pupils to do further work and make more rapid progress through the curriculum.

If they are to get maximum benefit from their work they need clear guidelines about how to carry out the task and some indication as to the nature of the product they are required to produce. We all have difficulty in managing our own time and pupils are no exception. Bearing in mind that pupils have other important things to do besides school work it is advisable to give a rough approximation as to how long they should spend on their homework. While it would not be true to say that pupils welcome homework, they do like to have a routine and it is helpful if teachers have a set pattern of delivering and collecting homework on a weekly basis. Not only does this build in a structure for the pupils but it should give the teacher a system that can be easily checked.

The HMI document *Education Observed 4: Homework*[13] reviews current practice and suggests ways of making homework a more worthwhile experience for pupils. In particular they point out that it should be clearly related to the work that children do in school. If pupils see that the work has a purpose then they are more likely to tackle it with enthusiasm.

You need also to be aware of pupils who consistently do not do homework either because of lack of parental support or because the pupil is disaffected with the school system. There is little you as an individual can do about the unsupportive parent but it might be possible to cajole the erring pupil to carry out some worthwhile tasks for you.

The following list gives some suggestions for homework.

1. Making personal notes from textbooks.
2. Answering questions on a worksheet using information they already have in their exercise books.
3. Writing up neatly an account where they only have rough notes of the work they have done in class.
4. Writing a piece of continuous prose, such as their opinions on particular environmental issues or a letter to a friend describing their work in science.
5. Carrying out a DART activity (see Chapter 6 for information on this activity).
6. Planning an investigation.
7. Carrying out a survey amongst family and friends, e.g. linked to classwork on the eye, pupils could survey a group of adults to find out if they wear glasses and what they use the glasses for.
8. Doing a science crossword or word search.
9. Finding out things about their home, e.g. asking about insulation and other energy saving devices use in the home.
10. Keeping a diary of their diet or the exercise they do for a week.
11. Preparing a poster.
12. Revising for a test.

Things to do

It is important that you have a clear picture with regard to the school policy on homework. You should find information about this in the school brochure and the documentation kept by the head of science.

Things to do continued

Try to find out:

1. What information does the school send to parents about homework?
2. How does the school encourage pupils to do homework and how does it equip them with the necessary study skills to carry out their tasks. Is this part of their PSE programme or is it achieved elsewhere?
3. Whether there is a standard procedure for setting and marking homework within the science department.

4.6 EXPEDITIONS AND FIELD WORK

Expedition may sound like a grand word for a half-day or a day visit to a place of scientific interest but to a parent or fellow teacher it sounds much more 'educational' than 'trip'. By its very nature there are examples of science all around us. The 'expedition' might be nothing more than a look at the school playing field or a walk around the nearest housing estate. Its purpose should be to open pupils' eyes and let them see things in a different light, for example: Why is that bridge shaped in that way? What building materials are used in a house? What is the distribution of plants on the school field? On a grander scale it may be a visit to a local industry, a local stream to sample the water life, a local museum to look at changes in land use over a period of time. Jennings[14] describes a whole host of activities that science teachers could do. Many of these cross traditional curricular boundaries and could be planned with other subject teachers. Whatever the event, field work should be seen as an important part of science. If properly planned it can be both rewarding and enjoyable for pupils.

Field work can be done in a double period if it only involves working in the school grounds. As time is a very precious commodity in schools these days you will need to justify using additional school time if you are planning a longer visit. You may find it possible to extend your lesson by using lunch or break time.

As with other lessons, success will only be achieved through careful planning. You will need to go through the activity that you wish the pupils to do. Note down things that you want them to observe, measurements to take and questions to answer. You should think of ways of keeping the pupils busy so that you can get the maximum amount of learning out of the time available. You will find it useful to have some follow-up activities planned for the next lesson so that the points learned can be reinforced.

If you are taking the pupils off the school premises you must consider their safety.[15] You should make sure that they are not likely to get into a situation where they can injure themselves. The following checklist will give you some guidance as to the procedures you should go through before embarking on your expedition. It is important that you obtain permission for your visit from the headteacher and also from the parents of the pupils concerned.

Planning checklist

Have you:

- Talked to the headteacher about the visit and obtained permission to go ahead?
- Clear aims and objectives for the visit?
- Worked out how much it is going to cost, taking into account:

(a) transport;
(b) entrance fees;
(c) essential publications;
(d) food;
(e) hire of equipment;
(f) insurance?

- Booked the transport well in advance of the visit and had a confirmation letter from the transport company?
- Booked the Field Study Centre, museum or other organisation and received written confirmation?
- Written to parents informing them of the cost and including a reply slip and consent form that has to be returned to you by a fixed date?

(a) you should give parents an address and/or a telephone number to contact you if you are going to be away for more than 24 hours;
(b) it is useful to have the name of the parent or guardian, address and contact telephone number for each pupil with you on your visit;
(c) you also need to know of any special problems a child might have, such as diabetes, hay fever and allergies.

- Carried out a preliminary visit to make detailed plans for the pupils' activities?
- Planned out the pupils' activities for the day, matching them to the objectives?
- Worked out a timetable for the activities?
- Checked about the toilet arrangements (both male and female) for the visit?
- Checked that you have the right ratio of staff to pupils and that you have mixed staff for a mixed group of pupils?
- Prepared a written briefing sheet for the pupils?
- Informed the pupils about what is expected of them in terms of:

(a) work to be completed?
(b) clothes to wear and additional clothes to bring?
(c) equipment to take?
(d) behaviour?

- Packed a first aid kit to take with you and checked that it is complete?
- Packed sick bags for the journey?
- Left work for those pupils that you would normally teach? This should be:

(a) written in a way that is clear and easy to follow;
(b) work that can be easily presented by a non-science specialist; and
(c) relatively easy for you to mark on your return.

- Planned follow-up work for the pupils when they return from their field work?
- Informed other members of staff that you will be taking pupils out of the school?

You will need to circulate a note to staff and put a notice on board in the staff room(s), listing the pupils by name and giving their form or tutor group. Members of staff will be very annoyed if they have prepared a significant piece of work for pupils and then find that they are absent from school.

NOTES AND REFERENCES

1. Lord Elton, (chair of the report), 1989, *Discipline in Schools. Report of the Committee of Inquiry*, HMSO, London.

2. The following books contain interesting reading about how pupils learn: Driver, R., 1985, *The Pupil as Scientist?*, Open University Press, Milton Keynes. Osborne, R. & Freyberg, P., 1985, *Learning in Science: The Implications of Children's Science*, Heinemann, London. Scott, P., 1987, *A Constructivist View of Learning and Teaching in Science*, Children's Learning in Science Project, Centre for Studies in Science and Mathematics Education, University of Leeds. Needham, R., 1987, *Teaching Strategies for Developing Understanding in Science*, Children's Learning in Science Project, Centre for Studies in Science and Mathematics Education, University of Leeds.

3. Shayer, M. & Adey, P. 1981, *Towards a Science of Science Teaching*, Heinemann, London.

4. Gagne, R.M., 1971, *The Conditions of Learning*, Holt, Reinhart & Winston, New York.

5. Bruner, J.S., 1969, *Towards a Theory of Instruction*, Belknap Press of Harvard University Press, Cambridge, Mass.

6. Ausubel, D. 1968, *Educational Psychology*, Holt, Reinhart & Winston, New York.

7. Adey, P., Shayer, M. & Yates, C., 1989, *Thinking Science: The Curriculum Materials of the Cognitive Acceleration through Science Education (CASE) Project*, Macmillan, London.

8. Bentley, D. & Watts, M., 1992, *Communicating in School Science*, Falmer Press, London.

9. Waterhouse, P., 1990, *Flexible Learning: an Outline*, Network Educational Press, Bath.

10. Foster, D., 1979, *Resource-based Learning in Science*, ASE, Hatfield.

11. National Council for Educational Technology, 1991, *Review of Flexible Learning in Schools (11–16)*, NCET, Coventry.

12. *The Advanced Physics Project for Independent Learning* (APPIL), John Murray, London. *The Independent Learning Project for Advanced Chemistry* (ILPAC), John Murray, London. *The Advanced Biology Alternative Learning Project* (ABAL), Cambridge University Press, Cambridge.

13. Department of Education and Science, 1987, *Education Observed 4: Homework, A Report by HM Inspectors*, HMSO, London.

14. Jennings, A. 1986, *Science in the Locality*, Cambridge Educational, Cambridge.

15. Department of Education and Science, 1989, *Safety in Outdoor Education*, HMSO, London.

CHAPTER 5

Practical work

5.1 THE NATURE OF SCHOOL-BASED PRACTICAL WORK

Why do we ask pupils to do practical work?

How often have you heard the phrase: 'Are we doing prac. today, Sir?' or 'Are we using the Bunsens today, Miss?' These are the frequent questions that teachers are asked at the start of many lessons. Science is seen as a practical subject and practical work is fun. Pupils think of practical work as less academically demanding and less like 'real work'. School practical work has been with us for some time[1] but science teachers' enthusiasm for it has waxed and waned over the last twenty years or so and you will find today that some teachers spend far more time on it than others. In recent years one of the major driving forces for increasing the amount of practical work was the introduction of the GCSE examination. These syllabuses required teachers to assess pupils' practical skills and submit the marks to the examination boards to be part of those used for the allocation of examination grades. This innovation helped to raise the status of practical work in schools and ensured that all pupils would have some practical experience during their GCSE course. The impetus for doing practical work has continued with the introduction of the National Curriculum, with one-quarter of the marks at KS4 being allocated to practical-related work.

There are a whole host of reasons for carrying out practical work in science lessons, some of which are listed below. Practical work:

- motivates pupils to do science and helps to keep them interested
- teaches skills to pupils (e.g. the ability to make accurate observations, manipulation skills)
- helps to promote logical thinking
- helps pupils to understand (or accept) the theory (i.e. the idea of seeing is believing)
- provides an opportunity for pupils to develop communication skills and to learn though group discussion
- provides an opportunity for pupils to work together as part of a team

It could also be said that the more practical work pupils do, the greater their skills will be and the higher will be their level or grade in any assessment scheme.

There is no doubt about it, experimentation is an essential part of a scientist's way of operating and it would be a very peculiar science course that did not contain an element of practical work.

Things to do

Write down a list of why *you* think pupils ought to do practical work. Use the reasons above if you wish but try to add some of your own. Once you have completed your list rank them in order of importance.

As you write down your aims of practical work and try to rank them in order of priority (as mentioned in the activity above) you may find yourself locked in some sort of mental conflict while you picture the different types of practical activity that are carried out in the classroom. Teachers use practical work in a variety of ways to enable pupils to learn more about science. At one level the pupils will be learning about how to use simple measuring instruments and at another they may be learning about controlling variables in an investigation. Clearly the pupils will be presented with a variety of types of practical work, but they should all fulfil three major aims:

- they should motivate the pupils to do science
- pupils should learn something from the experience, and
- they should be safe

Types of school-based practical work

Although a significant amount of time is allocated to practical work in schools in the United Kingdom, the nature of the type of practical tasks undertaken varies from classroom to classroom.

Practical work generally falls into one of the following four categories:

- learning basic practical skills
- illustrating a theory or concept
- proving a theory, and
- investigative work

1. Learning basic practical skills

Some teachers would argue that it is necessary to teach pupils some fundamental science skills before they can be allowed to carry out whole experiments. Lesson time has been allocated to sessions on such topics as the correct use of the Bunsen burner or how to read measuring instruments accurately. The majority of teachers, however, appear to be of the opinion that pupils will develop these skills as they carry out their practical exercises.

2. Illustrating a theory or concept

The assumption underpinning this approach to practical work is that pupils will have a better understanding of a scientific idea if they have observed an experiment to illustrate that idea. While this may be true in some cases it is certainly not so in all situations especially when the experiment does not yield the desired results and when the complexities of the task mask the end result.

However, illustrative experiments can often be a great motivator for pupils' learning and act as an initiating step for further work.

3. Proving a theory

This approach requires the student to generate the 'correct' scientific answer by carrying out experiments. The Nuffield Science schemes of the 1960s adopted this enquiry-based approach in their GCE O- and A-level courses. It is not expected that the pupils would be able to rediscover each individual principle in the syllabus but that they should be guided through the work and be expected to work and think like a scientist.

Woolnough and Allsop[2] express doubts over the intellectual honesty of this type of practical work. They argue that the pupil quickly realises that there is a 'right' answer and often becomes frustrated by the 'practical game' that they must play before the teacher tells them the 'correct' answer.

Many of the above types of practical tasks are presented to pupils as a list of instructions, usually on a worksheet or in a workbook. Using this method, pupils can carry out multi-step procedures with minimal help required from the teacher. Well-produced worksheet schemes can allow the student to progress at a rate corresponding to the individual's ability.

Critics of this approach would say that this reduces science to little more than 'cookery', with pupils ardently following a recipe.

4. Investigative work

Investigations, or explorations as they are sometimes called, incorporate a fairly new breed of practical activity. Scientific investigation is one of the four attainment targets of NC science. It differs from the types of practical work described above in a number of ways:

- it is more mentally taxing

- it involves more than just carrying out an experiment
- it requires the pupil to plan his/her own experiment
- the whole activity can span over two or more double periods
- it requires pupils to evaluate their experiments and suggest improvements
- it encourages pupils to question their own understanding of scientific phenomena, and
- it encourages pupils to search out information for themselves rather than relying heavily on the teacher

There are three phases to this type of practical activity: planning; implementing and concluding. Within these phases pupils will spend some time working in groups and sometimes working on their own. The process of scientific investigation is seen to be just as important as any product or result that the pupils may obtain from their experiment. Should the experiment not work or not give the desired results it is not a disaster, as it would be in illustrative type of practical work. With investigative work the pupil is encouraged to find out why the experiment did not work and how the procedure could be improved if the experiment were to be repeated.

In any school you are likely to see examples of each of these four types of practical work being used. The most common type of practical work has been (and perhaps still is) illustrative work. As far back as 1979, HMI were reporting that pupils were not doing enough of the more mentally taxing type of practical activity, investigative work.[3]

Many science teachers recognised the importance of practical work. They believed that students should have first-hand experience in laboratories in order to acquire skills in handling apparatus, to measure and to illustrate concepts and principles. Unfortunately practical work did not go further than this and few opportunities were provided for students to conduct challenging investigations.

Not everybody uses the term 'investigation' in the same way. In some textbooks you may find titles of experiments such as: 'Investigating the action of heat on metal carbonates'. Such experiments, which involve following a set experimental procedure leading to a predetermined outcome, would fall into the illustrative category described above. Most people are now using the term in its NC sense. Another term that sometimes causes confusion is that of 'problem solving'. There is obviously a clear distinction between numerical problems or calculations such as those that you might get at the end of a chapter in a textbook and practical problems. Investigative work is a type of practical problem solving but there are other practical problem-solving activities which do not neatly fit into the investigation category. 'Egg Race'[4] activities, for example, can be classified as problem solving but it is the element of designing and making something that makes them different from investigative work.

Things to do

Investigate the nature of practical work carried out with one class over a period of two weeks (longer if the class does not have frequent science lessons). This could be one of your own classes or one that you are observing. Comment on each experiment under the three headings:

1. What are the objectives?
2. How successful was the experiment in meeting these objectives?
3. Use the four categories of practical work listed above to classify each experiment carried out.

   Evaluate the amount and nature of practical work experienced by the class over the period of time.

5.2   PLANNING A PRACTICAL ACTIVITY

Careful planning is essential if you are going to maximise the learning from experimental work and all the experiments that the pupils carry out in the classroom need to be checked by you first. This includes investigations where you should consider the feasibility, practicalities and safety implications of the experiments that may be carried out.

   Whenever possible you should carry out the experiment well before the lesson using exactly the same materials as those the pupils are going to use.

   The starting point for every practical activity is to clarify in your own mind the reasons for doing the experiment. Remember that practical work can be costly both in terms of materials and, perhaps more importantly, lesson time. Before you begin the experiment you should be clear in your own mind about why you are doing it, i.e. what are your objectives? Use the practical work checklist below to help you to plan practical work.

Practical work checklist

1.	Objectives	Write down the reasons for doing this experimental work.
2.	Timing	It is difficult to judge how long pupils will take to carry out a specific activity. They may rush through the work in race-like fashion, trying to be the first to finish or they may prolong it so putting off the less attractive option of writing the work up. Assume you have a model pupil who will work through the practical thoroughly, achieving all your objectives. Make an estimate of how long you

think it will take him/her to complete the work then carry out the practical yourself and time how long it takes you.

3. Problems

What difficulties do you expect the pupils to have in doing this experiment?
(a) safety problems (COSHH risk assessment[5]);
(b) problems associated with the distribution of materials;
(c) problems concerned with manipulating apparatus;
(d) problems concerned with pupils making observations;
(e) other problem areas.

4. Introduction

You need to plan out carefully how you are going to present the experiment to the pupils. They must know the purpose of the work and what they have to do. There is nothing more frustrating than having a group of youngsters gathered round you asking you every few seconds, 'What do I do next?' Plan your work so that you avoid this.
How will you motivate the pupils to want to do it?
How will you give the instructions to the pupils (worksheets, textbook, oral instructions, etc.)?

5. During the experiment

Many pupils are not good at seeing what they are supposed to see during experiments. They need training in making observations. They also need to be trained in selecting what to record. You should consider ways of helping pupils to use their practical time most effectively. For example, it is unproductive to allow pupils to sit and watch while one group member takes all the measurements. Much idle gossip takes place during practical work while pupils are waiting for something to happen. Pupils should have their attention focused on some science activity such as making observations, discussing something related to the practical task or recording their work. They should also examine different methods of presenting their results.
How are you going to get the pupils to draw the conclusions from their results?

	How are you going to cope with the pupil question: 'Have I got the right answer, Miss?'?
6. Teacher situation	Make a list of questions you will ask pupils as you circulate around the class. Perhaps think about who you will give special attention to during this lesson. Are there opportunities for assessment?

Practical work, more so than any other teaching activity, requires that the teacher is organised. If you are not organised you could find yourself with a lot of extra work or your plans falling apart. One source of pressure in getting the equipment ready for the lesson will come from the technician.

Information for the technician

Technicians are very busy people, often having to serve a number of teachers. If you are to get your laboratory requirements on time and in the right place you must give the technician all the information plenty of time in advance of your lesson. This may involve handing in your list a week or more before you are ready to teach. It is not advisable to write your requirements down on the back of old envelopes as they have a tendency to get lost or thrown in the bin. Most schools have a system such as a diary, record book or record cards for you to fill in. It is advisable to be fairly explicit in your request, otherwise you may find you get the wrong size of the item you are using or parts of the apparatus are incompatible. If you limit yourself to writing statements such as 'the apparatus as on the worksheet' or 'the distillation of ink' then you should not be surprised if you get something rather different from what you had in mind. It is much easier for a technician to work off a list, where things can be checked and ticked off as they are put ready for you. Figure 5.1 illustrates one way of presenting your requirements. The method that you choose to use should at least include the following information:

- your name and the class name
- the date and time (or lesson period) you require the materials
- the room where the lesson will be held
- the quantities of chemicals, etc.
- the concentrations of solutions
- the numbers of each item required
- the size of items required (remember that test tubes, beakers and flasks come in a variety of sizes; the range of any meter used must be compatible with other apparatus), and
- where you would like the apparatus to be placed in the room

Teacher	A. Einstein	Class:	Y10P
Date of lesson:	1.10.99	Time:	1.45
Room:	Chem. lab	Expt.:	Investigating carbonates

Bottles of the following metal carbonates:
copper (II) carbonate; zinc carbonate; sodium carbonate; calcium carbonate

15 sets of:

4 hard glass test tubes
Spatula
Safety glasses
1 holed bung to fit test tube complete with right-angled bend tube
4 ordinary test tubes
Bottle of limewater (made up fresh)
Bottle of hydrochloric acid 1–2 mol dm $^{-3}$

In trays along the side bench, please

Figure 5.1 **Example of a requisition form for the technician**

Whenever possible, you should check through the equipment that has been prepared for you prior to the lesson. It is often the small things that catch teachers out, such as matches to light the Bunsen burners or test tube racks to hold the test tubes.

Things to do

Obtain feedback from the technician about the detail you are giving on your equipment requisition forms. Are you giving sufficient notice?

How do you check that all the equipment has been returned?

What is the procedure for breakages? How are these recorded and replacement items ordered?

In what way could the system for organising apparatus be improved? Could pupils be given more responsibility for getting their own equipment or even looking after a set of equipment that they use on a regular basis?

Setting out the equipment in the laboratory

Unless the equipment is set out in an orderly fashion around the laboratory you will find that eager pupils will rush and push to get the 'best' apparatus. You will find it helpful to have different parts of the equipment placed at different points in the room. This avoids all the pupils converging on one spot to get what they require. You should try to avoid any situation where the pupils are likely to bump into one another. This is particularly important when they are carrying hazardous chemicals or glass apparatus. One way of overcoming this problem is to insist on a one-way movement of pupils around the laboratory (say, clockwise) during practical work. Another ploy is to insist that only one person from each group will be responsible for collecting equipment and that person can only move when you say so. No matter how organised you think you are there will always be situations that catch you out. You should learn from these and gradually improve the efficiency of the distribution of equipment. The following paragraphs, taken from a report of a trainee teacher, serve as a timely reminder that all will not run smoothly straight away.

In my first lesson with this class I naively assumed that a brief outline of the practical work to be undertaken, including identification of the page to follow in the workbook, would be sufficient for pupils to start working, and that I would be free to walk around checking that everyone was clear about what they were supposed to be doing.

The resultant chaos as pupils tried to scramble for equipment, whilst clearly not knowing what they were going to do with it, resulted in frustration, for them and for me, but at least ensured that by the next lesson I had evolved a more effective strategy.

5.3   PLANNING DEMONSTRATION EXPERIMENTS

Demonstrations are an important part of a teacher's classroom repertoire. They are performed by the teacher when it is impossible for the pupils to do the experiment themselves. 'Performed' is a key word here, because for the demonstration to be effective there needs to be an element of stage management. As scientists we are all used to carrying out experiments for ourselves but we are not used to presenting an experiment to others so that they can see what is going on and be involved with the activity. Pupils should not be simply passive observers of the demonstration but should be actively involved, mentally and in some cases physically, in what is going on. Before you finally decide to do the demonstration, read through any instructions or description of the experiment and think about its usefulness by asking yourself the following questions:

- what is it for?
- why is it included in the course?
- what could the pupils learn from it?
- can it be used to teach any major ideas of scientific importance?

Once you are clear in your own mind about the purpose of the demonstration then you need to practise it. You will find it beneficial to practise the demonstration at the place you are going to perform it. This will give you the opportunity to consider the positioning of the equipment so that it is both safe and in a place where the pupils can get the best possible view. As a general rule demonstrations need to be big and bold. It is no use doing experiments in tiny test tubes that no one can see. If it is perfectly safe to do it in large beakers, then use large beakers. If there is part of the experiment that is difficult to see you should contemplate allowing pupils to come up a few at a time to make their observations. Alternatively, you could make use of the school video camera. This can be set up on a camera tripod prior to starting the demonstration and left to run. The video image can be displayed on a monitor while the experiment is in progress. Obviously the camera needs to be placed at a safe distance from the apparatus or be protected by a screen. Many schools will have a video camera that can be fitted to the top of a microscope, thus allowing pupils to see objects of microscopic size.

While practising the experiment, you should ask yourself the questions listed below and be prepared to modify the experiment in the light of your answers.

- Are the pupils protected from the experiment? Use a safety screen and eye protection, if appropriate. Make sure that the pupils are seated at a safe distance from the experiment. Make sure that you are suitably protected (safety spectacles, goggles or face shield, plus laboratory coat and gloves if necessary).
- What are the crucial observations that you would like the pupils to make? Write these down in your lesson plan.
- How could you improve the design, scale or positioning of the apparatus to make sure that pupils will see everything?
- What could you say or do to focus their interest on these points?
- What will the pupils do besides just listening and watching (they could get restless)? Could some of them act as assistants?
- At points where waiting is essential, can you set them worthwhile and interesting tasks?
- In what ways might the experiment go wrong on you?
- How long will it take?
- What would you get the pupils to do later in the lesson, which would (a) give them a feeling of achievement and (b) show you whether they have understood and can apply the concept taught?

You may need to do the experiment several times to gain confidence with the equipment and know how to cope when things go wrong. It is worth while remembering that when you carry out an experiment for yourself you become absorbed in what is going on and you have little concern for your surroundings. When you perform a demonstration, however, not only have you got to be concerned about the experiment but you also have to interact with your pupils. It is important that you try to create the right sort of atmosphere with your class so that this interaction can take place easily. This will involve bringing the pupils round the demonstration bench in an orderly fashion, indicating that misbehaviour will not be tolerated. The pupils should be comfortable during the demonstration and should preferably be sitting on stools. Pupils that are standing or sitting on benches tend

Do	Don't
– have all the materials carefully prepared and labelled	– leave dirty equipment lying around for others to tidy up
– try the experiment out beforehand	– give the answer away before the experiment is performed
– ask relevant questions	– use concepts that are too difficult for the class
– ask for student assistants and 'volunteers'	– forget to make careful notes so that when you do the experiment again it will be easier to organise
– require that the students make notes or answer questions	
– know why the demonstration is being performed	
– respect safety	

Figure 5.2   *A checklist for setting up a demonstration experiment*

to shove and push and occasionally thump one another. You will find it difficult if you have to deal with discipline problems at the same time as performing the demonstration.

Choose the site for the demonstration carefully. Think initially about the services you require (water, gas, electricity) and then about the positioning of the apparatus with respect to the pupils and yourself. The pupils need to be comfortable and safe. You also need to be safe and in a position where you are free to move quickly to any other point in the room in case of an emergency. If you choose to demonstrate on a raised teacher's bench, as found in many older laboratories, you should make sure that there are no pupils blocking your way at the end of the teacher's platform. It can be very awkward if you have to demonstrate on a side bench or in a fume cupboard and you will need to experiment to find the best possible position.

Things to do

The next time you carry out a demonstration experiment, ask someone to observe you and to make comments under the following headings:

1. The positioning of the pupils.
2. The visibility of the apparatus.
3. The introduction and presentation.
4. The nature of the questions asked.
5. The clarity of the science.
6. The appropriateness of the demonstration.

5.4 SCIENTIFIC INVESTIGATIONS

What is a scientific investigation?

In investigative work pupils are involved in the process of finding things out by enquiry. For the most part this will involve experimentation but it will also require the pupil to search out information in other ways. Through investigations pupils work in a scientific way to solve problems and so gain knowledge and understanding. The opening paragraph to Sc1 states:[6]

Pupils should develop the intellectual and practical skills which will allow them to explore and investigate the world of science and develop a fuller understanding of scientific phenomena, the nature of theories explaining these, and the procedures of scientific investigation.

Investigative work differs in a number of ways from the other three types of practical work. For example, investigative work:

- gives pupils the opportunity to test their own understanding of scientific phenomena
- encourages pupils to make statements that they can test
- allows pupils to plan their own investigation
- presents pupils with the opportunity for discussing their ideas with other pupils
- encourages pupils to think in a scientific way, consider the variables and carry out a fair test
- makes pupils think about the type of apparatus and measuring equipment they will need
- allows pupils to make decisions on what observations to make
- gives pupils the opportunity to decide on the most appropriate way of recording their results
- places pupils in a position where they have to interpret their own results, and can initiate further discussion and/or further investigative work

Investigative work is not *just* another type of practical activity, it encompasses a whole range of activities that are centred around helping pupils to learn. The first point in the list above, highlights the fact that pupils can 'check out' what they understand to be the truth. As mentioned in Chapter 4 (page 88) Driver and co-workers have shown that pupils come to science lessons with a whole host of different ideas about why things happen. Many of these do not fit the accepted scientific explanations. The process of changing from an original understanding to a scientific one is difficult and many pupils will pass through school still retaining their original ideas. They may even give 'correct' explanations for examination purposes while still retaining considerable doubt over the scientific reasoning. For meaningful learning to occur pupils must construct their own understanding by modifying their pre-existing ideas in the light of new insights gained from their performance and outcome of the investigation. This constructivist approach to learning is largely based on the work of the Children's Learning in Science Project (CLISP).[7]

NC science provides teachers with a framework for viewing (and assessing) scientific investigation in terms of the three strands of Sc1:

The activities should encourage the ability to plan and carry out investigations in which pupils:

i)   ask questions, predict and hypothesise
ii)   observe, measure and manipulate variables
iii) interpret their results and evaluate scientific evidence.

These three strands of an investigation are basically the three phases of activity that pupils are involved in during their work as well as forming the framework for the assessment for Sc1. Before considering the practicalities of carrying out an investigation you need to familiarise yourself with the principles of problem solving and the language associated with it. The first term you need to be familiar with is the difference between open and closed investigations. A closed investigation may be defined as one where there is a single way of approaching the task, whereas an open investigation can have multiple solutions or one solution with many approaches. All the investigations described here are open investigations as these are the type required for Sc1.

Using a problem-solving model in investigative work

There is no simple answer to the question of how pupils go about solving a problem. There will be a lot of guessing and trying things out, perhaps some journeys down blind alleys, perhaps some lucky breaks. More often than not it will take a number of false starts as the investigators come to terms with the problem and the equipment to solve the problem. How can such a haphazard sequence of events possibly form part of our orderly system of teaching? This is a dilemma that has faced the traditionalists amongst teachers since the introduction of the NC. In an attempt to introduce some order to problem solving and to help to get a feeling for the types of processes that are going on in pupils' minds, various groups have produced problem-solving models. Broadly speaking they are all very similar. Each of these models represents an idealised situation but they help us by providing a framework on which to build our teaching strategies. For this work we shall use the model that is most widely quoted in science education, the Assessment of Performance Unit (APU)

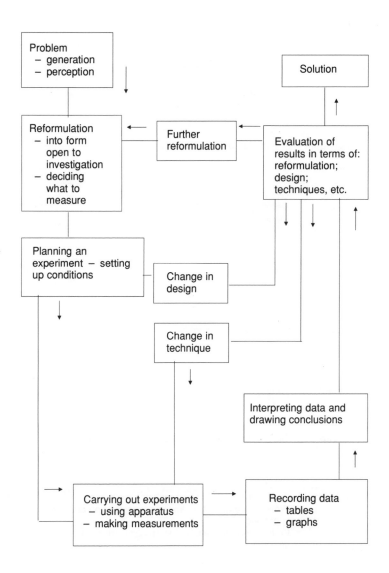

Figure 5.3 **A problem-solving model** *(based on Gott & Murphy, 1987)*

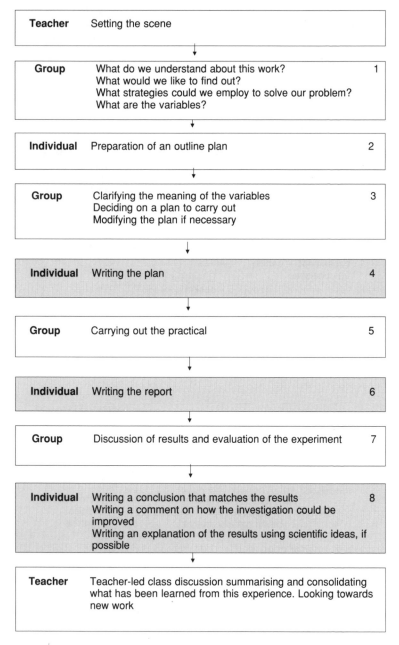

The shaded areas are occasions where pupils can be assessed on the three strands of Sc1.

*Figure 5.4   **Possible sequence of activities in an investigation***

problem-solving model as shown in Figure 5.3.[8] Basically, the three blocks on the left-hand side of the diagram represent the planning stage of Sc1. Following the arrows round, the next block is obviously the implementation phase. The blocks up the right-hand side represent the concluding phase. The central blocks show the cyclical nature of problem solving, how we need to keep revising our thoughts or our experimentation to come to an ever more accurate solution.

Before we move on to developing a teaching strategy, it must be pointed out that this procedure outlines only one approach to problem solving. There are others and they may work just as well. This method has the benefit of allowing pupils to work both individually and in groups. It also fits into the pattern of Sc1 and provides opportunities for individual pupils to be assessed (see the shaded areas in Figure 5.4).

Starting at the left-hand side and working our way round to the right, let us see how this model can help us to put together a teaching strategy.

The first stage in problem solving is identifying a problem to be solved. While on the surface this may appear simple, it is the key to a successful activity. If the problem does not match the ability of the pupils then they are likely to become frustrated. The pupils will have a greater commitment to the problem if they see it as their own rather than one that has been artificially introduced by the teacher. The pupils need to take their initial ideas from the carefully managed introduction of the teacher and begin to make them their own, through their group discussion, and devise a problem that they would like to solve (see area 1 in Figure 5.4).

The next key stage in the process is the important reformulation of the problem into a form that can be tested (see area 3 in Figure 5.4). The problem needs to be put into the form of a clear statement, e.g. 'I think that the strength of the electromagnet will increase if I increase the number of coils round the iron bar'. As the planning process proceeds pupils will start identifying the variables that are associated with their problem. For example, in the electromagnet investigation they may identify the following variables:

1. the number of coils;
2. the thickness of the iron core;
3. the number of cells;
4. the current through the wire;
5. the distance apart of the coils;
6. the length of the wire;
7. the type of plastic cover on the wire;
8. the distance of the coil away from the end of the iron core;
9. the material of the core.

In this list there are different types of variables, categoric, discrete and continuous. Table 5.2 gives the meanings of these terms and gives examples for two different investigations. For the electromagnet investigation the variables can be classified thus:

Categoric

2. the thickness of the iron core (i.e. thick or thin);
5. the distance apart of the coils (i.e. close together or far apart);
7. the type of plastic cover on the wire (i.e. thick plastic or thin plastic);
9. the material of the core (e.g. aluminium, iron, steel, lead, plastic).

Discrete

1. the number of coils;
3. the number of cells;
8. the distance of the coil away from the end of the iron core.

Continuous

4. the current through the wire.
6. the length of the wire.

In order to make a test fair the investigator must choose to change only one of the variables in any one experiment. This one is called the independent variable. All the others are kept the same or controlled (called the control variables). The variable that is measured by the investigator is called the dependent variable. The results will compare the dependent variable with the independent variable being investigated. It may be that the results will need to be mathematically transformed into a quantity normally used in science, e.g. temperature into thermal energy, height into potential energy, electric power into thermal energy. This type of variable is called a derived variable.

The third stage (area 5 in Figure 5.4) is the actual carrying out of the plan. There are two major challenges facing the pupils at this point, the difficulty of the experimental procedures and the conceptual understanding of the processes going on. There is a great temptation for the teacher to tell them what to do, either to speed the process up or to put the pupils out of their misery but it will be far more fruitful in the long term for the teacher to restrict his/her intervention to advice and encouragement. The APU[9] have shown that:

In practical tasks, the feedback that is available throughout the investigation assists in the development of appropriate procedural strategies.

The fourth stage firmly places the learning in the hands of the pupils. It is the pupils who discuss the results, not the teacher telling them what they should have got. This is the time that the pupils go back to their original ideas and check to see if they were true. But perhaps more importantly, were their explanations correct? This stage covers areas 7, 8 and the teacher-led discussion of Figure 5.4. It is hopefully the point where the pupil comes to terms with the 'correct'

Table 5.1 Types of variables

	Independent	Dependent	Control	Derived
Alternative name	Input variable	Output variable	Controlled variable	Calculated variable
Explanation	The factor that the investigator changes systematically	The factor that the investigator measures	The factors that the investigator keeps constant during the investigation	Calculated from the results of the experiment
Examples of the variables in an investigation on bouncing balls	• type of ball • colour of ball • the height the ball dropped from • the surface the ball is dropped on • temperature • mass of the ball	• the height the ball bounces to • the number of bounces	All the independent variables except one	e.g. potential energy (mass × height × g)

Table 5.2 Types of independent variables

Example	Categoric (A non-numeric quantity)	Discrete (Can only have whole number values)	Continuous (Can have any numeric value)
1. Investigation involving the insulation of a container	type of material used for insulation colour of the material hot or cold	number of layers	thickness of insulation measured in cm temperature measured in °C volume of water measured in cm^3
2. Investigation involving the dissolving of fizzy sweets in water	colour of the fizzy sweets shape of the sweets	number of fizzy sweets	temperature measured in °C volume of water measured in cm^3

scientific understanding or at least has a clearer grasp of the phenomena than s/he had before.

Preparing for investigative work

For years teachers have been used to the idea that if they wish to carry out an experiment with pupils, then all they have to do is to go to a textbook and find the instructions. With investigative work life is not so easy. However, there are books available[10] to help teachers in their preparation of investigations and I feel sure that during the next few years we will see many more. Examples of investigations are also given in some of the publications from SEAC for KS3.[11] For KS4 ideas you could turn to the examples given by the examination boards.[12]

The SoW for each group of pupils should highlight occasions for carrying out investigations. For individual lessons you will need to expand on this information so that you have a clearer picture of what is involved. Table 5.3 gives examples of six possible investigations showing the type of information that you require to start your planning. The first column indicates how the investigation fits into the SoW and the reference to the NC. It is important to have an approximate match between the maximum level you are aiming to assess in Sc1 and the level of work in the other attainment target. The advice from SEAC[13] with regard to this is:

There should be approximate parity between the level pupils are working at in Sc1 and the level of knowledge and understanding in Sc2, 3 or 4 required by the investigation.

The second column looks at a possible way into the investigation. This will be related to the work the pupils have done or are in the process of doing. It is important to try to set up the investigation in a context that has some everyday relevance or intrinsic appeal for the pupils.

The next two columns in the table list the possible variables pupils may wish to investigate. This list is probably best completed while the teacher is 'playing' with the equipment and materials and thinking about the suggestions that pupils may have for their investigation. It is important that you carry out some investigative work with the materials the pupils are going to use. It will help you to spot possible snags with experimental procedure or equipment and, while you may not do exactly the same experiment that the pupils will do, it will give you a rough guide as to how long to allow for the work.

The final column draws attention to the appropriate science theory on which the investigation is set. If pupils are to obtain level 6c and above they must explain their results in terms of a scientific model,

Table 5.3 Some examples of areas of the Science National Curriculum where investigative work can be carried out

Topic / NC ref.	Possible framework	Possible independent variables	Dependent variables	Example of related scientific theory
Digestion *Sc2/7a*	What factors affect the digestion of egg white?	• Temperature • Concentration of egg white solution • Concentration of acid added to egg white • Volume of acid added • Volume of pepsin added	Time taken for the cloudy suspension of egg white to clear	Pepsin digests egg white in acid conditions at temperatures round about body temperature (35–40°C)
Rate of reaction $CaCO_3(s) + HCl(aq)$ *Sc3/7f*	Limestone buildings being dissolved in acid rain	• Size of limestone chips • Mass of limestone • Concentration of acid • Volume of acid • Temperature	Volume of CO_2 liberated in specific time intervals	Rate of reaction is increased by: increase in temperature, increase in concentration, etc.
Gyrating wheel *Sc4 PoS for KS4 strand ii*	Pupils investigate spinning wheels	• Diameter of wheel • Length of spindle • Position of the wheel on the spindle • Intitial spin given to the spindle • Material used for the wheel • Material used for the spindle • No. of holes in wheel	Time the wheel will spin	Larger wheels store more energy and therefore spin longer

e.g. the kinetic theory, theory of genetics, theory of electrolysis. If an investigation does not involve two or more independent variables then pupils will not be able to reach level 7 in either strand (ii) or strand (iii).

It is unreasonable to assume that pupils will assimilate the skills necessary to carry out scientific investigations overnight. Teachers need to devote some time to teaching on how to think and work scientifically. Feedback to the pupils about how to improve their investigative skills is essential if the pupils are to achieve the higher levels of Sc1.

The final version of a teacher's planning sheet for investigative work may look something like Figure 5.5. This is where you could jot down information about the experimental procedure and ideas on how to introduce the work to the pupils. The sheet can also form the basis of an assessment plan for the work, as can be seen from the example in Figure 9.3. Judgements need to be made as to how much classroom time you are going to allow for the activity and how many, if any, homework sessions.

Setting up an investigation (the planning phase)

Using the approach described so far, there are four clear stages that lead up to the practical part of the investigation and these involve:

- the teacher setting the scene
- group discussion to initiate the investigation
- individual work to prepare a plan, and
- group work to clarify meanings and decide on a strategy

The teacher's involvement in setting the scene is crucial to the success of the work. Tell the pupils too little and they will not be able to proceed. Tell them too much and it will no longer be an investigation. The teacher must create an atmosphere of curiosity and develop a desire amongst the pupils to want to find something out. The OPENS[14] (Open-ended Work in Science Project) has carried out research into how teachers can plan their investigative work to make it as open-ended as possible. Their report gives examples of how teachers introduced investigations and discusses the problem of giving the pupils just the right amount of information. Probably the best approach to initiating investigative work is to do a lot of asking rather than a lot of telling. For example, pupils might be asked questions that require them to reflect on their understanding of work they have done previously. Interest may be generated by some background information or telling a short story putting the situation into an everyday context. Alternatively the stimulus may come from a demonstration (with no explanation from the teacher, perhaps) or a brainstorming session.

Topic: Electromagnetism	**KS:** 4 **Year:** 10

NC reference (PoS): strand i	**NC reference (SoA):** Sc4/7a
Pupils should study electromagnetic effects in common devices. Pupils should be given the opportunity to extend their quantitative study of electrical circuits	Understand the magnetic effect of an electric current and its application in a range of common devices

Setting the scene:	Previous work on passing an electrical current through a straight wire and a coil. Plotting the magnetic fields. Uses of electromagnets. What affects the strength of an electromagnet? How can we measure strength?

Possible independent variables:	**Possible dependent variables:**
Categoric	
· the thickness of the iron core (i.e. thick or thin)	Number of paper clips that the electromagnet can pick up
· the distance apart of the coils (i.e. close together or far apart)	
· the type of plastic cover on the wire (i.e. thick plastic or thin plastic)	Mass of iron filings that can be picked up
· the material of the core (e.g. aluminium, iron, steel, lead, plastic)	By lifting small masses
Discrete	
· the number of coils	
· the number of cells	
· the distance of the coil away from the end of the iron core	
Continuous	
· the current through the wire	
· the length of the wire	

Scientific ideas: Experiments show that, for a solenoid of any given length, the strength of the magnetic field can be increased by:	**Textbook reference:**
1. increasing the current	
2. increasing the number of turns	
The iron core increases the strength of magnetic field. It is about 1000 times stronger than the coil by itself	

Teacher's notes: Using cells is the most convenient way of carrying out the experiment but it does have a number of disadvantages:
· rechargeable cells can be quickly drained
· it limits the investigation with regard to changing the current

The wire can get quite hot if the current is left on

The length of wire in the circuit should be kept constant otherwise the resistance of the circuit will change

Figure 5.5 **An example of a teacher planning sheet for investigative work**

A starting point for the group discussion might be to ask each member of the group to write down questions that s/he would like the answer to. By doing this, they have all started to focus their minds on to the task and they each have something they can contribute to the discussion. The group would decide on the nature of the problem to be solved and start to pinpoint the variables involved. It would get the problem into a form that could be investigated and would discuss the practicalities of solving the problem. It would be up to the individual pupils to take sufficient information away from this group meeting to start writing his/her own plan. To help them with this process it is advisable to have some sort of guidance sheet. Examples of this type of sheet are given in Figures 5.6 and 5.7.

Before starting the practical task, members of the group need to satisfy themselves that they all agree over the exact meaning of the variables. It is useful to go through each one and ask the question, 'What do we mean by . . . ?'. For example, in an investigation involving bouncing balls, pupils would ask the question, 'What do we mean by large, medium and small balls?'. They may go on to ask, 'What is a bounce? Do we count the very small bounces at the end or has the ball got to reach a certain height before we count it?'.

Guiding the pupils (the implementation phase)

It has already been mentioned that the teacher should not fall into the trap of telling the pupils the answer at this stage. It is a time for guiding, asking questions, prompting and giving advice and support. Pupils, in their groups, should be encouraged to work independently from the teacher. The teacher is not there to tell them what to do. S/he is there as a resource along with the other resources such as books, computers and charts.

Pupils may need assistance in composing their report. They are notoriously poor at writing down what they observe, often abbreviating things to the point that it is almost meaningless and not making it clear what they are referring to. For example

some pupils write:	when they mean:
(a) it popped	the gas given off popped in a Bunsen flame
(b) it went yellow	a yellow precipitate was formed and the solution went colourless

Figure 5.7 illustrates a type of guidance sheet that covers all aspects of the investigation.

Investigation Planning Sheet

| Strand (i) level: | |

Name: _____

Science group: _____

Investigation title: _____

What are you going to find out? (I think that . . . because . . .)

_____

What do you think will happen?

_____

Why do you think this will happen?

_____

What are the variables?

_____

What will you change in your experiments?

_____

What will you measure/observe?

_____

What will you keep constant in your experiments?

_____

How many measurements will you take?

_____

What instruments will you use to make your measurements?

_____

How will you make sure that you carry out the experiment safely?

_____

Figure 5.6 **An example of a pupil planning sheet**

Remember

You will be marked on what you write down and not on the thoughts in your head

---

Planning

What are you going to investigate?
> Look at the apparatus/materials that are associated with your investigation.
> Talk this through in your group and write down a draft title.
> During the planning process you may need to change the title.
> Think about the work you have carried out on this topic.
> If there is anything you don't understand, ask your teacher or look it up in a book.
> Write down a statement in the form, 'I think that ... because ...'

Write down a list of variables.
> Brainstorm a list or ask each member of the group to come up with a list.
> Check that everyone in the group understands the exact meaning of each variable by asking the question 'What exactly do we mean by ...?' You must be precise.
> What are you going to measure? (What are you investigating?).
> What are you going to change? What are you going to keep constant in your experiments?

Use variables that change continuously if you can, e.g. mass, temperature, time, distance, area, volume.

If you can't, then use variables that change in steps, e.g. colour, hot and cold, thick and thin, number of layers.

Write down a list of the apparatus you will require.

Experimenting

> Check your plan for safety.
> What instruments will you require to make your measurements?
> What range of measurements do you expect to take?
> Do you need to take a number of readings and take an average?
> How are you going to record your results?
> Write down all your observations as the experiment proceeds. It is better to write too much than too little.
> Think about ways of improving the experiment if you were to do it a second time.
> Write down your possible improvements.

Concluding

> Describe your investigation. What changes did you make to your original plan? Have you described the effects of your variables?
> Present your results in a table if at all possible.
> Can you show your results as: a pie chart, a histogram or a line graph?
> Did your findings match your predictions?
> How can you explain your results? Is one explanation of your results better than others? Why?
> Write down clearly the conclusions that can be formed from the results.
> How could you improve your investigation (e.g. by making it more accurate or more reliable)?

---

*Figure 5.7   **An example of a support sheet for investigations***

Reviewing the experience (the concluding phase)

Pupils and teachers expend a lot of time and energy in any one investigation. It is, therefore, worth while spending some time to finish off the job well. Pupils will need help in sorting out their results and suitable ways of presenting them. They may not readily see the need to display their results graphically and will require guidance as to what type of graph to use.[15]

An essential part of the whole process of investigating is the establishing of ideas about science and the world in which we live. The consolidation of ideas is best done through group and class discussion at the end of the investigation. It will be a time for re-asking the key questions posed at the start of the task and looking for clearer understanding amongst the pupils. Time should also be put aside for an evaluation of the experience. 'What have we learnt from our work? What else do we need to know? What experimental skills do I need to improve?'

Progression in investigations

The nature of scientific problems set in schools can be extremely varied, from tasks that can be readily solved in a single science lesson to those that require work over many weeks. It is important that teachers have a clear understanding of the complexity of each problem to be tackled by pupils. If we wish pupils to make progress with their investigative techniques then we should provide them with tasks of increasing complexity. However, there are many facets to the complexity that confronts us when studying any investigation. The APU have carried out extensive research into pupil progression in problem-solving activities and have provided teachers with a useful insight into task difficulty.[16] Qualter et al.[17] have built on this work to provide teachers with a useful framework for reviewing progression in investigative work. There are two key areas of progression to consider:

- the complexity of the task set by the teacher, and
- the approach a pupil uses to tackle an investigation

Table 5.4 summarises the areas that need to be considered when planning for progression in investigative work. The SoAs for the levels of Sc1 give a picture of progression in terms of task complexity and it is easy to pick out references to increasing difficulty in terms of:

- the context in which the investigation is set
- the procedural demands of the investigation, and
- the conceptual demands of the investigation

Deciding on the context in which to set an investigation is not as straightforward as it might at first appear. Some teachers may believe that pupils will perform at their best when the problem is placed in an everyday context. The work of the APU has shown that this is not necessarily true. If a problem is set in a scientific context, pupils are cued in to working in a scientific way. This does not happen if the problem is based around more common household situations. It is also possible that in an attempt to make things more relevant to pupils' experience, teachers may introduce situations that favour one sex or pupils from one particular cultural background.

Another point worth considering is that the context of a problem may help pupils to recall certain previous experiences that will help them to make decisions about how to investigate and to decide on the detail of their investigation.

Children are likely to tackle a problem badly if it is overburdened with procedures. The sheer complexity of a task may cause some children to completely shut off and not even attempt the problem. The approach used by pupils will depend heavily on their previous experience, not just in science lessons but also from their everyday activities. It is worth bearing in mind that if pupils are presented with an array of apparatus from which to choose at the start of their work, they will obviously be influenced by the amount and type of equipment supplied

It has been mentioned previously that there needs to be an approximate matching of the level of Sc1 and a level in one of the other science attainment targets. The aim of the investigation is for the pupil to achieve a greater understanding of the scientific concepts s/he has learned. Pupils need to be taught to tackle their problems in an increasingly scientific way. They will learn by example from the teacher and from the detailed comments made on their investigation reports. The headings given under task approach in Table 5.4 can serve as a useful guide for such comments.

Things to do

Consider an investigation that you have recently carried out with a class and analyse the task for:

- procedural demand
- conceptual demand, and
- the context in which it was set

Table 5.4 **Areas of progression in investigative work**

	Type of progression	Lower and upper limits of progression	→
	Context	Everyday contexts	→ New and unfamiliar contexts
		Simple apparatus	→ Complex apparatus (including use of computer interfacing)
Task complexity	Procedural demands	Simple skills required	→ More complex skills with measurements taken to a greater degree of precision
		Single independent variable	→ Multiple independent variables
		Categoric independent variable	→ Continuous independent variable
	Conceptual demands	Based on simple ideas	→ Requires deep understanding of science concepts
	Overall approach	Trial and error with little formal planning	→ Structured plan, systematic approach, analysis of procedures
Task approach	Observing and collecting information	Subjective (non-structured) and qualitative judgements made	→ Quantitative measurements taken with accuracy at the appropriate time. Measurements repeated and average value calculated
	Evaluating	Limited	→ Make judgements on the appropriateness of the procedure. Able to comment on how the investigation can be improved
	Reasoning	Simplistic, unable to make generalisations	→ Ability to use abstract reasoning, make generalisations, use formulae and symbols

NOTES AND REFERENCES

In order to reduce confusion with the many SEAC KS3 documents, which all look very similar, their reference numbers have been given in addition to the normal information.

1. Gee, B. & Clackson, G., 'The origin of practical work in the English school science curriculum', *School Science Review*, 1992, **73** (265), 79–83.

2. Woolnough, B.E., & Allsop, R.T., 1985, *Practical Work in Schools*, Cambridge University Press, Cambridge.

3. HMI, 1979, *Aspects of Secondary Education in England*, HMSO, London.

4. Ideas for practical problem-solving activities are given in: *Ideas for Egg Races and Other Practical Problem Solving Activities*, 1983, British Association for the Advancement of Science, London. *More Ideas for Egg Races and Other Practical Problem Solving Activities*, 1983, British Association for the Advancement of Science, London. Davies, K., 1990, *In Search of Solutions: Some Ideas for Chemical Egg Races and Other Problem Solving Activities in Chemistry*, Royal Society of Chemistry, London.

5. Health and Safety Commission, 1989, *COSHH: Guidance for Schools*, HMSO, London. (See Chapter 3 for further information on COSHH regulations.)

6. Department of Education and Science and The Welsh Office, 1991, *Science in the National Curriculum (1991)*, HMSO, London.

7. Scott, P., 1987, *A Constructivist View of Learning and Teaching in Science*, Children's Learning in Science Project, Centre for Studies in Science and Mathematics Education, University of Leeds.

8. Gott, R. & Murphy, P., 1987, *Assessing Investigations at Ages 13 and 15*, APU Science Report for Teachers No. 9, DES, London.

9. Reference 8 (page 52).

10. The following books contain examples of investigations:

    (i) Gott, R., Welford, G. & Foulds, K., 1988, *The Assessment of Practical Work in Science*, Basil Blackwell, Oxford.

    (ii) Bryce, T.G.K., McCall, J., MacGregor, J., Robertson, I.J. & Weston, R.A.J., 1991, *TAPS 3 How to Assess Open-ended Practical Investigations in Biology, Chemistry and Physics*, Heinemann, Oxford.

    (iii) Strang, J., Daniels, S. & Bell, J., 1991, *Assessment Matters: No. 6: Planning and Carrying out Investigations*, SEAC, London (Ref: D/012/B/91).

(iv) Schools Examinations and Assessment Council, 1993, *KS3 Pupils' Work Assessed: Science (Four Pupils' Folders)*, SEAC, London, (Ref: A/065/B/93).

11. See reference 10(iv) and School Examinations and Assessment Council, 1993, *School Assessment Folder: Assessing Sc1*, SEAC, London (Ref: A/057/B/92).

12. All GCSE examination boards will supply examples of Sc1 work. See reference 17 in Chapter 9 for examples.

13. Schools Examinations and Assessment Council, 1993, *School Assessment Folder: Assessing Sc1*, SEAC, London (p. 15) (Ref: A/057/B/92).

14. Jones, A.T., Simon, S.A., Black, P.J., Fairbrother, R.W. & Watson, J.R., 1992, *Open Work in Science: Development of Investigations in Schools*, ASE, Hatfield.

15. Taylor, R.M., & Swatton, P., 1990, *Assessment Matters: No. 1, Graph Work in School Science*, SEAC, London.

16. *Assessment Matters: No. 5: Profiles and Progression in Science Explorations*, SEAC, London.

17. Qualter, A., Strang, J., Swatton, P. & Taylor, R., 1990, *Exploration: A Way of Learning Science*, Blackwell, Oxford.

CHAPTER 6

Reading, writing and talking

6.1 WHAT SHOULD PUPILS WRITE?

As science teachers we are reasonably clear about why we ask pupils to do practical work but are we clear about why we ask pupils to write in science? Is it because we see it as important that pupils have a good set of notes from which to revise? Is it because we see writing as a method of learning? Is it because we want to develop pupils' literary skills or is it a combination of these? Having a good set of notes for revision purposes is obviously essential but how should these notes be compiled? In the past some science teachers have helped pupils to obtain good notes either by dictating to them or getting them to copy their notes from the board or from a sheet. It was not uncommon a few years ago to find that thirty minutes or more of a lesson were given over to taking down dictation. There are those who would argue that pupils will learn best from notes written in their own hand rather than from a set of typed notes, although I am not sure there is any research findings to support this idea. Teachers have always been faced with the conflict that if they allow pupils to make their own notes then inevitably they will make mistakes and, therefore, learn incorrect science. One way of overcoming this has been a move towards the workbook approach where pupils fill in gaps or answer questions. The amount of pupil writing is fairly limited and one could argue that the workbook acts as a good revision aid since all the important points have been typed in correctly by the teacher.

While considering the status of writing in science lessons it is also worth bearing in mind how the work is going to be marked. If pupils were to compile all their own notes they would need to be checked for correct science and presumably for correct use of grammar and spelling. Such a task would drive even the fittest of teachers to an early grave. A key factor in deciding the type of writing that we are going to ask pupils to do must be the feasibility of marking the work.

Pupils' ability to write will vary considerably in any one mixed-ability class, from those that are able to write with confidence to those who have difficulty stringing a few words together. Indeed there may be pupils in the class who have learning difficulties and find writing very hard. They may view science as an interesting subject where they can find out things through experiments. If they are asked to write copious amounts in science lessons they may quickly become demotivated and lose all interest in their work.

The amount of time allocated to science lessons is also an important factor when considering how much writing pupils should do. Teachers feel under a lot of pressure to get through the work prescribed by the NC and other examinable courses. If time is so important then we need to look at how other activities in our science lessons use up time. Is the time spent doing certain practical activities worth while? Sutton[1] argues that practical activities can become so prominent that little time is left for pupils to reflect on the meaning of ideas. As mentioned in Chapter 5, you need to think carefully about the aims of the practical task and decide if it is a worthwhile activity.

One way of looking at writing is as a means of helping pupils to learn. Copying or taking down dictation is not going to help pupils to learn. They will only learn if they get the opportunity to think about ideas in science, reflect on them and put them down in their own words. They may be able to memorise a law or principle in science but have no understanding of what the words really mean. It is only when they have to use the principle in a new context that their knowledge is tested. Looking at writing from this standpoint is obviously different from thinking about writing as a means of compiling accurate notes for revision. This type of writing is a learning activity, involving the pupil in cognitive processes rather than mindless copying.

The NC encourages teachers to set pupils tasks that will develop their reading, writing and oral skills. For example, the following section is taken from the general introduction to KS3:

Communication: pupils should be given the opportunity to extend their use of scientific and mathematical conventions and symbols. They should be encouraged to read purposefully an extended range of secondary sources. They should take increasing responsibility for selecting resources. They should be encouraged to express their ideas and to respond to those of others and to record their work.

Where does all this leave us when we consider what should pupils write? A balance is called for between notes, whose sole purpose is for revision, and writing exercises to help pupils to learn. Many pupils enjoy their science because of the practical work and it would be unfortunate if pupils became demotivated towards science by being asked to carry out writing exercises that they saw as pointless and boring. Pupils should see time spent on writing as time well spent. The APU[2] have shown that the great majority of pupils see learning to write as one of the most important activities in school and enjoy at least some forms of writing (fictional narrative in particular). Copying and dictation are listed amongst those forms of writing that are particularly disliked by pupils. Pupils should gain experience of using a variety of modes of writing. At one extreme is the traditional, formal

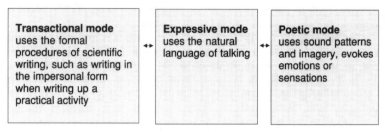

*Figure 6.1   **Modes of writing***

mode of expressing oneself in science, the transactional mode, and at the other end of the spectrum is writing that is full of expression and feeling, the poetic mode.

Most pupils will feel most comfortable writing in an expressive mode, which is much nearer to normal talking and is far less structured than formal writing. One of the problems that pupils have when considering how to express themselves is: *'Who am I writing for?'* Many pupils see themselves as writing for the teacher[3] and therefore tend to try to adopt a transactional mode and, because of their difficulties of expressing themselves in this form, they tend not to do as well as they might if they were encouraged to use an expressive mode. Table 6.1 gives some suggestions for writing exercises.

Things to do

The next time you ask your pupils to carry out a writing exercise consider the following:

- What is the purpose of the written task?
- How can the task be framed in an attractive way for the pupils?
- Are the pupils going to work on it individually or in groups?
- How are you going to help the pupil with spelling, punctuation, handwriting and grammar?
- How are you going to mark it?

Learning through writing will not be new to pupils. They will have come across the technique in other subjects and it is up to you to take advantage of your pupils' ability to manipulate words and to help them to develop this skill in the field of science. You should seek advice from colleagues in the English department and find out if the school has a teacher who has been given the responsibility of co-ordinating language work across the curriculum. Just as you would expect pupils to learn skills in practical lessons that could be used elsewhere, the skills learned through writing exercises go well beyond those required for the immediate science lessons. In particular, this type of exercise will help pupils to develop study skills and enable them to become less

Table 6.1 **Ideas for writing exercises**

Idea	Notes
Writing up an experiment	Does this have to be in the traditional style of method, results, conclusion? Is it necessary for the pupil to repeat information given in the instructions? Can pupils be given the opportunity to draft and then redraft their reports?
Making notes from a textbook	If pupils are not to copy the text word for word they will need guidance on how to identify key information targets and how to compose the new passage
Writing a letter to a pen-friend about the work you have done in science	Allows pupils to use a range of language not normally associated with science, perhaps helping the pupil to think of science as an everyday activity
Convert a diagram or flow-chart into words	The process can also be done in reverse
Prepare a newspaper article on the science investigation carried out by the pupils	Using the computer and suitable software pupils are able to prepare a polished product
Prepare a summary of the topic just completed	Requires the pupil to pick out the key points from a piece of extended writing
Rewriting jumbled-up text in the correct order	This activity can be fun. It is best carried out by pupils working in groups, discussing the sequence of the sentences or paragraphs.
Restoring 'damaged' text	For example, the teacher can present pupils with text that has been partly 'destroyed' by an acid spill or by fire. The pupils have to use their knowledge gained from the topic they are covering to reconstitute the document
Writing from the position of being a fantasy figure	For example, the pupils can write a story from the point of view of a gas molecule, a water droplet, a person on another planet or any other make-believe situation. You may be surprised at the degree of imagination some pupils have and, as long as the science is correct, this is a perfectly legitimate way of learning
Preparing a report for an organisation	For example, pupils could write a technical report describing the qualities of a substance or material. Alternatively they may outline the arguments for and against sighting a factory at a particular location in preparation for a class discussion or role play
Writing quiz questions on the topic covered	Why not get the pupils to write the questions for a test?
The teacher selects a number of key words from the topic and the pupil has to write a sentence in explanation of each of them	This helps to highlight the main points of a piece of work

dependent on the teacher as their main source of information. A combination of reading and writing exercises over a period of time will provide pupils with the necessary skills for preparing their own notes. The following seven sections outline how writing exercises can be used in imaginative ways in science lessons. Most of the initial work may be carried out using a pen but the teacher should look for opportunities for using either a word processor or desk-top publishing package (see page 173) to take the tedium out of redrafting and to produce a well-finished product.

Draft and redraft

There must be very few writers who are able to run off a polished article the first time round. Most of us muse over our first attempt and contemplate how we might improve our expressions. There may be several attempts before we produce a product that we are satisfied with. We do not appear to give the privilege of being able to redraft materials to our pupils, usually blaming it on lack of time. In the process of redrafting, pupils are put in a position where they have to think about the meaning of what they are writing. They have to ask themselves questions such as: *'Does it make sense? Do I understand what I have written? Would someone else be able to understand what I have written?'*

One example of using this technique is in the writing up of a practical exercise. All too often pupils stand around watching an experiment and then write it up afterwards or worse still at home. The time delay can often mean that important aspects of the experiment are forgotten. Pupils will quite rightly argue that they cannot keep an eye on the experiment and write up a report at the same time. It is, however, well within their capabilities to write down notes about how they set up the equipment, their observations and an evaluation of the procedure as the experiment progresses.

Another opportunity for this type of work arises when teachers ask pupils to prepare some notes using resources from the school library. As well as developing pupils' ability to search for information in a library, this type of activity teaches them to sift through the literature and select only that which is relevant to their work. Initially pupils will find it difficult to select the appropriate items of information and probably write down everything they find that is remotely connected to the topic. A number of carefully worded, pertinent questions should be prepared to guide the pupils to the relevant work in the literature. The draft notes could be subjected to peer group review to check that the main points have been covered and that the writer has not deviated too much from the key issues. This task not only helps to improve the quality of the notes but serves as a focus for group discussion about science and areas of misunderstanding can be brought to the fore.

Pupils should regard the initial draft as valuable a document as the final one. Although it may look untidy, with crossing out and lines drawn all over it to show the movement of sentences, the draft should not be written on a scrap of paper. For one thing, scraps of paper can easily be mislaid but it is also useful to have a record of the process of redrafting so that pupils can learn from their experience. One solution is to allow pupils to use the left-hand side of their exercise book for the rough draft and the right-hand side for the final copy. Another is to have an exercise book set aside for draft work.

Writing letters

With a little imagination, letter writing can be a most enjoyable way of learning science. There are many different characters pupils can write to, some real and some fictional. Pupils will benefit from learning about the art of constructing a letter. They should write in a manner that is not discourteous or libellous and which presents only the facts as they see them. Table 6.2 outlines some suggestions for letter writing. Environmental and health issues are topics that concern young people and this can lead to a high degree of motivation for preparing letters. You might choose to send examples of certain types of letter to the named individual to increase pupil motivation. Others may just be read by you or they may be exchanged with another class doing the same topic who could be asked to reply. Some schools carry out similar work to this in class tutorial or PSE lessons and you may find it useful to talk to the relevant class teacher about the type of work carried out.

Newspaper articles

This gives pupils the opportunity to experiment with a completely different style of writing and makes them think about how they can present the information in an attractive and understandable way. They will need to examine newspapers and discuss in their groups how the writer attracts the reader to the article and how s/he constructs the passage so that people will want to read it. Desk-top publishing packages give pupils the opportunity to experiment with layout and to include pictures and graphics. For example, they can write about: environmental issues; keeping healthy; fictional journeys into space; their discovery following an investigation; a result of a survey they have carried out; and almost anything else they do in their science lessons. *Which?* type reports are useful in getting the pupils to consider the claims of the manufacturers and to prepare a balanced argument based on their research findings.

Table 6.2 **Examples of different types of letters**

Correspondent	Potential topic for a letter
Political figures	A letter to the Energy Minister pointing out the limited amount of energy resources that are available to us and making suggestions for energy conservation and future use of energy
Local community figures	Outlining the arguments either for or against the siting of an industrial organisation in the locality
Environmental organisations	Pupils could describe how environmental groups might instigate the cleaning of an area of land or water that is familiar to them
Manufacturers	Following an investigation into a product, pupils could write to the manufacturer commenting on the claims made in advertising the product
Parents	One of the suggestions for improving home–school links (page 236) is the production of a class newsletter. This could contain letters from pupils describing the work they have recently carried out in their lessons
School personnel	Following an investigation into the properties of rust removers, pupils could write a letter to the headteacher advising as to which product would be most suitable to remove the rust from the bike stands
Friends	At the end of a topic a useful revision exercise would be for the pupil to write a letter to a friend describing what s/he had found out in her recent lessons
Newspapers and magazines	A letter about issues such as smoking, alcohol abuse or drugs with suggestions as to how the problem might be reduced
Beings from another planet	The alien being has never been to our solar system. Write a letter describing it to him

Diaries

Diaries give pupils the chance to write down what they understand about a topic. They differ from an exercise book insomuch as they will be written in the pupils' own personal styles and they will not be penalised if they write down things that are scientifically incorrect. Indeed the diary should be seen as something rather personal containing ideas and thoughts that can only be shared with the teacher as confidant. For example, as you approach the teaching of the topic of light you may ask the pupils to write an account in their diaries of how they see themselves in a mirror or what role light plays in seeing another object. This diary entry could be used as the basis for your discussion with individuals as the teaching of the topic progresses.

Prose

Some pupils can feel stifled when asked to continuously write in the formal science method. They feel inhibited and their writing may hide some of their misunderstandings of scientific principles. A more open approach to writing, giving pupils the opportunity to express themselves, can be very revealing. They question their own thoughts and beliefs when asked to construct a passage in their own words.

The last two examples of methods of writing, which are described below, are also ways of encouraging pupils to express themselves orally in science. Further examples of oral work in science are given in Section 6.4.

Poetry

Poetry is not often seen as a way of writing in science. However, it is a method of expression that appeals to many young people. Using poetry gives pupils the opportunity to voice their opinion on issues and to present things from an emotional point of view rather than the dispassionate standpoint often taken by scientists. With a little imagination poetry can be used in almost any area of science. The following list represent a few examples:

The wonder of birth
The colours of the spectrum
The devastation of environmental pollution
The warmth and comfort of man-made materials
The beauty of structures (both man-made and natural)
Particle movement (Brownian motion)
Energy

Plays

Mini plays are frequently used in primary schools to illustrate an aspect of the curriculum but the adoption of this teaching mode in the secondary school has been limited. However, science and drama have been successfully blended together in some secondary schools. The performances may be restricted to one class or may be part of a presentation for an assembly, school concert or Eisteddfod. Professional theatre groups (e.g. The Kinetic Theatre Company) sometimes arrange performances with a science base. Such groups tour round the country and may be booked for a performance in your school.

Plays can be used to illustrate an historical event in science giving the pupils the opportunity to place themselves in a scientist's shoes and helping them to understand some of the dilemmas s/he may have had to face. Alternatively, pupils can work completely in the abstract and act out science processes such as food digestion or the movement of particles as a solid changes to a liquid and then to a gas.

Things to do

Below are three extracts from the PoS for KS3. Choose one of them and devise a writing exercise for pupils based around the topic.

Sc2, strand i	Pupils should extend their study in which healthy functioning of the human body may be affected by diet, lifestyle...
Sc3, strand iv	They should investigate some natural material (rock or soil) and link the properties of minerals and rocks to their uses as raw materials in construction.
Sc4, strand ii	Pupils should survey national and global sources of energy.

It may be that having read this section, there are some trainee teachers who are still sceptical about the advantages of using writing exercises in science lessons. A response from this type of trainee would include the argument the s/he had asked his/her pupils about the type of writing they preferred and they had said that they liked copying. Copying is easy, it does not involve the pupils in thinking about what they are doing. Copying at home can be done while playing pop music very loudly. Writing of the type described here helps pupils to organise their thoughts and leads them to a clearer understanding of science concepts. It may not be an easy process but then learning of any sort requires the learner to make an effort. Writing exercises can be fun to do and as such can help to reduce the pain and tedium of learning.

6.2 INCLUDING READING TASKS IN LESSONS

At one time or another most of us have read a passage from a book and at the end have had little idea about what the work meant. This may not have anything to do with our ability to understand the text but may simply be associated with the fact that our mind was not fully concentrating on the words on the page. Effective learning takes place when readers have to 'take in' or 'digest' what is written down and then have to 'put in their own words' or reformulate it and use it themselves. Teachers have often said to one another that they only came to really understand a topic when they had to teach it and this same principle is equally true for pupils. One of the most influential reports on language in education, the Bullock Report,[4] emphasised the importance of this reflection and reordering of information.

It is a confusion of everyday thought that we tend to regard 'knowledge' as something that exists independently of someone who knows. 'What is known' must in fact be brought alive afresh within every 'knower' by his own efforts.

In Table 4.2 reading was listed as an active learning activity rather than a passive one but it can only be active if the pupil is instructed to do something with the information s/he has read. Many science books now contain reading exercises with a passage to be studied and questions to be answered. Some science books have been written containing only reading exercises for pupils.[5]

Things to do

- Look through three or four science textbooks written for KS3 pupils and locate the reading exercises. You will find these under clear headings like 'Readabout', but also in exercises such as 'Try these' or 'And for homework'.
- How frequently do they appear in each textbook?
- Choose two of the exercises and try to identify what the pupils would learn by carrying out the reading task. How would you present the tasks to pupils? Would you expect pupils to discuss the work with other pupils in class time or would you think it more appropriate for the task to be carried out by the pupils at home?

Preparing reading activities

From 1978 until 1982 a major research project into reading for learning in the secondary school[6] was carried out under the directorship of Eric Lunzer and Keith Gardner. They made a detailed study of the different ways that pupils could be actively involved with reading texts. Of particular interest to science teachers is the work carried out by the two project officers, Florence Davies and Terry Greene, into the study of science texts. The research group designed activities that focused pupils' attention on to their reading and made them reflect on the content. They used the term 'directed activities related to text' (or DART) for their exercises. DART exercises can be found in SATIS books and some modern textbooks. As can be seen from the following five sections describing examples of DART activities, they are easy to prepare and generally fun for pupils to do.

Cloze

Cloze procedure is used extensively in both primary and secondary schools. It is commonly referred to as 'filling in the blanks'. Pupils have to predict the missing words, using their knowledge of the subject and by talking through the text with other members of their group. There are many ways of presenting this type of exercise. A common approach is to omit words at regular intervals. Alternatively all the words related to the topic being taught are left out. Sometimes clues are given, such as a list of the missing words at the bottom of the page or the first letter of each missing word is left in place. Figure 6.2 shows a variation on the usual theme. Another interesting way of presenting this type of exercise is to remove parts of the text, using white correction fluid. Care must be taken not to remove so much text that it makes the task of replacing the missing letters an impossibility. The worksheet can then be presented to the pupils along with the story line that a chemical has been spilled on the paper, destroying part of it. Can they find the missing letters. A development could be to take the worksheet and slightly burn the edges of the paper and present it to the pupils as a photocopy of a fire-damaged manuscript.

Sequencing

These are very easy to produce and can be most effective in getting pupils to talk about science. A piece of text is divided up into a number of sections, ranging from about 6 to 12. These are then shuffled and presented to the pupils in their jumbled format. This can either be done by presenting the pupils with a photocopy of the mixed-up format or by giving each group the text on a set of papers that have to be physically rearranged into the correct sequence. This second method is preferred as it gives the pupils the opportunity to experiment with the sequence as the debate over the order is continuing. Its obvious game-like characteristics can make it very popular with pupils.

Labelling

Putting labels on parts of text or on diagrams encourages pupils to ask questions about the text and to search for any hidden meaning. If pupils are presented with a piece of writing on a science topic, which covers most of an A4 page, they generally have difficulty locating the information they require. The pupils could be asked to read through the passage carefully and then read through it a second time, labelling the areas (paragraphs) with a phrase that characterises its meaning. Such passages could be designed by the teacher or photocopied from a textbook (subject to copyright restrictions). This type of activity

Something seems to have gone wrong with my computer and it has written in some funny faces instead of letters. Please help to unravel it by discussing the meaning of the passage in your groups and then write out a correct account of the work in your exercise books.

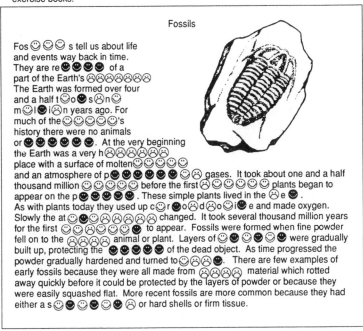

Fossils

Fos ☺☺☺ s tell us about life and events way back in time. They are re 😊😊😊😊 of a part of the Earth's 🙈🙈🙈🙈🙈🙈 The Earth was formed over four and a half t☺o😊s🙈n☺ m☺l😊i😊d🙈o☺i😊n years ago. For much of the ☺☺☺☺☺'s history there were no animals or 😊😊😊😊😊😊. At the very beginning the Earth was a very h 🙈🙈🙈🙈🙈🙈 place with a surface of molten☺☺☺☺ and an atmosphere of p😊😊😊😊😊😊☺🙈 gases. It took about one and a half thousand million ☺☺☺☺ before the first 🙈☺☺☺☺ plants began to appear on the p😊😊😊😊😊. These simple plants lived in the 🙈e 😊. As with plants today they used up c☺r😊o🙈d🙈o☺i😊e and made oxygen. Slowly the at ☺😊🙈🙈🙈🙈 changed. It took several thousand million years for the first ☺☺🙈☺☺😊 to appear. Fossils were formed when fine powder fell on to the 🙈🙈🙈🙈 animal or plant. Layers of ☺😊☺😊☺😊 were gradually built up, protecting the 😊😊😊😊 of the dead object. As time progressed the powder gradually hardened and turned to☺🙈🙈😊. There are few examples of early fossils because they were all made from 🙈🙈🙈🙈 material which rotted away quickly before it could be protected by the layers of powder or because they were easily squashed flat. More recent fossils are more common because they had either a s☺😊☺😊☺😊🙈 or hard shells or firm tissue.

Fossils

Fossils tell us about life and events way back in time. They are really a part of the Earth's history. The Earth was formed over four and a half thousand million years ago. For much of the Earth's history there were no animals or plants. At the very beginning the Earth was a very hostile place with a surface of molten rocks and an atmosphere of poisonous gases. It took about one and a half thousand million years before the first simple plants began to appear on the planet. These simple plants lived in the sea. As with plants today they used up carbon dioxide and made oxygen. Slowly the atmosphere changed. It took several thousand million years for the first animals to appear. Fossils were formed when fine powder fell on to the dead animal or plant. Layers of powder were gradually built up, protecting the shape of the dead object. As time progressed the powder gradually hardened and turned to rock. There are few examples of early fossils because they were all made from soft material which rotted away quickly before it could be protected by the layers of powder or because they were easily squashed flat. More recent fossils are more common because they had either a skeleton or hard shells or firm tissue.

Figure 6.2 **A different approach to cloze**

involves the pupil in careful analysis of the text and thus requires similar cognitive processes to those required for the highlighting of text.

Another labelling strategy is to ask pupils to search for information in a text and use this to label a diagram. Alternatively, the text could contain missing words that are to be found on a diagram with the

How fast is starch broken down?

In this experiment you are going to study how fast amylase breaks down starch. Work quietly in your groups.

1. Read through the first paragraph about the amylase in saliva. All the words beginning with 's' in the paragraph have been omitted. Once you have decided on the missing words, write the full paragraph in your exercise books.

2. The instructions for the experiment have been mixed up. Your first task is to decide the correct sequence.

3. Write down a list of apparatus that you will require.

4. When you have had your plan checked you can proceed with the experiment.

5. Consider how you are going to present your results.

6. What do the results tell you about the reaction between amylase and starch?

7. In what way could you make the experiment more accurate?

What happens to food in your mouth?

Just thinking about food often makes your mouth water. This liquid has a special name, ******, ****** is produced by the ****** glands that are connected to the mouth cavity by ducts. ****** contains an enzyme called amylase. This acts on *****, breaking it down into malt ***** (maltose).

Experimental instructions

☐ With a teat pipette place one drop of the amylase–starch mixture to a drop of iodine solution on the white tile.

☐ Take a white tile and place one drop of iodine solution in each of the hollowed out sections.

☐ Add one drop of starch solution to one of the drops of iodine solution on the white tile. A blue-black colour indicates starch. This will act as your control.

☐ Collect test tubes containing: starch solution, amylase solution and iodine solution along with the other equipment you require for the experiment.

☐ Pour the amylase solution into the starch solution, stopper and shake quickly.

☐ Add further drops of the amylase–starch mixture to separate drops of iodine solution at half minute intervals. Note the colour given each time.

*Figure 6.3   **An example of a sequencing exercise***

Sexual reproduction in flowering plants

A flower contains the parts of a plant that enable it to reproduce. It contains both male and female parts

Male Parts
The male sex cells are contained in the pollen grains. The pollen grains grow in the anther and when they are fully grown the anther splits open.

Female parts
The female sex cells are contained in the ovules, which grow in the ovary. Extending from the ovary is the style, which is expanded or divided at one end into the stigma.

Other parts of the flower

The bright colours of the petals attract insects to the flower to assist in pollination. The sepals are usually green and small and they protect the flower while it is in bud

Nactaries are glandular swellings at the base of the ovary, which produce a sugary solution called nectar.

Pollination

Pollination is the first step in reproduction. A flower is pollinated when a pollen grain lands on a stigma. Each pollen grain grows a tube down the style. When the pollen grain tube reaches the ovule, nuclei from the male cell travel down the tube. When the male nuclei meet the female nuclei in the ovule they join. This process is called fertilisation.

Figure 6.4 **An example of a labelling activity**

object of the exercise being to use the labelled diagram as a guide to finding the missing words. Figure 6.4 illustrates this type of activity.

Highlighting

Highlighting or text marking involves pupils in locating and marking parts of the text that have a certain meaning or provide the reader with a piece of information. It is an analytical technique and as such requires the reader to think very carefully about the text. What does this really mean? What is it referring to? This type of exercise involves pupils working through a text highlighting or underlining words, phrases or sentences that have specific meaning. There may be a number of different information targets in the text, which the pupil would have to highlight in different ways, e.g. different coloured pen, different number of lines, different shape of lines (squiggle, dotted, etc.).

Even the simplest underlining involves classification of some kind, e.g. cause and effect. Text marking is an ideal starting point for tabular or diagrammatic representation. Figure 6.5 gives a very simple example of highlighting text combined with a labelling activity. Most modern science textbooks for 11–16 year-olds do not lend themselves readily to this type of exercise. Using modern printing techniques they are able to highlight parts of text and use different colours to attract the reader to various sections. This should not be seen as a reason for excluding highlighting from your teaching repertoire but as an incentive for the pupils for learning the skill of producing clear, unambiguous text.

Summarising information

It is useful to be able to extract the most important items of information from a piece of text and present them in a summary form. This is often achieved by producing either a flow chart or a table of key points. An opportunity for using this technique arises when pupils are asked to carry out a practical activity. Many teachers will report that pupils do not read their practical instructions and will constantly ask what they have to do. Before asking pupils to embark on a multi-step practical task for which you have given them some written instructions they could be asked to produce a flow chart identifying the sequence they must follow. This should help them to become more organised and eliminate the problem of not knowing what to do next. Flow charts can also be used to summarise processes such as the stages in development of a living organism, an industrial process and the sequence of electronic devices required to carry out a particular task.

Lightning conductors

Read through the following paragraphs. Read them through a second time, underlining the word *charge* in red each time it appears. Write down all you know about positive and negative charges. Underline in blue any word you don't understand. Talk about these words in your group and write down what you think they mean. Label the diagram to show how a lightning conductor works.

In order to save tall buildings from damage by lightning they are fitted with a lightning conductor. This consists of a strip of copper attached to one side of the house. At the bottom it is buried into the ground and at the top there are a number of spikes pointing upwards.

Thunderclouds carry electric charges, either positive or negative. A negative charge on the cloud would induce a positive charge on the roof of a building. The force of attraction between these two charges may be sufficient to produce a sudden flow of electrons from the cloud to the roof. We say that the roof has been struck by lightning.

The lightning conductor helps to reduce the risk of damage to the building in two ways:

1. Electric charge leaks away from a sharp point. Charged air molecules can flow from the spikes of the lightning conductor thus reducing the induced charge on the roof and cancelling out some of the charge on the cloud. This reduces the chances of lightning striking the building.

2. If the lightning does strike, the lightning conductor provides a route for electrons to pass into the ground without damaging the building. The ground can absorb a large amount of charge.

Figure 6.5 **An example of highlighting text together with diagram labelling**

Industrial manufacture of iron

Iron is made in a **blast furnace**. Suitable amounts of iron ore and coke are mixed together and preheated. These small lumps of material are called 'sinter'. The sinter is then mixed with limestone and poured into a blast furnace from the top. Hot air is blown in from the bottom of the furnace. The following reactions take place:

1. The coke reacts with the oxygen in the air to give carbon dioxide.

   _____

2. The limestone decomposes when heated to give calcium oxide and carbon dioxide.

   _____

3. The carbon dioxide reacts with more coke to give carbon monoxide.

   _____

4. The carbon monoxide reacts with the iron oxide in the iron ore, giving molten iron.

   _____

5. Calcium oxide reacts with the impurity in the iron ore, sand (silica), to form calcium silicate (slag).

   _____

Write in the equations for the reactions. Complete the flow charts below to show the major processes.

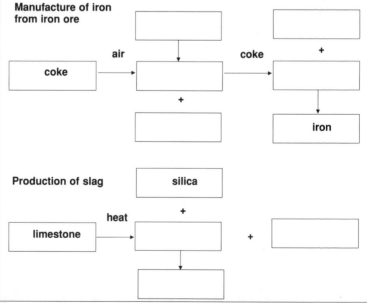

*Figure 6.6 **Producing a flow diagram to summarise information***

Figure 6.6 is an example of using a flow chart to summarise an industrial process.

Tables or summary lists are useful aids for revision but the process of producing them is also an effective way of learning. The first stage in this process may be highlighting the important points that you wish to summarise in the text. This could be followed by a decision-making process as to the headings for the rows and/or columns of the table. Once this has been done it is simply a matter of placing the summary statements in the cells of the table in a suitable form.

Things to do

Prepare a number of DART activities and try using them with your pupils. You will probably find that cloze activities are the easiest to prepare. Once you have used them ask the pupils for feedback. Ask them if they prefer this method to other methods of presenting them with notes. How do they think your activity could be improved?

6.3 TALKING TO PUPILS

When a sergeant-major addresses his squad of troops he does so in a certain style. When lovers talk to each other they also have a style, quite different from the brusque approach of the sergeant-major. As a teacher, you will need to adopt a style when talking to your classes. This will be different from the way you talk to your friends, different from the way you would talk to a group of adults and certainly different from the sergeant-major approach.

There are many occasions when it is necessary to address the whole class, such as an introduction to a new topic or the giving of instructions or the summing up of a period of work, but rarely these days would you find an experienced teacher talking to the class for prolonged periods of time. This is mainly because you cannot ensure that all the pupils are paying attention to what is being said and in a mixed-ability situation it is difficult for the teacher to gauge the language so that it caters for individual needs. When talking to the whole class you should stand in a position where you can be seen and where you can clearly see all the pupils. A good idea is to gather the pupils round you in a semicircle before you begin your talk. This will make interactions between you and the pupils easier and more relaxed. Eye contact is very important and you should ensure that you move your head around looking at the faces of the pupils. In this way you will be quick to spot signs of puzzlement or the look of understanding when a pupil has grasped a particular concept.

Observing an experienced teacher give an exposition may give you the impression that there is little difference between talking to a group of pupils and talking to an individual. What you cannot observe is the preparation and years of practice that has gone into making the task look so easy. Successful teacher presentations are well planned so that you can sound and look confident. Below are a few points that are worth considering if you are going to give a competent presentation:

- Position yourself where you can be heard and where you can see everybody.
- Remember to sound and look confident and relaxed. If necessary, hold something firmly, rather than fiddle with things like paper-clips or parts of your clothing.
- Try not to refer to your notes too often. Remember, eye contact is very important.
- Make sure that you have the attention of the class before you start and that they are sitting comfortably. Your first few sentences should be structured to catch their attention.
- Keep your voice level to the minimum necessary. A low voice level creates a feeling of expectancy, gives a sense of importance to the occasion, and creates a mood of mutual confidence.
- Vary the volume and pace to give variety.
- Use precise terms rather than vague ones, for example try to avoid terms like 'a couple of'.
- Repeat important points and put them up on the board. Define any new terms that you use and summarise these on the board.
- Make sure that the pupils never lose sight of the structure of the whole presentation, e.g. have frequent pauses and invite a pupil to summarise the arguments so far.
- Take great care in the use of language. Look out for pedantic language, avoid jargon, use concrete rather than abstract words, beware of verbosity and be alert to overworked metaphors (see the section about 'words' below).

If you find it difficult to talk to groups of people then you will need to build up your confidence slowly. Initially you will find it helpful to write down every word you are going to say. Reading your script through several times before the lesson and familiarising yourself with the sequence of points will boost your confidence. As your confidence develops you will find that you can manage with a simple flow sheet showing the order of points you are going to make. As well as considering the words you are going to use, you should spend some time thinking about when you should pause. If you are so unsure about your presentation that you have to read from your script then remember to look up at your audience from time to time and scan their faces. If your confidence does not rapidly improve then you need to look for an alternative career!

Any talk should be interspersed with questions to check that the pupils are following your line of argument. It is no use relying on questions that you will think up while you are making your presentation to the class although, of course, you will need to think on your feet and respond to the development of the discussion. You should plan several key questions as part of your overall lesson plan, thinking carefully about the purpose of the questions. These can vary from straightforward recall questions such as asking the pupils about the last lesson's work to asking pupils to suggest reasons why things happen in the way that they do. You will need to think about how you are going to involve as many pupils as possible in the question-and-answer session. If the session becomes mainly a dialogue between you and one or two individuals in the class, you will find that all the other pupils rapidly lose interest. Inexperienced teachers are often anxious about getting the right answer as soon as possible and may often miss valuable teaching points. They may direct the question to pupils who they think are likely to give them the correct answer and when they get their reply be quite content that the concept has been understood by all the class. In reality, of course, there may be quite a number of individuals in the class who have little understanding of the work. Another tactic used by inexperienced teachers is to give the correct answer themselves if the first response they have obtained from pupils is incorrect. Rather than act in haste the teacher should consider:

1. Alternative ways of phrasing the question.
2. Putting a simpler question to the pupil on the same topic perhaps linked to a clue (e.g. *'Well OK, you can't answer that but just think about what we said earlier on about the pull of gravity on the Earth. What do you think will happen to our two objects initially?'*).
3. Asking other pupils the question.

You should try not to discourage pupils by asking them questions that are too difficult or by embarrassing them in front of their classmates by making disparaging remarks about incorrect responses. If the answer you get is incorrect, try looking for elements of the correct answer and give some credit in terms of a positive comment to the pupil. You will quickly have pandemonium if you throw the questions open to the class and have no system for who is going to respond. One way of overcoming the problem is to insist that the pupils put their hands up to answer, another way is to ask pupils directly by name. You will find that the time spent in learning pupils' names when you first meet a class is very worth while. Some suggestions as to how you might do this are given on page 83.

Table 6.3   Oral questioning checklist

Before you start writing down your questions think about:

Why am I asking these questions?

Am I:

- checking to see if they remember last lesson's work?
- creating interest in the lesson?
- checking that they are making the correct observations?
- trying to determine how they are tackling a problem?
- seeing if they can weigh up a situation?
- finding out what they know already about a topic?

How am I going to involve as many pupils as possible?

Will I:

- be able to check that **all** the pupils understand the work?
- insist that the pupils put their hands up?

Questioning skills

When planning your questions think about the following:

1. Pitching the language and content level of the questions appropriately for the class. Are the questions clearly phrased?

2. Distribution of questions around the class. Don't just ask questions of the pupils sitting in an arc directly in front of you. Eye contact is important as is the use of names.

3. Prompting and giving clues when necessary. Can you use non-verbal clues, such as puzzlement, enthusiasm or just an appropriate smile to help pupils answer questions?

4. Using pupils' responses (even incorrect ones) in a positive way. What praise are you going to give for correct answers?

5. Timing questions and pauses between questions.

6. Learning to make progressively greater cognitive demands through sequences of higher-order questions.

Words

Pupils often become confused over words that sound or look similar. They will also have difficulty with words that have one meaning in everyday use and another, sometimes completely different, meaning in science. It is not just the scientific and technical words that should concern us but it is also worth reflecting on all the language we use. Cassels and Johnstone[7] have carried out extensive research into pupils' understanding of non-technical words and the following list indicates some of the words pupils have difficulty with:

Word	Some pupils' views on the meaning of the word
Abundant	'scarce', 'shortage', 'poor supply'
Accumulate	'take from', 'use up', 'accommodate', 'calculate'
Complex	'natural', 'simple', 'clever', linked to 'complexion'
Composition	'*how* it is made', 'forcing together'
Conception	pupils generally unsure about the meaning
Constituent	equated with words to which it is normally attached, e.g. mixture
Contract	'get larger', 'become longer', 'become slacker'
Emit	mixed up with 'omit' and 'admit'
Excess	a lot of guessing as to the meaning; common choices: 'essential', 'very good', 'except', 'dilute', 'just right'
Immerse	'float', 'wipe with oil', 'coat'
Initial	'with greatest care', 'best effort', 'crucial', 'final'
Linear	confused with 'liner', 'linen', 'ascending', 'descending'
Negligible	'a lot', 'most important', 'great', 'less than nothing', 'negligent'
Omit	'put in', 'collect in', 'repeat', 'finish off', 'admit'
Spontaneous	'quick', 'vigorous', 'steady', 'loud', 'long'
Stimulate	'end', 'slow down', 'deactivate', 'smother', 'stop'
Tabulate	'interpret', 'allocate', 'solve', 'construct'
Valid	no pattern of responses

If pupils have difficulty in understanding these non-technical words then you can be sure that they will have difficulties in understanding the rather specialised vocabulary that we use in science. Bentley and Watts[8] point out that it is not just a matter of clearly defining these words when pupils first come across them in their science lessons but of giving pupils the opportunity to talk about their understanding of what the words mean and to offer them the opportunity of using the words in different situations.

Things to do

Tape record the next time you make a presentation to a class. When listening to the recording in the quiet of your study analyse it for:

1. Length (overall length and length of and frequency of pauses).
2. Style (pace and level of voice).
3. Number and type of questions asked.
4. Number of new terms used.
5. Difficulty of language (ask a colleague to discuss this with you).

6.4 PUPILS TALKING

Why use talk?

You may feel that you spend a lot of your time trying to stop pupils from talking, so why would you want to read an article that promotes pupil talk. The aim of this section is to examine strategies that encourage pupils to be involved in purposeful talk about science. Talk is a common way of testing out our understandings. Speech makes it easy for us to try out new ways of arranging what we know and makes it easy to change our ideas if they seem inadequate. Barnes[9] highlights the importance of being able to talk to one another, collaborating and trying out new ways of thinking.

Listening and talking should generally be inseparable. Bulman[10] reminds us that pupils need to be involved in 'active listening' such as in conversations where the pupil is expected to respond to what is being said. 'Active talking' increases the pupil's participation in his/her own learning and decreases boredom and frustration. Working in small groups will create the maximum opportunity for each pupil to be involved in 'active talking'. Section 4.5 outlines the principles of group work, showing how they can be set up and managed. Here the emphasis is on learning and how we can foster a better understanding of science by giving pupils the opportunity to talk about it.

Some teachers object to group work saying that it encourages pupils to 'share ignorance'. In order to overcome this, pupils need to be properly briefed for the group activity. For example, it would be unproductive to ask pupils to discuss 'the problem of the hole in the ozone layer' without any background information. A non-structured discussion would perpetuate pupils' misconceptions rather than lead them to greater understanding of the subject. There is a clear responsibility for the teacher to make the purpose of the group work as explicit as possible.

Forrestal[11] presents teachers with a useful model for learning through group work. He proposes that there can be five stages of learning within the group activities. These are illustrated in Table 6.4 along with the types of processes and activities that could take place during the group work. It would be wrong, however, to think that this sequence was followed in every group discussion session. For example, it is quite likely that there will be more than one stage where pupils are involved in the process of clarifying the issues and, in a way, coming back to the start. The main activity itself may consist of a number of stages as the pupils transform from an active learning mode to a presentational mode. In any event the teacher's role should be seen as a facilitator, a person who sets up the situation for learning to take place.

Table 6.4 **Stages of group work**

Stages	Pupil activities and thought processes	Teacher role
Setting the scene	What is the purpose of the exercise? Clarification of issues. A sharing of ideas. Looking towards the eventual outcome	Give the learners a sense of direction. Provide members of the group with appropriate information. Create a sense of excitement for the work
Exploration	Clarify their own thinking in a non-threatening situation	As and when required. Keeping an ear on the situation to check that pupils remain on task
The main activity	Putting together their thoughts in preparation for the presentation. Time for checking on understandings before the presentation	As and when required
Presentation	Drawing together the ideas from the group. Each member of the group to check that the reporter is accurately reporting on the findings of the group	Listening carefully to what is said. Not interrupting the flow of ideas but being prepared to take up issues later
Reflection	What have the pupils learned?	Taking up some of the points made in the presentations. Drawing conclusions, if appropriate. Leading the pupils into further learning experiences

Different types of talk

There are plenty of opportunities for setting up situations where pupils are involved in purposeful talk. Some of these will involve pupils working in small groups. Sometimes it may involve a pupil talking to the whole class but on other occasions it may simply be one pupil talking to his/her neighbour. Table 6.5 lists occasions when pupils can be directed to talk about science. All too often opportunities are missed. Pupils 'do' some science but teachers do not give them the time to think and talk about the meaning of what they have done. If this is not done, the opportunity for internalising the information and making it their own is lost.

Table 6.5 **Opportunities for pupil talk in science lessons**

Idea	Notes
Planning an investigation	Brainstorming ideas for an investigation. Clarifying the meaning of the variables. Determining a strategy for carrying out the experiment
Focusing attention on an experiment	Focusing in on key observations. What do the observations tell the pupil about what is happening during the experiment?
Discussion of results of practical work	One group report their experimental results to another group. Differences in results are noted and the pupils attempt to explain the differences. The two groups attempt to interpret the results
Role play	Can reveal many hidden talents amongst pupils. Particularly good teaching method for dealing with issues where there is likely to be a difference of opinion. Pupils are not necessarily expressing their opinions and therefore have the opportunity for viewing things from another standpoint
Discussion groups	It is best to have a clearly defined task with a definite outcome, which is to be achieved in a fixed period of time. Assigning the roles of chairperson and secretary within the group will help to ensure that the task is completed and that everyone gets the chance to speak
Presenting a play	Short plays written by pupils can be used to illustrate science concepts. They can also present a simulated TV advert, perhaps based on the results of an investigation, e.g. an advert based around 'Buy Ricochet Balls. Tests show that they bounce higher than any other ball, on any surface you care to mention'
Reading poetry	Reading the poem to a group rather than the whole class reduces embarrassment. Pupils should be encouraged to question each poet as to why they wrote what they did[12]
Rap	This approach can have popular appeal. The rap could be written by individuals or by groups of pupils. Pupils are likely to remember the rap because of its rhythm and because it is a novel way of learning science[12]
During work on the computer	When pupils are working together on a science computer program they talk naturally about the science involved

What has been said previously in terms of the problems pupils face in writing for different audiences is mirrored in the talk situation. It is fairly obvious that the spoken language we use is dependent on the audience listening. Pupils are conscious of who they are talking to and will attempt to adjust the style of talking to suit the situation. Under the stress of a formal presentation a number of things can happen. For example, the pupil may try to act the fool in an attempt to overcome embarrassment or to belittle the situation. When asked to make a presentation to the whole class other pupils may try to use unfamiliar vocabulary so as to impress and as a consequence become tongue tied. In order to get the best out of the pupils, the teacher should attempt to create a situation where there is the minimum of stress and where the pupils are allowed to use language that is familiar to them. One way of doing this is to ask one group to report to another group. As well as reducing the stress factor this situation has the advantage of reducing the amount of class time taken up with reporting.

Organising and running this type of work is another occasion where science teachers can learn from colleagues in the English department. To finish off this section there is a description of a type of language work that has increased in popularity in science lessons over recent years, role play.

Role play

Rather than have a fully scripted play some teachers prefer to use role play, where individuals are given background details of the role but no script to read from. The role players have to respond to the conversation as it develops. In order to do this they must be aware of all the relevant issues and have an understanding of the science involved. Therefore, for a successful role play, briefing sheets must be prepared for each role. This type of activity gives pupils the opportunity to test their own understanding of their scientific knowledge and to explore their own views, feelings and attitudes towards certain issues. The benefits of role play are many, such as

- it is a way of teaching the social, economic and environmental aspects of NC science
- it encourages co-operative learning
- it involves active learning
- it is a useful way of simulating real-life situations
- it provides an opportunity to practice oral skills, and
- it can be fun

If it is to be effective role play must be carefully planned and the following sequence of events illustrates the planning stages that should take place.

Planning for role play

Lesson 1

Pupils require a thorough briefing that should include:
- a reminder about the relevant science
- pointing them in the direction of appropriate reference material, and
- details of the role they are to play

The number of roles will be less than the number of pupils in the class. In order to ensure that everyone plays an active part in the exercise, pupils should work in pairs or groups of three preparing and rehearsing their roles. Some of this will be also done for homework and the final preparations will be at the start of lesson 2.

Pupils should be allowed to elaborate on their roles and bring in 'props'. They will need time to plan this.

Pupils should be told that they must not prepare long speeches (2–3 minutes at the most). This will help to remove the anxiety from quieter pupils.

It may be that your normal laboratory is unsuitable for role play and therefore you will have to arrange to hold the lesson in another room, e.g. the drama studio.

Lesson 2

From each group that has prepared a role, select one pupil to act it out. Remember to select a different pupil next time you do a role play. Involve those who are not selected in some way, e.g. as audience, as extras.

Try to set the scene and create the right sort of atmosphere for the situation. Once the role play is under way, step back and let it run. If you think it is losing direction then intervene, but 'in role' rather than as a teacher. Only intervene as 'teacher' if the situation gets out of hand.

Follow-up work is essential, such as:
- Discussion out of role (How did you feel? What have you learned?)
- Summary by teacher (What are the key issues? What are the main arguments of the debate?)

Lesson 3 (perhaps)

Use the role play as a stimulus for further work, e.g. a review of the play in the 'newspaper'.

There are examples of role play activities in the SATIS units, e.g. in 'The retrial of Galileo' pupils take the parts of Galileo, his supporters and representatives of the Church. On the one hand we have Galileo who believes that the Earth is not the centre of the Universe and on the other there is the Church that considers this point of view to be heretical.[13] Guidance on setting up the role play and planning the all-important follow-up work are provided in the teachers' notes to the unit. Harrison and co-workers have carried out extensive work with teachers on role play and other aspects of active learning in science and have prepared a range of materials for school use.[14]

Things to do

Plan a group task based on work you are currently doing with one of your classes. Prepare briefing sheets for members of the group. You would also find it interesting to talk to the members of the group about the frequency of contributions and about what they think they have learned. However, it is not always easy to quantify the learning.

NOTES AND REFERENCES

1. Sutton, C., 1992, *Words, Science and Learning*, Open University Press, Buckingham.

2. White, J., 1986, *The Assessment of Writing: Pupils Aged 11 and 15*, APU, NFER/Nelson, Slough.

3. Martin, N., D'Arcy, P., Newton, B. & Parker, R., 1976, *Writing and Learning across the Curriculum 11–16*, Ward Lock (Schools Council), London.

4. Bullock, A., 1975, *A Language for Life*, Report of a Committee of Enquiry under the Chairmanship of Sir Alan Bullock, HMSO, London.

5. For example: Berry, M. & Kellington, S., 1986, *Reading About Chemistry*, Heinemann, London (other books are available in this series).

6. Davies, F. & Greene, T., 1984, *Reading for Learning in the Sciences*, Oliver & Boyd, London.

7. Cassels, J.R.T. & Johnstone, A.H., 1985, *Words that Matter in Science*, Royal Society of Chemistry, London.

8. Bentley, D. & Watts, M., 1992, *Communication in School Science: Groups, Tasks and Problem Solving 5–16*, Falmer Press, London.

9. Barnes, D., 'The role of talk in learning' in Norman, K. (ed.), 1992, *Thinking Voices: the Work of the National Oracy Project*, Hodder & Stoughton, London.

10. Bulman, L., 1985, *Teaching Language and Study Skills in Secondary Science*, Heinemann, London.

11. Forrestal, P., 'Structuring the learning experience' in Norman, K. (ed.), 1992, *Thinking Voices: the Work of the National Oracy Project*, Hodder & Stoughton, London.

12. Keay, K., 'Raps, poems and pistons', *Talk*, 1989, **1**, 37–39, National Curriculum Council, York.

13. Solomon, J., 'The retrial of Galileo', *SATIS 16–19 unit 1*, ASE, Hatfield.

14. Centre for Science Education, Sheffield City Polytechnic, 1992, *Active Teaching and Learning Approaches in Science*, Collins, London.

CHAPTER 7

Using information technology

Information technology (IT) is the broad term used to cover all aspects of transmitting or manipulating information using some sort of technology. However, in schools the term is usually restricted to using microcomputers. Most, if not all, schools are now equipped with microcomputers of one sort or another. The most common form of arrangement is to find the majority of the computers situated in one room, the IT room, with a few computers in key teaching rooms. The computers in the IT room are often linked together or networked so that information can be centrally stored and retrieved from a central computer called a file server.

Already you will have realised that the world of computing is full of jargon, which along with the high-tech nature of the work can quickly turn people off and send them scurrying back to chalk and the blackboard. However, it does not take long to master simple computer use and when you see the fascination on pupils' faces, their sheer enjoyment of working with computers and, quite often, the improvement in classroom control, you will be convinced that your effort was well worth while. By the time pupils start their secondary education they will have had considerable experience of using computers. In the primary school they will have used them as word processors, databases, for drawing pictures, devices for controlling other machines, educational games and probably a lot more. In addition, many pupils have their own computers or games machines at home and are quite familiar with much of the jargon used. In fact, it is not uncommon to find a pupil in your class who knows a lot more about computing than you do. If you find yourself in this situation you should turn it to your advantage by reinforcing the fact that the teacher is not the fount of all knowledge and it will certainly help to raise the self-esteem of the computer-literate pupil. You do not need any special skills such as the ability to write computer programs to be able to use computers. The vast majority of programs produced for schools will run very smoothly from a menu on the screen and the minor skills required will quickly be assimilated.

7.1   THE HARDWARE AND THE SOFTWARE

Types of microcomputers used in schools

Because computers are expensive items it has often been left to the LEA to decide which type of machine to buy for all the schools in the county and, as one might expect, different authorities have used different criteria to decide on their purchases. As a result you will find that even neighbouring counties will often have different machines. Those in common use at the moment are:

APPLE Macintosh (Macs)
Acorn Archimedes A series
IBM (or IBM compatible)
Nimbus PC
BBC B and BBC master

All have the same parts, a keyboard, a monitor, a disk drive and a processor unit, and operate in very similar ways. The software (program) is generally specific to each computer type but you will find that software manufacturers will make several different versions of the same program to match each of the computer types in common use.

Software

Teachers rarely have the time or the even the expertise to write software for use with their classes. It is therefore common practice to buy software from educational suppliers. The software needs to be of the appropriate type for the machine used and with some computers you also need to consider the size of the floppy disk drive, either 3½ or 5¼ inches wide. The old BBC B and BBC master computers have an additional complication as they can be fitted with a disk drive that works on either a 40-track system or an 80-track system. The more modern computers are generally fitted with a hard disk drive in addition to one or more floppy disk drives. Software may be loaded from the floppy disk drive on to the hard disk and stored there. Once the program is on the hard disk it will remain there even when the computer is switched off. A program that is loaded into the working memory of the computer from a floppy disk will be lost once the machine is switched off. It is a matter of convenience to have all your most frequently used programs stored on the hard disk of the computer.

Things to do

- Find out where the computers are kept in your school and who is responsible for them. Make sure that you know how to switch the network on and how to operate the system. You may need to have a password.
- Find out if the science department has any microcomputers and ask to be shown how to operate one.
- Find out what science software is available in the school.

How many computers do I need for my class?

Getting thirty youngsters round one small computer monitor is not the best way of using information technology. If you are confronted with the situation of having one computer in your laboratory to service the needs of all your pupils, there are a number of ways of overcoming the problem. Whatever method you choose it is important to remember that the computer is there to help stimulate the learning of science. The pupils may learn from the machine itself but they will also learn from talking together in groups about the information they are going to put into the computer and the response the computer makes to their commands. One possible method is to link the output from the computer to a large television monitor, perhaps the one that is normally used for showing videos to pupils. In this way you can use the computer as an electronic blackboard. The teacher or pupils can input information and the results can be seen by all. A second strategy is to have the computer situated in one corner of the room and allow pupils to access it on a rota basis. The computer can act as a source of information alongside the teacher and books.

Some activities are best carried out in the computer room with all the pupils working on the same task at once. This situation may arise when you want the pupils to prepare a document using either the word processor or desk-top publishing packages. Alternatively you may wish to teach the whole class using a particular piece of software. Working in the computer room rather than the laboratory brings with it new challenges. Pupils are very keen to press the keys, any keys, and see something happen on the screen. In order to make the most of the visit to the computer room you will need to be very familiar with the program and, of course, have a detailed plan of what you are going to do. You may find it useful to consider the following:

- holding the whole lesson in the computer room rather than have the disturbance of moving the pupils from the laboratory during lesson time
- giving a simple explanation of what they should do, without the computers switched on and with all the class facing you

- preparing a simple flow chart to show the procedures to be followed
- how you are going to capitalise on the fact that the pupils are working in groups of two or three on a computer
- try to free yourself from technical problems so that you can walk round and talk to pupils about science

7.2 WAYS OF USING THE MICROCOMPUTER IN SCIENCE LESSONS

Microcomputers are not restricted to number-crunching work and it would be wrong to think of them just in terms of being super-calculators. On a very simple level they can be seen as being yet another aid in the classroom to help the pupil to learn but they can also be used in many ways that reflect their use in the wider world outside the classroom.

The main uses of microcomputers in science lessons are:

- as a learning aid
- to simulate situations that cannot otherwise be carried out in a school laboratory, e.g. experiment with the operation of a simulated nuclear reactor
- as a device for storing and manipulating data
- as a device for presenting information (word processing, desk-top publishing and graphical packages), and
- as a device for controlling and monitoring experiments

Information technology is one of the 'key competencies' of the NC and as such needs to be part of all pupils' work. Pupils will use IT in many of their subjects but science has a key role to play in raising pupils' awareness of the uses of computers.

Information about what is required as far as the NC is concerned is given in the NC science and the NC technology documents.[1] At present the technology NC is being revised from the original five ATs to three ATs. The AT that deals with IT in the 1990 version of NC technology is Te5, whereas it is Te3 in the revised (1992) version.[2] The content of the AT has not changed between the two versions, only the number. The relevant areas to look at in the documents are:

- in the paragraphs headed **Communication** in the introduction to the PoS for each KS and in the PoS for Sc1 in the Science document, and
- in **Attainment Target 5: Information technology capability** (Te5) in the Technology document

Complementary statements are made in the different documents as illustrated in Table 7.1. The non-statutory guidance produced by both the NCC and CCW is very helpful in indicating how IT can be incorporated into lessons.[2]

Table 7.1 **Related statements from the science National Curriculum and technology National Curriculum documents for key stage 3**

From the science PoS	They should begin to use information and data accessed from a computer and be able to identify the main features of an information transmission system and the way in which data are coded, handled and transmitted
From the technology PoS	Pupils should know that information technology is used to monitor physical events and conditions, and to process, present and to respond to collected data
Example from the technology document	To monitor the dampness of the soil around house plants, with a view to developing a self-watering system
The SoA for assessment purposes to be found in the technology document	Te5/7c: Pupils should understand that the results of experiments can be obtained over long or short periods or at a distance using data logging equipment

This interlinking of the two NC documents requires science teachers to work very closely with their colleague in charge of computing in the school as this person will have to collate pupils' abilities in IT from a whole range of different subject specialists.

Things to do

Below are two statements of attainment from the NC technology. Match the statements with the PoS in the Technology document and locate the relevant examples. From KS3:

Te5/6a: Pupils should be able to use information technology to combine and organise different forms of information for a presentation to an audience.

From KS4:

Te5/9a: Pupils should evaluate a software package or a complex computer model; analyse the situation for which it was developed; access its efficiency, ease of implementation and appropriateness and suggest refinements.

Look for areas in the science document that could relate to the example given.

One problem about writing about IT in schools is the rapid pace of development in this field. New and more powerful machines are being introduced on to the market almost weekly. Prices are staying the same or in some cases coming down. New and more flexible software is being introduced all the time and so it is inevitable that what is written one minute is out of date the next. The following sections outline the principles of computer use in science lessons together with examples of software currently in use.

Some software packages are very sophisticated, particularly the word processing and desk-top publishing packages. Both teachers and pupils should not feel that they need to acquaint themselves with all the facilities the software can offer before they can start using them. Most people will learn as they use the software, picking up skills as and when they are needed.

The computer as a learning aid

Many of the early computer programs were designed as drill and practice exercises. Some were routine and tedious with little advantage over pencil and paper exercises. The better programs have game-like characteristics and may present pupils with an interesting screen display. They may involve sound effects or allow a pupil to build up points in competition with others. The motivational factor of working on a computer often encourages pupils to make greater effort.

An example of this type of program that is currently popular with pupils is 'Forensic – a Case to Solve' published by Chalksoft where each pupil is presented with a 'murder case' to solve using his/her knowledge of simple chemical analysis and the properties of compounds. Using simulated tests (on the computer screen) the pupils must identify substances found on the shoes of the suspects. By finding out who is lying, and also by looking for a substance found at the scene of the crime, they can identify the murderer.

Using the computer to simulate situations

There are a number of topics on the syllabus where computer simulations help to bring the situation alive and make it more meaningful for the pupil. This is particularly valuable when discussing industrial processes or evaluating the reasons for siting an industrial plant at one location rather than another. Difficult or dangerous experiments can be illustrated through computer simulations with the pupils given the opportunity to alter the conditions. The following software is in common use:

Millikan's Oil Drops and the Electron's Charge (AVP)
The Nuclear Reactor Simulation (Longman)
Iron and Steel (Mercury)
Graphic Hearts (BHFCP)

Simulations can help to introduce environmental and economic considerations into lessons. The Iron and Steel simulation program, for example, examines a number of possible processes that could be used to manufacture iron. If the process selected by the pupil is either too costly or environmentally unsound the screen display highlights the problem with a flashing box.

Most of the simulation packages that are available have been produced for low-power machines such as the BBC series. Few have been produced for the present generation of computers.

Things to do

Try out a simulation program for yourself. A good one to choose would be the Nuclear Reactor package as most science teachers are likely to have to teach some aspect of nuclear power. Look up the relevant SoA in the NC technology document (1990), i.e. Te5/7f. As you work through the program consider:

- what briefing would you give the pupils in order to motivate them for this work?
- how will you ensure that the pupils work together in their computer groups and that each member actively participates?
- what follow-up activity, such as a role play exercise, could you have to consolidate the ideas presented in the program?
- what other resources are available for this topic, e.g. SATIS units?

Using the computer to store and manipulate data

Computers are particularly good at remembering large amounts of data and have the ability to sort it into useful categories. The collection and manipulation of data is usually done through a database program. Common examples used in schools are:

GRASS (Newman College, Birmingham)
ViewStore (Acornsoft)
Quest (Advisory Unit)
Microsoft Works (Microsoft)
Key Plus (Mercury)

Pupils can either use a bank of data that has been prepared for them by the publishers or they can build up their own database. The information is placed under a series of headings called *field names* or just *fields*. There can be many fields but there will be an upper limit depending on the memory size of the computer. Each set of data is called a *record* and the set of records is called the *data file*. Most databases will allow the operator to present the findings of their search in a variety of ways, such as numbers or percentages, as histograms, pie diagrams, scattergrams or line graphs. Building up a database is also a useful experience for pupils and there are many opportunities for doing this during their secondary science course.

The following examples show how databases can be used in science:

- Pupils could interrogate a database containing a list of the elements with some of their properties, such as melting point, boiling point, year of discovery, abundance on the Earth.
- Pupils could build a database from measurements about themselves such as height, weight, handspan and eye colour (see Things to do, below).
- A record of the planets in the solar system with information such as their size, gravity, surface temperature, mass, distance from the Sun could be explored.
- Pupils could prepare a database of the many different types of polymers, their properties and uses.

Operating a database is very simple once you have got to grips with the terms that come up on the screen menu. From the search data command you will need to select which fields you wish to search and what your limits are going to be. There will be the opportunity to include AND or OR commands in your search to make it more specific. You will need to spend some time 'playing' with the database to get used to all the functions available.

Things to do

Build up some data on a class that you teach. Pupils will find it interesting to manipulate the information and produce statistics on the group as a whole.

Headings for the fields might be: Sex, eye colour, hair colour, roll tongue, height (m), weight/N, leg length (m), arm length (m), maximum stride distance (m), distance can jump from standing position (m), favourite drink.

Pupils can then use the data to answer questions and see if there is any relationship between items of data, for example: (a) Is there a relationship between: height, weight, leg length, arm length, stride distance and the distance you can jump from a standing position? (b) Is there a relationship between: favourite drink and the ability to roll your tongue? (c) Is there a relationship between: leg length and height?

Spreadsheets

Spreadsheets are useful whenever we want to make a large number of routine calculations in science. A spreadsheet is a matrix of rows, labelled with numbers, and columns, labelled with letters as shown in Figure 7.1. Each unit of the matrix, called a cell, can be identified by

For the reaction: $H_2 + I_2 \Leftrightarrow 2HI$

Students input data for the concentrations of hydrogen $[H_2]$, iodine $[I_2]$ and hydrogen iodide $[HI]$ as supplied by the teacher for the three experiments (given in rows 01, 02 and 03). The spreadsheet calculates the values in row 01 for columns D, E, F and G by inputting the following formulae:

For D: C01*C01 (take the number in cell C01 and multiply it by itself)
For E: A01*B01 (take the number in cell A01 and multiply it by the number in cell B01)
For F: C01/E01 (take the number in cell C01 and divide it by the number in cell E01)
For G: D01/E01 (take the number in cell D01 and divide it by the number in cell E01)

A simple copy command will allow the formulae to be reproduced in the other rows.

	A	B	C	D	E	F	G
	$[H_2]$	$[I_2]$	$[HI]$	$[HI]^2$	$[H_2] \times [I_2]$	$[HI]/[H_2][I_2]$	$[HI]^2/[H_2][I_2]$
00							
01	4.56×10^{-3}	0.74×10^{-3}	13.54×10^{-3}	1.83×10^{-4}	3.37×10^{-6}	4.02×10^{3}	54.3
02	3.56×10^{-3}	1.25×10^{-3}	15.59×10^{-3}	2.43×10^{-4}	4.45×10^{-6}	3.50×10^{3}	54.6
03	2.25×10^{-3}	2.34×10^{-3}	16.85×10^{-3}	2.83×10^{-4}	5.27×10^{-6}	3.20×10^{3}	53.7

The results show that the formula given in column G gives a value that is approximately constant for the 3 sets of experimental results. This is called the equilibrium constant for the reaction in terms of concentrations, K_c.

$$K_c = \frac{[HI]^2}{[H_2][I_2]}$$

Figure 7.1 Example of using a spreadsheet in A-level chemistry

the column letter and the row number, e.g. E03 is the cell in column E and row 03. You can enter text, numbers and formulae into the boxes of the spreadsheet. You would choose to enter text when you are putting in the headings for each of the columns as you set up the system. Each set of data can be inputted into columns in the spreadsheet. Further sets of data could be inputted into separate rows. Common spreadsheet packages used in schools are:

GRASSHOPPER (Newman College, Birmingham)
EXCEL (Microsoft)
EUREKA (Longman)
LOTUS 1–2–3 (Lotus)

Things to do

Practise using a spreadsheet by carrying out an exercise on reaction times with a class. Pupils will work in pairs with one holding the top of a ruler and the other with his/her thumb and finger on each side of the bottom of the ruler. When the first pupil drops the ruler the second pupil must catch it as soon as possible. The experiment is repeated three times and all the results are entered into the spreadsheet under the following column headings:

	A	B	C	D	E	F	G	H	I
00	Name	Height	Age	Right or left handed	Result 1	Result 2	Result 3	Average	Reaction time

The formula for column H line 01 will be (E01+F01+G01)/3.

The formula for column I is derived from the formula
$s = ut + \tfrac{1}{2} at^2$

where u = the initial velocity, 0 m s^{-1} in this case
        t = the time
        a = acceleration, which in this case is the acceleration due to gravity, i.e. 10ms^{-2}
        s = distance measured in metres

Therefore, the reaction time, t, can be calculated from $t = \sqrt{(s/10)}$. In terms of the spreadsheet cells, for row 01 this translates as Sqr(H01/10).

   The next time you find that the pupils have to manipulate data using a simple formula, take the opportunity of introducing them to the use of spreadsheets in science. They may already be familiar with the technique from their mathematics lessons.

Things to do continued

Other opportunities arise for using spreadsheets when working on the following topics:

- heat (using the formula $\Delta H = ms(\theta_2 - \theta_1)$)
- Ohm's law (using the formula $V = IR$)
- mole calculations (using the formula no. of moles = mass/formula mass)
- light (measurement of angle of incidence and angle of reflection and calculating)
- $\sin i / \sin r$

There are more openings for using spreadsheets in post-16 courses than pre-16 courses.

Using the computer to present information

We have probably not reached the stage of computer development where a teacher would ask pupils to write up all their work on their word processors. Although who knows, computers may be commonplace on pupils' desks in a few years time, replacing the old pen and ink. In the mean time it is not unreasonable to expect pupils to produce written items using the computer occasionally. Pupils should have reasonably free access to computers in either the IT room or the laboratory and these should be equipped with the appropriate software. There should be a simple word-processing package that will allow pupils to set work out neatly and possibly check their spelling. One advantage of using a word processor is that the document can be written over a period of time by saving the work on disk at the end of the work period and recalling it when you are next ready to write. In addition to adding new work, the order of the work can be changed by simple computer manipulations. Pupils should also have access to a desk-top publishing (DTP) package. This will enable them to present work in an attractive form with different type faces and graphics. It needs to be said that when pupils (and teachers) are first exposed to this new device they tend to overuse the array of available fonts and clip art and need to be advised towards restraint. DTP packages can be used for presentations of reports but are probably best kept for larger scale items such as posters or newspapers. There are plenty of opportunities for these two uses in science lessons, such as:

- preparing a poster on the results of an investigation
- writing an advertisement for a scientific product or type of healthy food
- writing an article on a famous scientist
- presenting a report on a survey carried out by the class.

Things to do

Familiarise yourself with the word-processing package available in your school by preparing a worksheet for a group of your pupils. Be content at practising a few of the selection of facilities available to you on your first visits to the computer. Obviously, the more you practise, the more proficient you will become. When you are reasonably happy about word processing try out the desk-top publishing package used in the school. If you want pupils to be able to use them, then you should be able to use them.

Using the computer to control or monitor experiments

As any visit to an industrial site will show you, many industrial processes are monitored and controlled by computers. The equipment is available in schools for pupils to make similar interactions with their experiments. In addition to the computer, pupils will need appropriate sensors, an interface and suitable software to run the system. This may sound more complicated than the other uses of computers in science as it involves more wires and boxes but the manufacturers have gone to a great deal of trouble to make the systems as simple to operate as possible. These devices open up a whole new area of experimental science that has not previously been possible in the school laboratory. It is possible to take measurements over a very short period of time, e.g investigating the discharge of a capacitor, examining the waveform of a musical note or over a long period of time, e.g. the growth of a plant, the rate of a slow reaction. There are many different measurements that the computer can deal with, such as:

- measurement of speed
- changes in light level
- electrical conductivity
- movement
- temperature
- amount of oxygen dissolved in water, and
- measurement of radioactive decay

Basically any measurement that can be converted into a voltage can be monitored by a computer. With a little ingenuity it is possible to convert what would initially be seen as an impossible task for the computer into a possibility. For example, volumes of gases can be measured by attaching the end of a gas syringe to a movement sensor. As the volume increases the plunger of the syringe moves out, pushing the lever of the movement sensor and this information is passed to the computer which can be calibrated to read the data in terms of volume.

The information received from any sensor, via the interface box, must be processed by software. Most software packages are specific to the interface used but are common to all the sensors that can be used with that interface. Common control and monitoring packages used in schools are:

Sense and Control (Educational Electronics)
First Sense (Philip Harris)
Blue Box Sensors (Philip Harris)
LogIT (Griffin & George)
Simple Logger (Unilab)

Most of the experiments using this type of equipment involve monitoring the experiment rather than controlling it. This type of activity is often referred to as data logging. The control aspect is used more frequently in technology, where computers can be used to switch devices on and off and sequence events. Computer control could be used in science experiments in circumstances where fixed amounts of a quantity need to be administered at predetermined time intervals. This sort of activity requires a different type of interface and software.

Some data loggers can be used to collect data without being attached to the computer. They are battery powered and the information received is stored on a chip. The data can be reviewed by means of a display panel on the logger (similar to that on a calculator) or it can be downloaded to a computer. Software can be used to manipulate the data into a suitable form such as a graphical representation. Common portable data loggers are:

Sense and Control (Educational Electronics)
VELA (Versatile Laboratory Aid) (Educational Electronics)
EMU (Easy Memory Unit) (Philip Harris)

Each of these devices has its own peculiar characteristics and some are much easier to use than others. CLEAPSS[4] have produced a *Which?* type review, which should give you an indication as to the device that would best suit you.

Textbooks usually give only the broadest of outlines on how to carry out data logging and some of the written material produced by the manufacturers can be daunting for beginners. However, there are a number of publications, such as those produced by NCET[5] and the ASE,[6] which give simple instructions for data-logging experiments.

7.3 DEVELOPING AREAS OF COMPUTER TECHNOLOGY

Interactive video

Interactive video (IV) is the interplay of computer software with a video disk. In addition to the normal computer you will need a video

Experiment	Probe	Sensor	Connecting wires	Interface	Interface cable	Interface
Energy released from seeds (i) Using Sense & Control (Educational Electronics) Two batches of seeds, one killed by boiling in water, are placed in separate vacuum flasks	A temperature probe is placed in each vacuum flask. The probe is calibrated against a mercury-in-glass thermometer	The probe is connected to the Sense and Control unit	The communicating cable is connected directly to the computer			Practical Science with Micro-computers software is used to run the procedure
Rate of reaction for the thiosulphate + acid reaction (ii) Using Blue Box and Universal Interface from Philip Harris. Various concentrations of sodium thiosulphate are reacted with dilute hydrochloric acid	A light probe is used to monitor the reaction. As the reaction proceeds the precipitate of sulphur that is formed gradually reduces the amount of light that can pass through the reaction flask	The probe is connected to the sensor unit	4 mm leads connect the sensor unit to the Universal Interface	Universal Interface	A cable connects the interface to the computer.	Datadisc software is used to run the procedure
Weather monitoring (iii) Using an Easy Memory Unit (EMU) from Philip Harris. Air pressure, light, humidity and temperature can be measured over a period of time	The four probes are connected to their sensor boxes and each box is connected to one of the four channels on the EMU. All connections are via 4 mm leads. The EMU is battery driven and will record the data without being connected to the computer		Calibrate the Datadisc software using the sensors and a four-way box (fitted with its own lead to the computer) Connect the EMU to the computer using the interface cable. Each channel can be downloaded in turn			Datadisc software is used to run the procedure

Figure 7.2 Apparatus required for control and monitoring using a computer together with examples of experiments using different data-logging systems

disk player and an appropriate chip fitted into the computer. With this package quality TV pictures and sound can be mixed with computer graphics. The operator can interact with the sequences of the program and can replay section if s/he desires. Such a system can act as a valuable learning module where the pupil can watch a topic being illustrated and then answer questions, utilising the normal computer mode, on the work immediately afterwards.

In 1990 the Royal Society investigated the use of IV in school science[7] and found that there were few science-related IV disks readily available. In addition the equipment and the disks themselves are very expensive.

CD ROM

This involves fitting a computer with an additional chip (a ROM) and linking the computer to a special compact disk (CD) player. Instead of having music on the CD it can contain large amounts of information and images. Data can be accessed quickly and easily. Encyclopaedias and other large banks of information are available on CD making this a valuable device when pupils are asked to carry out research for project work. This type of equipment is most likely to be found in the school library.

NOTES AND REFERENCES

1. Department of Education and Science and The Welsh Office, 1990, *Technology in the National Curriculum*, HMSO, London.

2. Department for Education and The Welsh Office, 1992, *Technology for Ages 5–16 (1992) Proposals*, HMSO, London.

3. See Chapter 2 reference 17.

4. CLEAPSS, 1990, *Stand-alone Dataloggers*, School Science Service, Brunel University, Uxbridge.

5. National Council for Educational Technology, 1990, *Practical Science with Microcomputers*, NCET, Warwick.

6. Frost, R., 1992, *The IT Science Book of Datalogging and Control* (A compendium of ideas for using sensors and control technology in science), ASE, Hatfield.

7. Royal Society, 1990, *Interactive Video and the Teaching of Science*, Royal Society, London.

Science for all

Equality of opportunity

Prior to the introduction of the 1988 Education Reform Act science was one of the optional subjects that could be 'dropped' at the end of the third year (year 9). Pupils in their fourth and fifth years in school would take one of the following combinations: all three sciences, any two of the sciences, one science, a general science course, or no science at all. The introduction of NC science brought with it science for all, from the age of 5 up to 16. It can now be said that there is equality of opportunity for all pupils to study science in schools. However, the equality is only there in the sense that there is a common programme of study that all pupils must follow. What we need to consider is the way in which that programme is delivered. How can we ensure through our teaching that science knowledge is equally open to all pupils, allowing them to develop to their full potential?

In this chapter three areas of equality in science teaching are reviewed:

- teaching pupils who have difficulty learning either because of physical or mental disabilities
- teaching pupils from different cultural backgrounds, and
- equality in terms of gender

Things to do

It may be that at this point you are debating the significance of this chapter to your own situation. Thoughts may be running through your mind such as:

'It doesn't matter about the less able, they won't remember anything you teach them anyway.'
'I don't need to know anything about teaching in a multicultural school. All the pupils in my school are white.'
'I treat boys and girls the same.'

If these are your thoughts you may find it useful to take a fresh look at the aims of education or more specifically the aims of science education. You are first and foremost a teacher of pupils and your job is to prepare pupils for the world beyond school. Part of this work will be to engender tolerant behaviour amongst your pupils and a respect for the rights of individuals.

No scheme of work or set of curricular materials can hope to meet the needs of all the individuals in a class. It is the presentation and the sensitivity of the teacher to pupils' needs that will help to ensure that there is equality of opportunity. Teachers must become aware of their own attitudes towards groups of individuals in the class and how these affect their expectations of pupils' performance. Science education has its part to play in shaping the future. Although it may sound very grand, it is true to say that we are all involved in helping to create the society of tomorrow. The quality of that society will rely heavily on people having the skills that science can offer together with understanding and respect for other people's opinions. The attitudes we help to develop in pupils today will have a major influence on the way in which they think and operate when they reach adulthood.

8.1 TEACHING PUPILS WITH SPECIAL NEEDS

The term 'special needs' covers pupils with a whole range of abilities and those with a variety of physical problems. There are pupils in mainstream schools who may be classified as having special needs because they have learning difficulties or because they have emotional or behaviourial problems. Some teachers may also describe exceptionally able pupils as a group having special needs. In addition to those in mainstream schools there are pupils with more profound and multiple learning difficulties who attend special schools. All of these pupils are entitled to a broad, balanced science curriculum and are expected to follow NC science and will be assessed against all attainment targets unless specifically disapplied.[1] Science makes an important contribution to their learning experiences, in particular science offers pupils:

- opportunities for developing manipulative skills
- guidance in developing a better understanding of the world in which we live
- opportunities to develop their communication skills
- the chance to work together as a team, and
- help in acquiring problem-solving skills

There is a danger that the recent changes in national educational policy concerning the publication of test results at KS3 and KS4 may have an adverse effect on the teaching of less-able pupils. There is a risk that schools that wish to achieve a high ranking in the examination league tables may concentrate their efforts on the most able, leaving the less able marginalised. Failure to meet the needs of the less able is a significant failure in our duties as teachers.

Identifying the special needs

Rather than group all pupils with special needs together it is best to consider their specific learning problems. The following categories of needs have been identified:

- Pupils with exceptionally severe learning difficulties, e.g. pupils who are both blind and deaf.
- Pupils with mild, moderate or severe learning difficulties (some of these pupils may have a Statement describing their special educational needs and the special provision required, the term Statemented is used to categorise them).
- Pupils with specific learning difficulties, e.g. language problems.
- Pupils with emotional and behaviourial difficulties.
- Pupils with sensory impairment, e.g. pupils with hearing problems, pupils who have visual difficulties.
- Pupils who are physically challenged, e.g. pupils in wheelchairs, pupils who have difficulty with speech.

There are pupils with special needs in all schools but only a small proportion of these (about 2% of the school population) is likely to fall into the category where their disabilities are so great that they have to have a formal Statement of the pupil's special needs and the special provision required. Each school will have its own policy for grouping special-needs pupils. Some integrate these pupils into the mainstream classes whereas others will group the pupils together in one class. The decisions are generally made on the basis of the pupil's level of need and what is thought would be best for the individual. If the integration approach is adopted then it is common for the classroom teacher to have the support of an additional member of staff from the Special Needs department during the lesson.

Things to do

Contact the Special Needs department in your school and enquire about the nature and level of support that they are able to offer. What resources have they got and are you able to borrow them? They may have devices such as a concept keyboard that will allow pupils to work with a computer using simple, perhaps pictorial, commands. They may have simple lap-top computers for children who have difficulty in writing. Can they give you advice on how to deal with certain individuals in the school? They will be able to tell you about the level of work you can expect to get from some pupils.

The low ability of some pupils can come as a shock to trainee teachers. It is worth while talking through some cases with experienced teachers to get a feeling for what pupils can do.

Teaching pupils with learning difficulties

There is no single reason why a pupil might have learning difficulties. Jenkins[2] has identified five possible causes for low educational attainment:

- intellectual factors (such as limited educational development)
- home background (leading to poor language development, emotional insecurity and poor attitudes to education)
- personality factors (which, for example, prevent the growth of satisfactory relationships with teachers and other pupils)
- physical factors (such as below-average health and physical development)
- school factors (such as characteristics of the headteacher and staff, the organisation of the school, and the classroom procedures)

Whatever the cause of the difficulty in learning there is always some way of helping the pupil to progress and develop. For the most part, the teaching techniques used with other classes will be appropriate for those containing pupils with special needs. The difference that might be observed are in terms of:

- the longer time required for pupils to master skills and concepts
- the use of support staff
- greater emphasis on important points, and
- the need to keep bringing them back to the key point of the lesson

In planning courses for these pupils you will need to consider a list of goals that you would like your pupils to achieve. As with other pupils you will need to build on their prior knowledge and experiences and look for strategies that will help to develop the pupil through the medium of science. You might find it helpful to think of science as the vehicle for helping pupils to mature and to gain an insight into the world in which they live. As you prepare a list of goals or aims that are specific for less-able pupils you should contemplate the contribution science can make to the pupils' development. For example, a school science course might have the following points listed amongst its aims:

- pupils should be able to form increasingly mature relationships with adults and peers
- wherever possible the science should be related to the immediate interests of the pupils and in particular to leisure activities, e.g. photography, pets, bird watching
- pupils should develop a growing awareness of science in society
- pupils should develop the skills of communication and number work through practical experiences

It is worth while spending time pondering over your aims so that the targets you set for pupils are ones that they can achieve and where you will be able to reward for their efforts. In planning for individual lessons where there are pupils with special needs you have to consider ways of building pupils' confidence and self-esteem such as those outlined in Table 8.1. Because the needs of the individuals are so diverse there is no one answer to producing the model lesson. You will find a range of materials that have been especially written for low-ability pupils that will be helpful in your preparation.[3] The NCC have prepared some guidance for teaching special-needs pupils with examples of work in each of the attainment targets at both KS3 and KS4.[4] In the long term the best approach is to make small changes to your existing techniques and see if they work.

Table 8.1 *Ideas for helping pupils with special needs to learn*

Teaching resources	They should be attractive and easy to read. It is no use using materials that were designed for a younger age group. They will find these demeaning
Laboratory equipment	Make sure that they are provided with good quality equipment. They should not be of the opinion that they are always given the rubbish whereas the top set get the best. If the group is small it opens up the possibility of individual practical work and the use of equipment that is in short supply
Rewards	The pupils will respond well to praise. Show the pupils that you appreciate that they are trying. Display pupils' work. Occasionally, invite another member of staff (possibly the headteacher) to come and see the good work and give additional praise. Use a Record of Achievement to highlight the progress in learning. Use school-prepared certificates (easy to do with a desk-top publishing package) to reward specific events
Setting tasks that match the pupil's ability	Some science departments have the policy that all pupils in each year group will follow exactly the same work. If this policy is pursued then the less-able pupils will always fail. They need to experience success. It is pointless setting them tasks or end-of-topic questions that are way beyond their capabilities. They will benefit from being set tasks that are differentiated according to their ability. Carefully judge the amount of writing you require from them
Room layout	Consider where the pupils are going to sit. Remember that eye contact is important. A semicircle or circle of chairs is a good arrangement, with the teacher sitting on a stool within the circle
Links with the home	Encourage the parents to take an interest in their child's learning by getting parents to comment or be involved with homework. Ask the pupils to show their work to their parents. Give the parents a warm welcome on parents' evenings
Language	Pupils can be 'turned off' science because of its difficult technical vocabulary. Simplify the language so that they can understand. They are not going to be scientists. Do they need to know specialised scientific terms?
Repetition of key ideas and concepts	If pupils are to grasp the key ideas they will need to revisit them as the course progresses. This does not mean that the work should be repeated but that the idea should be re-presented in a different context

If pupils have difficulty in writing then they could record their results using a tape recorder or present them pictorially. You could also pre-record instructions for activities so that pupils can work at their own rates and listen to the tape as often as they need to. You should take advantage of all the new technology that is available to you to make life as easy as possible for those pupils with special needs.

Reading may also pose a problem for some pupils. Teachers have attempted to overcome this by providing pupils with worksheets where the information is given pictorially rather than in words. Reid[5] points out that although this may serve our immediate purpose, it does not aid the long-term solution of developing pupils' reading skills. You will need to plan out a long-term strategy to gradually remove the support of the special worksheets and the tape recorder in order to help pupils to function more independently.

Things to do

Find out what science courses pupils with learning difficulties follow in your school. Locate other materials that have been specially written for the less able.

Evaluate the resource materials or books using the following list of questions:

- Are they visually attractive?
- Is the level of language appropriate to slow learners?
- As far as you can tell, do you think the content of the packages is relevant to pupils?
- On the basis of your answers to the first three questions, do you think that pupils would be motivated to read the materials?
- Do they give examples of investigative work?
- Do they provide pupils with a broad science curriculum?
- In what way could the materials be used to encourage the development of self-esteem?
- What skills and processes are developed in the schemes you are considering?
- In what way would you improve one or both schemes so that they meet the needs of young people with learning problems?

Teaching physically challenged pupils

Some pupils can be very cruel and treat all individuals who have some sort of disability in the same demeaning manner. Terms such as 'thickies', 'rems' (for remedials) and other derogatory names are used. It can be very disheartening and discouraging for pupils to be labelled in this way but particularly so for those who may only have some physical or sensory disability. These pupils may be slow at manipulating pens and scientific apparatus but that does not mean that they are slow at thinking. One way of helping to overcome the problem of acceptance by their peers is to fully integrate pupils with such difficulties into mainstream lessons so that it can be shown that they can achieve as well as anyone.

Practical work will require that extra bit of thought and attention to detail. Special equipment may need to be purchased or borrowed that is easier to manipulate. Jones[6] describes many practical tasks that can be undertaken by pupils with physical disabilities. Conventional laboratory benches are high off the ground and access by wheelchair is impossible. A lower table with space to manoeuvre will provide a better working environment.

Always adopt a positive stance towards the work of the disabled pupils using phrases such as: '*I want you to do the timing in this experiment. Here is the stop clock. Now practise switching it on and off*', rather than: '*I know you can't do this John, but we'll find something for you to do in a minute*'.

You should not draw attention to the disability and you should think carefully about what you say.

Teaching pupils with hearing problems

When we are not able to hear exactly what has been said in a particular situation we can generally get the sense of the statements and mentally fill in the missing words and phrases. For a hearing-impaired pupil the situation can be quite different. Even with the hearing aid on, the reception may be akin to listening to a person who is almost out of earshot. The hearing aid will amplify all sounds, making it very difficult for the pupil to concentrate if the classroom is noisy. In addition the pupil's command of langauge is unlikely to be sufficient for him/her to be able to fill in all the gaps and grasp the meaning. The problem is further compounded in science lessons where some of the language will be technical and, therefore, unfamiliar to the pupil. Some pupils require the teacher to wear a microphone and radio transmitter in order to be able to hear the teacher clearly. While these can be a great aid to the pupil, it is worth remembering that anything you say will be heard by the pupil, right down to the smallest burp! The following points are worth bearing in mind when teaching hearing-impaired pupils:

- The pupil needs to be able to see the teacher's face if s/he is going to be able to lip read. Let the pupil sit near enough to the front of the class to see clearly without strain. The second row from the front is ideal.
- Let the pupil sit near the window side of the room, so that the teacher's face is not in the shadow. It is very difficult to lip read when the light or the window is behind the teacher.

- To use the hearing aid to advantage keep the pupil within 2 metres of the teacher whenever possible. For individual work, speak as closely as possible into the aid.
- Let the pupil turn round to see and hear others talking.
- Make sure that you have the pupil's attention before you speak.
- Give a definite clue to the subject of any class work or discussion by a quick word on the blackboard. If at all possible let the pupil read in advance about any new subject.
- Write important new words on the blackboard.
- A hearing-impaired person will probably not be able to listen and write at the same time.
- When the pupil fails to understand what is said, try rephrasing the statement to bring in new word patterns.
- Talk as normally as possible and try not to shout as this noise is distorted by a hearing aid.

The problem of sensory impairment is often compounded by the fact that a weakness in one area can lead to a weakness in another. For example, pupils with hearing impairment can often have difficulties with reading, writing and talking.

Teaching science to visually handicapped pupils

Teaching science to pupils with visual impairment is particularly challenging when so much of the information we give them is in written form and the success of many practical activities is dependent on careful observation. Safety can be a special worry and all practical activities must be carefully assessed for possible risk to the experimenter and his/her classmates. You may think that chemistry, with all its dangers, might be an area of practical activity best avoided by visually handicapped pupils but Betts[7] provides us with an array of ideas of how these pupils carry out work in chemistry using their other senses.

The Royal National Institute for the Blind have produced some very useful guidance material for teaching science to visually impaired pupils.[8] The following list, taken from their work, highlights points that you should consider when teaching classes containing such pupils:

- ensure that the pupil is very familiar with the working environment (the laboratory), the exits, the layout of the benches, the position of all the services
- present apparatus on a tray so that it is all close to hand
- make sure that the pupil can get close to the apparatus and chemicals
- present written material in a large type face (easy to do when the worksheet has been written using a word processor)
- use special bright lights to shine on work areas

- allow the pupil to use vision aids, e.g. magnifying glass
- make apparatus easier to see by sticking luminous tape around parts that will not be heated
- use digital apparatus with a large number display
- use 'talking' apparatus (such as an electronic balance interfaced to a computer fitted with appropriate speech software), and
- use volumetric apparatus with special raised marks

It is also worth bearing in mind that colour blindness will affect how a pupil observes and records certain chemical reactions. You need to know which of your pupils are colour blind so that you do not penalise them unfairly.

8.2 MULTICULTURAL ISSUES

All too often science teachers shun their responsibility to educate pupils to become responsible, well-informed citizens of a multiracial society. The main culprits are those teachers who teach in all-white schools where they see this issue as being somebody else's problem. As science teachers, we all have an important role in helping our pupils to be aware of the variety of approaches there are to life and to make them question any in-built prejudices that they may have. Britain is a multiracial and multicultural society and all pupils must be enabled to understand what this means. On the surface it is perhaps easy to comprehend why many teachers deny any multicultural dimension in their lessons.

Attitudes such as:

'Atoms are neither black nor white, there is no cultural diversity in science'

'I have no children from ethnic minorities in my class so it doesn't concern me'

'I've got enough to worry about teaching the National Curriculum'

persist in many classrooms. This narrow and limited view of science teaching has to be changed if science is going to make its proper impact on the education of the whole child. The most significant document in recent times on multicultural issues for teachers is the so-called Swann Report. This report, published in March 1985 and officially called *Education for All,*[9] was the result of a working party's investigations into the education of ethnic minority students led by Lord Swann. The committee was primarily concerned with changing people's behaviour and attitudes towards the ethnic minorities. Society is faced with a dual problem: eradicating discriminatory attitudes of the white majority and evolving an educational system that ensures all pupils achieve their full potential. The problem then is not one of how to educate children of ethnic minorities but of how to educate all children. It is necessary to combat racism, to attack inherited myths and stereotypes and the ways they are embodied in institutional practices. Multicultural understanding has to permeate all aspects of a school's work. It is not a topic that can be welded on to existing practices. There are many opportunities in science where teachers can help pupils to understand the diversity of society and the contributions different cultures have made to our existing body of scientific knowledge. In considering multicultural issues the teacher should be concerned that s/he provides all pupils with opportunities to:

- question the reasons underlying inequalities between peoples and nations, and relate such issues to those of interdependence
- question and challenge racist attitudes and assumptions
- examine positive images of people from other cultures and avoid stereotypes of peoples places and times, and
- consider science as a world-wide activity

In addition, where there is a mixture of cultures in the school, teachers should:

- build on the pupils' own cultural backgrounds and experiences, and
- value and develop their own linguistic repertoire

Things to do

What do you understand by the following terms: multicultural; ethnic groups; and antiracist approach to teaching?

A science course that proclaims to offer equal opportunities should build on both the culture and the ethnicity of the pupils in the school. Hoyle[10] and Dennick[11] provide useful definitions of these terms.

Racism

Pupils have all sorts of mixed ideas about why individuals differ from each other and why they behave differently. Their opinions are formulated by listening to comments from their parents, peers or from the powerful influence of the media. All too often pupils come up with racist ideas based on a concoction of pseudo-scientific theories about hierarchical differences in intellect and ability. Science teachers have a vital responsibility to challenge such ideas and to ensure that pupils are fully aware of the scientific explanations of why people differ. NC science offers an excellent opportunity to discuss this issue when covering strand (ii) of Sc2:

KS4 Sc2 strand (ii) They (the pupils) should consider the interaction of genetic and environmental factors (including radiation) in variation.

Some teachers are altogether unhappy about using the concept of 'race' as they consider it a completely false method of classifying people. They would argue that there may have been a time in the distant past history of the world when groups of people were isolated from one another and as such could be classified as a 'pure race'. However, as soon as populations began to migrate and encounter one another the concept of race began to lose its meaning. We are all part of one race – the human race – within which there are different breeding groups, which vary in the frequency of one or more genes. These groups of populations are more accurately referred to as genogroups rather than races. Variation is a continuous phenomena and its importance as a climatic adaptation should be a foundation for understanding the differences in physical characteristics of human beings. Science teachers have the opportunity to expose the inadequacy of the concept of 'race' in the context of human variation and appropriately equip pupils to counter racial stereotyping. They can do this by exercises, such as the ability of pupils to roll their tongues, in order to stress the differences within the same genogroup as well as examples of differences between different genogroups.

Things to do

Study the way a science (biology) textbook deals with the topic of variation. List examples of exercises that you think would be useful in terms of getting your class familiar with the idea of variation.

Consider how you might deal with the data from any survey that the pupils might carry out, e.g. blood groups of all members of the class. Perhaps you might consider presenting it in chart form as a poster for the laboratory wall or you might put it on a computer database for analysis.

The 'west is best' attitude

It is no wonder that many pupils from ethnic minorities become alienated towards science when all that they hear of in their science lesson is the success of western scientists and how this is linked with progress, industrial development and wealth. This is often contrasted with the poverty, illiteracy and starvation in the home countries of many of the ethnic minority students. It is vitally important that pupils are made aware of the contributions made to scientific knowledge throughout history from other cultures. Much of today's scientific research involves teams of people from all over the world working together. While, sadly, there is illiteracy and starvation on a massive scale in the third world we ought not to ignore the fact that there are similar pockets of peoples in the so-called western civilization. It is perhaps western culture and traditions along with abundant resources and a moderate climate that have all contributed to our current success but who knows what the future may bring.

The language problem

Pupils whose home language is not English can have a great deal of difficulty with any school subject but the difficulty is exacerbated in science because of the large number of technical terms we use each lesson. Just consider for a moment what it would be like for you to sit in a class in a French or German school and try to understand the science lesson. While your 'school' language lessons would provide you with an understanding of a smattering of words it is unlikely that you would be in a position to come to terms with the finer points of the subject. Some ethnic minority students are in a much worse position than this and require considerable help if they are to make any progress. As well as encouraging these pupils to use a bilingual dictionary during lessons it is helpful to build up your own list of key words. This can be done through your own dictionary work, by help from a colleague who speaks the language or from past pupils. It is worth considering producing some worksheets bilingually. The fact that you are making an effort to get the pupils to learn will have a tremendous effect on their motivation and morale.

Teaching opportunities

On the surface, most syllabuses, including NC science, give the impression that there is little of a multicultural nature to include. This could not be farther from the truth. In fact most aspects of NC science can be opened up to include a multicultural dimension. However, it would not be appropriate to introduce multiculturalism artificially, rather it should arise naturally as the circumstances warrant it. The examples given in Table 8.2 illustrate how teachers can introduce a multicultural slant to their science lessons.

Table 8.2 **Examples of how National Curriculum science can be given a multicultural slant**

NC reference and PoS	KS3 Sc1: Scientific investigation
	KS4 Sc2 strand (i): They should explore how the internal environments of plants and animals are maintained, including water relations, temperature control, defence mechanisms, solute balance ...
Teaching ideas	The production of different crops in different climates, e.g. a comparison of wheat farming with the production of rice or sugar cane
Resources	An investigation that could be used with this topic is **bean sprouts**, details are given in *The Assessment of Practical Work in Science* (page 121) (Blackwell)[12]

Table 8.2 continued

NC reference and PoS	KS3 Sc2 strand (i): They should study life processes, feeding (including digestion and assimilation), respiration, removal of waste, movement behaviour, growth, reproduction and sensitivity, particularly as they relate to human beings
Teaching ideas	World diets in comparison with UK diet
Resources	1. SATIS unit 703: *Vegetarianism*[13]
	2. *Fibre in your Diet*, *Food, Glorious Food* and *Feeding the World* (Birmingham Education Authority)[14]
	3. Unit 6 in *Humans as Organisms* (Simon & Schuster)[15]
	4. Chapter B6 in *Nuffield Co-ordinated Sciences – Biology* (Longman)[16]
NC reference and PoS	KS3 Sc3 strand (iii): Pupils should investigate a range of types of reaction, including thermal and electrolytic decomposition, ionic reactions in solution, salt formation, oxidation and reduction, fermentation and polymerisation and, where possible, relate these to models and to everyday processes such as corrosion and the manufacture of new materials
Teaching ideas	Pupils could investigate the fermentation of many starch- and sugar-containing plants, e.g. millet, grape juice, cassava, sugar cane. Pupils could study how industrial alcohol is used as a fuel (Brazil) and as a chemical feedstock. Pupils could investigate the corrosion of metals in different environments
Resources	1. Unit 7.12 (page 208) in *Chemistry for GCSE* (Heinemann)[17]
NC reference and PoS	KS3 Sc4 strand (ii): Pupils should be introduced to the use of fuel/oxygen systems as concentrated forms of energy in living things, engines, heating systems and other devices. Pupils should survey national and global forms of energy. They should consider energy from the Sun, nuclear energy, the origin and accumulation of fossil fuels and the use of biomass as a fuel
Teaching ideas	Pupils could compare different fuels such as charcoal, peat, coal, gas and oil. They could study methane digesters and biomass production
Resources	1. SATIS Unit 201: *Energy from Biomass.*
	2. SATIS 16–19 Unit 20: *Energising an Indian Village.*
	3. SATIS 16–19 Unit 22: *Prospects for Wind Energy*
	4. SATIS 16–19 Unit 63: *Biogas*[18]
	5. Energy and fuels (page 148) in *Science Scene Book 1* (Hodder & Stoughton)[19]

Things to do

Further examples of NC science teaching ideas involving a multicultural approach are given in Table 8.3. Identify suitable teaching resources that could be used for each part of the PoS. You may have to spend some time searching, consulting with teaching colleagues in other departments (particularly geography) and may even have to send off for material but your efforts will be well rewarded.

Strang et al. warn us: 'If we only access investigations in a few restricted contexts we may tend to favour one group.'[20] Are the investigations that you have carried out set in a variety of contexts?

What is the science departmental policy on multicultural education? Is it time it was reviewed?[21]

Table 8.3 **Further examples of National Curriculum science that can involve a multicultural approach**

NC reference and PoS	KS3 Sc2 strand (iii): They should study the effects of human activity, including food production and the exploitation of raw materials, on the purity of air and water on the Earth's surface
Teaching ideas	Pupils could discuss issues related to global conservation. They could carry out a case study of pollution in one particular part of the world
NC reference and PoS	KS3 Sc3 strand (i): Pupils should carry out a more detailed study of selected elements and their compounds, covering metals and non-metals, in order to understand the limitations and different ways in which elements can be classified and ordered in the periodic table
Teaching ideas	Pupils could prepare a map of the location of the key deposits of certain minerals. They could study the historical development of the periodic table. They could carry out a case study on the discovery and isolation of an element
NC reference and PoS	KS3 Sc4 strand (v): Pupils should further develop their study of the solar system through observation and secondary sources. They should consider ideas about the position of the Sun and the planets in the solar system, and the position of the solar system in the Universe
Teaching ideas	Pupils could study historical ideas from different cultures. They could discuss the influence of religion on the development of our understanding of space

8.3 GENDER ISSUES

In the days before balanced science[22] it was not uncommon to see fourth and fifth form groups (now years 10 and 11) where the physics groups were made up mainly of boys, the biology groups mainly consisted of girls and the chemistry groups had roughly equal numbers of boys and girls. Many theories[23] have been presented to explain this gender imbalance, from biological and genetic effects to peer-group pressure. Some of the theories are in direct conflict with one another and there appears to be no clear explanation at the moment as to why girls favour the biological sciences and shy away from the physical sciences. There are, however, some ideas that are worth developing and in the late 1970s and the 1980s there were many attempts to improve the situation through the in-service training of teachers, reports and special projects. Some of these projects are on-going (e.g. the use of the Women in Science and Engineering (WISE) bus that travels around schools encouraging girls to take up careers in science or engineering).

There will be those who will argue that this situation is not really a problem, saying that pupils should have the freedom to choose whatever science subject they like and if girls prefer doing biology they should be allowed to do it in preference to physics. However, by removing the physics component from the curriculum for some girls, we would be denying them their entitlement to a balanced science education. In addition, we would be reducing the career opportunities open to girls when they eventually leave school. Pupils of either sex will always have their favourite science subject but it is up to teachers to ensure that we make all aspects of science as inviting as possible.

Although the problem of subject choice in science at the end of year 9 has now disappeared, teachers are still faced with the difficulty of encouraging girls to develop their interest in all branches of science with the hope that greater numbers will continue to study the subject to a higher level. The numbers of females that go on to study the physical sciences at university is disappointingly low (see Table 8.4). Unfortunately, there is still a tendency amongst some teachers and pupils to believe that physics is a boy's subject. Somehow it has become labelled and the label has stuck. Part of our role as teachers should be to help to remove this label and show that subjects are not gender dependent.

Table 8.4 **The percentage of female first degree university students (in the academic year 1990–91)**

Subject	% Female
Biology	57.4
Chemistry	35.7
Physics	15.6
English	66.9
French	78.9
Maths	33.0
All subjects	44.4

Source: *Statistics of Chemistry Education*, 1992, Royal Society of Chemistry, London

There may be some readers who, having got this far, are feeling very smug with thoughts running though their minds such as, '*I treat boys and girls the same, to me they are all individuals*'. If so, well done, but it is almost certain that, quite unconsciously, you will be reacting differently to each sex. The aim of this section is to enable you to review your current practice and, hopefully, to encourage more female pupils to study science post-16.

In many ways we are confronted with a daunting task. Boys and girls come to us with fairly clear ideas about what they like and what they dislike. They, like us, have been subjected to the influence of the media, trends, fashions and other changes in society but young people in particular build their ideas of what is the acceptable thing to do from the images they see. The powerful persuasion of television programmes, particularly advertising, play an important part in setting the stereotypical images of the day. The problem of gender stereotyping may originate as far back as the child's early development when parents, friends and relatives give children toys that they think are most appropriate for the sex of the child. Mechanical toys are given to boys and the soft, cuddly toys to girls. This presents boys with the opportunity to manipulate their toys and to find out how they work, thus acquiring confidence and adeptness in skills that will stand them in good stead later in their science lessons. Traditional girls' toys do not lend themselves to this sort of active involvement. Obviously, it is not possible for teachers alone to overcome the fixed stereotypes that are present in our community, but it should be regarded as part of our role to challenge existing views about the parts that men and women play in society. Attitudes are changing and many young people starting secondary school have a better understanding of equality than their predecessors and a great deal of credit for this should go to the excellent work being done in primary schools. Nowadays most primary schools will start to combat the problem of sexism by ensuring that all tasks are carried out by both boys and girls. Primary school teachers start the ball rolling in creating enthusiasm for science in all their pupils and there is no distinction between different types of science.

We should not underestimate the influence we have on pupils' attitudes towards science that is transmitted through our own personal behaviour, teaching style and willingness to challenge sexual discrimination. The teaching approach used can have a direct bearing on the attitude the pupil takes towards a subject. Using the ideas presented in earlier chapters in this book will lead to science lessons that will promote interest in science for both boys and girls. In order to get the maximum benefit from your lessons it is worth while considering a number of additional points.

Why should girls find certain topics in science particularly difficult or unattractive? Kelly[24] describes three main reasons why girls are put off the physical sciences:

- a lack of self-confidence and the fear that science is too difficult
- the masculine image of physical science, and
- the remoteness of science from girls' everyday concerns.

No one likes to be shown up in front of their friends, and girls, in particular, form very strong friendship groups. Girls then tend to lack self-confidence in science and can be reluctant to volunteer a contribution to a whole class discussion, particularly if they feel that the teacher may ridicule them in front of their peers. Boys brush off their inability to answer questions correctly more readily and quickly return to the cut and thrust of questions and answers. This calls for a more sympathetic approach from the teacher and possibly a greater emphasis on group work rather than whole class teaching.

Many researchers have found that both male and female teachers tend to spend more time talking to boys rather than girls in a class. We need to make a conscious effort to divide our time equally between the sexes and to consider the nature of the interactions with pupils so that we do not reinforce stereotypical perspectives.

Careful examination of textbooks over the last ten years or so will show that few, if any, females were pictured carrying out scientific tasks. If there was a picture of a female, she would generally be portrayed in a glamorous role or doing some menial task such as working on a production line or in a supermarket. This helped to reinforce the idea in some pupils' minds that men are involved in the important process of manufacturing materials such as washing powder, cosmetics and sophisticated electronic equipment to improve the lot of women. Most modern textbooks now depict female scientists and girls, as well as boys, involved in scientific activity.

Much of school science is about things rather than people. It is impersonal and dispassionate. On the whole, girls tend to be more caring and emotional than boys and see little of the characteristics that are important to them in the physical sciences. We encourage pupils to write up their reports of scientific investigations using the traditional, dry, detached method. Although this is a method of writing that may need to be learned during science courses, there is no reason why it should be the sole method for writing up practical work. A study of the life of the famous scientist who has contributed to the work pupils are studying will help to bring the work alive, particularly if this is done within the framework of the contemporary historical background. Many modern science courses (e.g. *Salters' Science*[25]) and resources (e.g. SATIS books[13, 18]) have tried to introduce the idea of looking at science from a social and humanistic context.

Table 8.5 **Suggestions for making science more girl-friendly**

Classroom environment	• Use attractive posters around the laboratory • Display posters of female scientists • Display photographs of girls who have gone on to study science at a higher level • In displaying pupils' own work, ensure that there is an equal amount girls' and boys' work
Teacher delivery	• Involve boys and girls equally in your interactions • Do not relate examples to a particular sex, e.g. 'Come on boys, you should know how a car engine works' • 'Stamp on' noisy boys and encourage girls to make contributions to whole class discussions • Do not tolerate sexist comments from pupils • Emphasise that achievement does not depend on gender
Group work	• Pupils work best in groups where they feel comfortable and, for the most part, this will be in single-sex groups At the reporting stage boys will see that the girls have achieved at least as much as they have
Practical work	• Be aware that girls may have had little experience of practical activities when they start year 7 • Be patient and encouraging • If necessary, show the girls what to do but do not do it for them • Make sure that girls get a fair share of the apparatus
Textbooks	• Do not use textbooks that have a sexist approach
Role modelling	• Arrange visits from working female scientists and engineers • Give examples of the contributions made by female scientists wherever possible
Assessment	• Use a variety of assessment strategies

Assessment plays a key role in pupil motivation and it is worth while considering the effect your assessment scheme may have on each sex. For example, it has been shown[26] that boys are more successful than girls in multiple-choice type questions, whereas girls are more successful than boys on essay-type questions, and papers carrying structured questions are answered equally well by both sexes. An effective and fair assessment scheme would, therefore, involve the use of a variety of techniques.

Things to do

Is there an equal opportunities policy statement for use within the science department? Review the document with a few science colleagues to check that it meets the needs of staff and pupils in the present climate of science education.

How does the science policy statement relate to the whole school policy on equal opportunities? Whose job is it to check that the policy statements are being implemented?

NOTES AND REFERENCES

1. National Curriculum Council, 1993, *Special Needs and The National Curriculum: Opportunity and Challenge*, NCC, York.

2. Jenkins, E.W., 1973, *The Teaching of Science to Pupils of Low Educational Attainment*, Centre for Studies in Science Education, Leeds.

3. Jones, A. & Purnell, R., 1992, *Specials* (a series of photocopiable materials for children at key stage 3 who experience learning difficulties), Folens, London.

4. National Curriculum Council, 1992, *Curriculum Guidance 10: Teaching Science to Pupils with Special Educational Needs*, NCC, York.

5. Reid, D.J., 1987, *Science for All: Teaching Science in the Secondary School*, Cassell, London.

6. Jones, A.V., 1983, *Science for Handicapped Children*, Souvenir Press, London. Another useful document for helping to teach handicapped pupils is: CLEAPSS, 1987, *Handicapped Pupils and Practical Science, L77*, Brunel University, Uxbridge.

7. Betts, F., 'Chemistry for pupils with visual impairments,' in Atley, M., Bennett, S., Dutch, S., Levinson, R., Taylor, P. & West, D. (eds), 1992, *Open Chemistry*, Hodder & Stoughton, London.

8. Information and guidance for teaching visually impaired children can be obtained from: The Royal National Institute for the Blind, Outreach Service, RNIB, New College Worcester, Whittington Road, Worcester, WR5 2JX. Useful books from the RNIB are: *Safety in Practical Lessons: Guidelines for Working with Visually Impaired Pupils in Science and CDT*; Minett, S., 1989, *Science Equipment List*; Pill, B.J. (revised by Herring, F.), 1991, *Teaching Science to Visually Impaired Children*.

9. *Education for All*, The Swann Report. The Report of the Committee of Inquiry into the Education of Children from Ethnic Minority Groups, Chairman Lord Swann, HMSO, 1985.

10. Hoyle, P., 'Science and equal opportunities', in Watts, M. (ed.), 1991, *Science in the National Curriculum,* Cassell, London.

11. Dennick, R., 'Analysing multicultural and antiracist science education', *School Science Review*, 1992, **73** (264), 79–88.

12. Gott, R., Welford, G. & Foulds, K., 1988, *The Assessment of Practical Work in Science*, Blackwell, Oxford.

13. Science and Technology in Society (SATIS), a series of twelve books plus SATIS update 1991. Each book contains ten units. Published by ASE.

14. Shan, S.J., a series of booklets entitled *An Antiracist Approach to Science Teaching* including *Fibre in your Diet, Food, Glorious Food*, and *Feeding the World*, Birmingham Education Authority.

15. Carrick, T., 1990, *Humans as Organisms*, Simon & Schuster, Hemel Hempstead.

16. Monger, G. (ed.), 1988, *Nuffield Co-ordinated Sciences – Biology*, Longman, London.

17. Johnson, C., 1991, *Chemistry for GCSE*, Heinemann, Oxford.

18. SATIS 16–19, a series of three files, each containing twenty-five units. Published by ASE.

19. Hill, G. (ed.), 1991, *Science Scene*, Hodder & Stoughton, London.

20. Strang, J., Daniels, S. & Bell, J., 1991, *Assessment Matters: No. 6 Planning and Carrying Out Investigations*, Secondary Examinations and Assessment Council, London.

21. A useful INSET manual for reviewing issues of race, equality and science teaching is: Thorp, S. (ed.), 1991, *Race, Equality and Science Teaching*, ASE, Hatfield.

22. Note: Balanced science was introduced in some schools prior to the science National Curriculum (see Chapter 2).

23. Physics Education Committee, 1982, *Girls and Physics*, Royal Society and the Institute of Physics, London.

24. Kelly, A., 'Why girls don't do science' in Kelly, A. (ed.), 1987, *Science for Girls?*, Open University Press, Milton Keynes.

25. The materials for Science: The Salters' Approach Consists of 4 unit guides and 4 student books, for example: Campbell, B., Lazonby, J., Millar, R. and Smyth, S., (1990), *Science: The Salters' Approach Key Stage 4 Book 1*, Heinemann, London.

26. Harding, J., 1983, *Switched Off: the Science Education of Girls*, Longman, London.

CHAPTER 9

Assessment techniques

If you were to ask yourself the question 'why do we assess pupils?', you would probably come up with a multitude of responses such as: to place the pupils in rank order of ability, to show them where they have gone wrong, to keep a check on their progress. In addition to the many purposes of assessment there are a large number of different ways of testing pupils. The purpose of this chapter is to give you a clearer insight into the reasons for using assessment and to guide you through a range of techniques for carrying it out.

Assessment should be an integral part of teaching and learning. Without it we would not be able to determine what the pupils had learned and would have no clear indication of the effectiveness of our teaching. Assessment should fulfil four main aims. It should:

- assist and support pupils in the learning of science (*it should be formative*)
- assist in identifying strengths and weaknesses (*it should be diagnostic*)
- assist science teachers in evaluating their teaching and learning programme (*it should be evaluative*)
- provide information about progress and achievement of individual pupils for themselves, parents and a range of other people (*it should be summative*)

Not many of us like to be measured, weighed or judged, particularly if that judgement compares us with others and we come out as the lesser mortal. While there will be judgement days in the lives of pupils, much of the assessment that goes on in the classroom will be of a formative nature. The teacher will support the pupil's learning by carefully identifying what has been learned and plan the way forward to new learning situations. A good assessment scheme will determine whether individuals have fully grasped the science concepts taught. When the teacher diagnoses that the work has not been fully understood, remedial action can be prescribed. If we get a clear message that a number of pupils have not grasped the concept we are trying to teach, then it is clearly time for us to review our approach and consider alternative ways of teaching the topic. At various times during the pupil's career in school we will want a snapshot view of how well s/he is doing. This might be at the end of a topic or the end of a term but might equally be at the end of some important lesson's work. This snapshot will give us an indication of the sum total of the knowledge that the pupil has on a particular area of the subject at a particular time. To many, this is seen as the most valuable outcome of assessment. It can be easily understood by parents, governors, school administrators and people outside the school system.

9.1 GENERAL PRINCIPLES OF ASSESSMENT

Measuring what a pupil knows, understands or can do is not always an easy process. The way we shape or phrase our measuring instrument may affect the response we get from our pupils. Is the question that we are asking clear? Does it contain any gender or cultural bias?[1] How are we going to record all the information we obtain through assessing our pupils?

Any assessment system used in schools should be:

- readily understood by both pupils and teachers
- reliable and valid
- positive
- compatible with external requirements (NC, examination boards), and
- easy to use

It is no use devising a complex method of assessment that involves recording the multiple attributes of each individual in the class as it would be impossible to keep it going. On the other hand, if the assessment scheme is reduced to comments such as, 'A – good', you will be left wondering what was good, the presentation, the understanding or some other aspect of the work. A mark out of ten can be just as meaningless, unless you (and the pupil) has some understanding of what the mark means. We will look at some ways round this problem in the section on marking pupils' books later on in this chapter.

Pupils are very quick to tell teachers if their assessment is not fair. 'I've done just as much as Jane has and you've given her 9/10 and you've only given me 7. Last time I labelled the diagram you gave me a mark for it. You haven't given me anything this time'. As teachers, we need to be seen as being as fair and as just as possible. The two factors associated with fair testing are the validity and the reliability of the test. An assessment is valid if it does what it sets out to do. If the pupils are told that the test they are about to sit is about the names and location of the organs in the human digestive system, and the questions are, in fact about the functions of the organs, then the pupils would be justified in complaining that the test is not valid. Just as we expect a balance used in science lessons to be reliable and give us the same reading each time we place a 1 gram mass on it, we expect an assessment-measuring instrument to give us the same reading each time we apply it to work of equal standing. There is, of course, a major difference in the unchanging 1 gram mass and the complexity of samples of pupils' work, however, the principle is the same. The 'tighter' the mark scheme the teacher writes then clearly the more reliable will be the results. The problem of putting a very tight mark scheme into operation with large classes is that it becomes too time consuming to be practicable. Teachers need to work towards a system of assessment that can be applied as accurately as possible within the constraints of the time available.

Another important aspect worthy of consideration when planning your assessment strategy is that of praise. You can imagine the disappointment of a pupil who has tried very hard with a piece of work only to be told that his/her effort is poor. It can be easy to fall into this trap if we are not aware of the pupil's innate capabilities or if we make the mistake of comparing his/her work with that of other pupils in the class. We should be concentrating our efforts at looking for progression from the individual rather comparing one individual with another. Rather than belittling the work of a weak pupil, the teacher should look for ways of making positive comments, praising successful achievement and making helpful suggestions for improvement. Pupils like to know that they have achieved something, even if they have not obtained complete mastery of the subject.

An assessment scheme cannot be prepared in isolation. It must be compatible with the departmental scheme, the school system and the requirements of the external examining agencies. For example, the school may require you to comment in the end-of-term report on a pupil's ability to work as a member of a team. If this was the case, you would need to build this into your assessment strategy so that you can monitor pupils' progress in this respect throughout their course. It is also vitally important that you bear in mind what is required of you by NC science and the examination boards. Course work forms a key component of most science courses and it is important that you are familiar with the timing and criteria for the assessments. An outline of the information required for NC science is given later on in this chapter. Post-16 courses generally involve some aspects of the assessment of practical work and may have other assessable course work requirements. Each board is slightly different from the others and only by careful reading of the syllabus can you be sure that procedures are carried out correctly.

Assessment objectives

In Chapter 3 mention was made of writing specific objectives for lessons in terms of what you would like the pupils to be able to do at the end of the lesson. These objectives go on to form the basis of your assessment scheme. There are three areas of objectives, called domains, and these are:

- the cognitive domain (involving thought processes)
- the psychomotor domain (involving co-ordination of the brain and muscular activity)
- the affective domain (involving attitudes to a task)

An illustration of behaviour within these three domains can be stated in terms of measuring the temperature of a cooling liquid at specific time intervals:

Cognitive domain:	identifying the time on the clock when the readings have to be taken and linking the time to a temperature reading.
Psychomotor domain:	knowing where to place the thermometer in the liquid and reading the temperature to sufficient accuracy at the appropriate time.
Affective domain:	seeing the exercise as sufficiently important to bother to do it at all.

A number of people have attempted to categorise objectives into certain groups and then to examine the level of difficulty of the various types of objectives. One such person was Benjamin Bloom who, with his co-workers,[2] produced taxonomies or lists of objectives from simple to complex with the underlying principle that objectives at any one level built on objectives at lower levels. Bloom's taxonomy sets the foundation for all the assessment schemes used in science as it helps to clarify the exact nature of what we are assessing. Using a framework such as this leads to a much greater precision in assessment and guides teachers towards testing for a wide range of skills and abilities. In terms of the cognitive domain, Bloom has identified six major categories of objectives. These are listed below in order of increasing intellectual demand together with examples of the types of verbs that you would use when writing assessment objectives in each category:

Knowledge   Knowledge is defined as remembering previously learned material, i.e. recall of facts. (Statements would include verbs such as: define, describe, identify, list, name, state.)

Comprehension Comprehension is the ability to grasp the meaning of material. This may be shown by translating material from one form to another (e.g. words to numbers), by interpreting material (e.g. explaining or summarising) and by estimating future trends (e.g. predicting consequences or effects). (Statements would include verbs such as: classify, explain, give examples, identify.)

Application   Application refers to the ability to use learned material in new and concrete situations. This may include the application of such things as rules, methods, concepts, principles, laws and theories. (Statements would include verbs such as: calculate, construct, demonstrate.)

Analysis   Analysis is the ability to break down material into its component parts so that its organisational structure may be understood. (Statements would include verbs such as: examine, inquire, investigate.)

Synthesis   Synthesis refers to the ability to put parts together to form a new whole. (Statements would include verbs such as: deduce, describe, design.)

Evaluation   Evaluation is concerned with the ability to judge the value of material for a given purpose. (Statements would include verbs such as: criticise, distinguish between, explain, select.)

Such a taxonomy is there to help stimulate the teacher into asking different sorts of questions and to help to review assessment tasks. It should not be read as a prescriptive or comprehensive list of statements into which all questions and tasks can be classified. Other factors, such as the circumstances in which the task is set, the prior learning and the relationship between the age of the pupil and nature of the task, are all important when determining the degree of difficulty.

Keeping records

It is very important to keep accurate records of pupils' work so that you can report with confidence to pupils, parents and senior staff in the school. Your mark book should be organised so that it is easy to access data and transcribe it into any form needed for reporting. You will need to use some shorthand notation in order to reduce the amount of writing on your mark sheet. However, this should be kept as simple as possible and should not involve too many characters as you may find that you forget what each one means. Each list of entries should be dated and given some sort of title so that you can cross reference it to other records that you keep, such as your lesson plan or SoW.

Table 9.1 **Suggestions for entries in a teacher's record book**

Useful information to record	Comment
Attendance at your lesson	You are able to account for everyone if there is an emergency. Helps to identify patterns of non-attendance. Highlights areas of work that pupils have missed
Whether or not homework has been handed in	Helps to avoid arguments with pupils when they insist that they have handed in their book when, in reality, they have not
Lateness in handing in work	Helps to identify those pupils who regularly hand in work late
Completeness of work	You need to know if pupils are up to date with their work. Is there important work they must complete?
Grades or marks for written work	Consider the nature of these marks and how meaningful they are in terms of your objectives
Grades, marks or levels for practical work	Will probably require a separate record from that kept in a mark book
Marks or levels for tests	Cross-reference to a master copy of the test with full mark scheme

In order to avoid lengthy discussions with pupils about whether or not they were present when the homework was set or if they handed in their homework to be marked, you will find it useful to keep a record of attendance and a check of work handed in. Once pupils know that you are 'on the ball' you will find that most will get their work in on time. You may find it useful to keep your mark book for the day-to-day account, simply recording a series of ticks, marks or grades for which you would know the meaning. Table 9.1 gives some examples of the type of entries that could be included in a mark book.

In addition to the mark book it is advisable to have a record card for each pupil, which should contain space for more specific comments and show progress on a level basis through the ATs. Such cards have been prepared by many schools and one such example for levels 3 to 6 is shown in Figure 9.1. A larger amount of space is available for reporting on pupils' investigations in order that detail about progress in the strands can be documented (the full form would contain space for additional investigation titles). When a pupil is working towards a particular statement of attainment a diagonal line can be placed in the box and when the pupil has achieved the statement this can be converted into a cross.

Keeping records can be tedious but it is an essential part of your teaching role. Obviously, thorough records lead to accurate reporting to others on the various attributes that you regard as significant. It should go without saying that the records should not be kept secret from the pupils since part of the purpose is to motivate them to work harder. The next section examines ways in which pupils can take more responsibility for their own learning by being involved in the assessment process.

Things to do

You should have a clear and consistent policy on what action you are going to take if your records show you that pupils are underachieving or are not behaving as they should. For example, consider what you would do in the following situations:

- How will you deal with pupils who hand in homework late? How does this differ from pupils who do not hand in work at all?
- What will you do if a pupil's standard of work suddenly deteriorates?
- How often are you going to mark the books and what system are you going to use for grading the work?
- How are you going to deal with incorrect work?
- How are you going to ensure that all the books are handed in?

Pupils' involvement in the assessment process

There are three broad areas where pupils can be involved in the assessment process:

- self-assessment and target setting
- keeping records of progress, and
- the selection of evidence to support levels of attainment

In the past, assessment has been the sole preserve of the teacher. Apart from the odd test that might have been marked by pupils to save the teacher some time, all other assessments were carried out by the teacher. Now, as teachers begin to take on board the formative nature

Name:_____ Group(s):_____ Starting date: _____

	a	b	c	Comment
				Sc1
3				
4				
5				
6				

Investigation titles   Date   Comment

1._____   _____   _____

2._____   _____   _____

3._____   _____   _____

	a	b	c	d	e	Comment
						Sc2
3				▓	▓	
4					▓	
5					▓	
6						

	a	b	c	d	e	f	g	h	Comment
									Sc3
3				▓	▓	▓	▓	▓	
4					▓	▓	▓	▓	
5				▓	▓	▓	▓		
6									

	a	b	c	d	e	f	g	Comment
								Sc4
3					▓	▓	▓	
4					▓	▓		
5								
6								

Completion date:

Figure 9.1 **Example of a pupil record card showing progress in the science National Curriculum**

of assessment, there is a growing number who involve pupils in the assessment process. This practice is encouraged by SEAC in their publications for KS3.[3] For some years, various science schemes and textbooks have encouraged pupils to carry out self-assessment at key points throughout the work. For example, the co-ordinated science syllabus developed in Suffolk[4] has checkpoints at the end of each topic where pupils are asked to review their progress. *Advanced Level Practical Work in Chemistry*[5] requires pupils to judge their practical ability for themselves using a set of criteria.

Pupils have a right to know what is expected of them so that they have clear goals that they can work towards. By involving pupils in the assessment process you can increase their motivation, make learning more effective and thereby raise their academic standards. The process must involve occasions where pupil and teacher sit down together to discuss what each pupil has achieved and make plans for the future. To facilitate this process the pupils will need to have some knowledge of the assessment targets written in a form that they can readily comprehend. For example, some teachers have rewritten the SoAs for Sc1 in a language that can be readily understood by pupils. This allows pupils to understand what is required of them if they are to progress up the levels of attainment. Another area of pupil involvement is where pupils are encouraged to check their spelling and grammar. This is a subject that often hits the headlines with various groups of indviduals moaning and groaning about low standards. If teachers were to set themselves the task of correcting all aspects of English they would find that the time spent on marking would be doubled or even tripled and the effect on pupil morale could be crippling. One step towards improving the situation is to encourage pupils to monitor their own work periodically, reviewing presentation, grammar and spelling. An example of a review sheet is given in Figure 9.2 showing areas of work that could be monitored every four lessons. There is no intention that this type of exercise should completely remove the need for the teacher to check pupils' work but it should reduce the burden on the teacher and the two should go hand in hand to encouraging pupils to make progress.

We all get a sense of achievement when we complete a task, particularly if it is one that has occupied us for a considerable period of time. A-level pupils like crossing off parts of the syllabus that they have been taught and, as teachers, we look forward to the sense of satisfaction when the last end-of-term examination paper is marked. It should be part of a teacher's regular duties to give feedback to their pupils about their rate of progress through their work. However, if in addition pupils are required to keep their own record of progress it provides them with an opportunity to reflect on their own mastery of the topic and sets an anchor point from where they can feel secure in the knowledge that they have understood a piece of work. Having their own record system shows them where progress is being made and gives the pupils greater confidence in their own ability.

Name: Group:	1 Date	2 Date	3 Date	4 Date
Review the last four pieces of work by answering the questions below with a Y or N. Finish off by writing a comment saying how you could improve.				
1. Is your work in the right order?				
2. Have you put a title and date?				
3. Are the headings underlined?				
4. Have your labelled all the diagrams?				
5. Is your presentation neat and tidy?				
6. Have you checked the punctuation and spelling?				
Comment:				

Figure 9.2 **A pupil's personal checklist on the presentation of written work**

Selecting your best piece of work from all that you have done can sometimes be a difficult task for a pupil but it is time well spent if they reflect carefully on the work they have done and think about ways that they could improve. The NC requires teachers to keep evidence of pupils' progress in each of the attainment targets and, therefore, decisions have to be made as to what pieces of work need to be stored. There is a temptation to restrict the evidence to tests and reports from investigations. However, pupils achieve on a day-to-day basis and it would be wrong to restrict the monitoring of progress to test results alone. Pupils can be involved in building up a portfolio of their best work, which can be used as evidence of achievement. Periodically pupils could be asked to review the evidence stored in their portfolio and asked about replacing it with work that shows a higher level of achievement. In addition to its NC use, such a package could be the basis for discussion with parents when they are invited to the school for parents' evenings.

For many teachers, involving pupils in assessment is a new venture and as such they tend to be a little wary of its consequences. There is no doubt that pupil involvement in this way can strongly support learning but it must be said that it is a time-consuming process.

Norm-referencing and criterion referencing

Everyone is familiar with the traditional grading system used at both GCSE and GCE A-level but there is a certain mystery about how the grades are awarded. It is based on a system called norm-referencing. With the large population of pupils that sit any one of these examinations there is likely to be a normal distribution of marks. The examiners and assessors take this distribution and make decisions as to the percentage of candidates that will lie in each grade range, based on past experience of where the grade boundaries were placed. It is possible that a mark of $X\%$ may have given a pupil a grade C in one year but the same mark in another year may give a grade B because of the way in which the marks are distributed on the normal curve. If, as is usually the case, the population of pupils in any one year is very similar in ability range to the population in any other year then this system of awarding grades is generally fair. Where it falls down is when you start to think about what is actually meant by each of the grades. A grade C, for example, can be obtained by different pupils in different ways and what one grade C pupil knows may be quite different from what another grade C pupil knows. An alternative, and perhaps fairer system, is to give credit to pupils who achieve fixed criteria. In this criterion referencing approach to assessment it is theoretically possible for all the population of pupils sitting a test to meet the criteria and, therefore, all to be awarded the highest level. In reality we are likely to obtain a normal distribution of pupils who have achieved specific levels but this time we will know that all those pupils who have reached level X have met the criteria for that level. This means that we have a clear picture of what a level X pupil knows and can do and we can distinguish him/her quite clearly from a level $X+1$ pupil who will have met further criteria. NC science is based on the principle of criterion referencing so that once a pupil has fulfilled the criteria as set out in the SoA then s/he can be awarded that level. It should not be assumed, however, that criterion referencing is the answer to all our problems. Rowntree[6] points out that on the one hand we need to write criteria to a high degree of precision so that we know exactly what test to apply but on the other hand they need to be flexible enough to work in a variety of situations.

9.2 ASSESSMENT STRATEGIES

Examination boards and science teachers have used a wide range of assessment techniques over the years in order to try to measure the many attributes that science courses can inculcate. Table 9.2 on pages 210 and 211 lists the main methods currently used.

Assessing oral contributions

To consider stopping the class after you have received a brilliant answer from a pupil to say that you must make a note of the achievement in your mark book, is obviously downright silly. In most question-and-answer sessions the rapid flow of interactions prevents you from carrying out any formal assessment. Oral questioning, however, plays a key role in formative assessment. The teacher is able to pick up any area of work that has not been fully understood by individuals and, through shrewd interplay with other members of the class, is able to check on understanding from a wider group.

There are, however, times when it is appropriate to assess pupils orally rather than by using the written word. Many pupils have difficulty in expressing themselves in written form but can get their ideas across orally, if given the right sort of help and guidance. For example, certain pupils with special educational needs might benefit from recording their answers using a tape recorder rather than writing them down. It is also worth considering ways of giving pupils credit for their contributions to activities such as group work, role play and oral presentations to the class. This need not necessarily be part of your formal check on the understanding of science concepts but may be part of your wider role in helping pupils to develop their communication skills and as such could be included in their pupil profile report.

There is one further area where it is appropriate to take cognizance of pupils' spoken words and that is in the area of assessing Sc1. SEAC[7] advise that:

Because a good deal of information is ephemeral, teachers will need to make brief notes of discussions and other evidence in order that essential information about pupils' attainment is not lost. This is particularly important for pupils with special educational needs.

Assessing day-to-day written contributions

Marking pupils' exercise books is an important element in the monitoring of their progress. It must be done on a regular basis if it is to be effective. If a set of exercise books is not checked for several weeks, the amount of writing will mount up to such an extent that marking becomes unmanageable. Pupils deserve to have their work checked and, indeed, you will find that some can get quite indignant if you have not given them credit for their hard work. Marking a class set of books can take a considerable amount of time if it is done properly. Rather than go through the work blandly giving a tick to each page that you think looks satisfactory, you may find it profitable to concentrate on certain pieces of writing that have been composed by the pupil rather than copied from the board or a worksheet. You will find it useful to consider the following points when devising your system for marking books.

• How are you going to correct mistakes made by the pupils?

Table 9.2   *Methods of assessment and how they can be used in science lessons*

Assessment strategy	Areas of use	Ways in which the strategy meets the aims of assessment	Problems with this mode of assessment
Assessing oral contributions	• Day-to-day oral question-and-answer session • Assessing a pupil presentation to a group or a class discussion	Useful as a tool for formative assessment. Immediate feedback from the teacher helps to sort out problems or misunderstandings quickly	Not a useful technique for summative assessment as it tends to be unreliable and subjective
Assessing day-to-day written contributions	• Marking written exercises (classwork and homework) • Marking project work • Marking a poster	Indicates progress (or lack of it) over a period of time	Can be very time consuming to keep a thorough check on progress. There is a need to separate out work that is done collaboratively from that which is done by an individual
Multiple-choice/ objective test	• Testing cognitive areas • Determining pupils' attitudes	Can assess a wide range of topics and objectives in a relatively short period of time	Although the questions are easy to mark they are very difficult to set. Does not appear to be a method of assessment favoured by the writers of statutory NC tests
Short answer/structured questions	• Testing cognitive areas	As above. In addition, pupils have to devise a response rather than select one from a list. Questions can be structured so that easy parts come first, making it possible to set a paper for a range of abilities. This method of assessment is favoured by writers of the statutory NC tests	Easier to set than multiple-choice questions but care is still required with the language used. Takes far more time to mark than multiple-choice tests

Technique	Purpose	Uses	Limitations
Essay-type questions	• Testing cognitive areas • Testing communication skills	Assesses pupils' ability to organise their ideas and write them down in a logical form. Can help to identify misconceptions	There is the possibility of penalising pupils whose science knowledge may be quite good but who are poor at expressing themselves in writing. Marking essays can be time consuming and subjective if a rigorous mark scheme is not used. Neat presentation may influence the marker to give a higher mark than the work deserves
Numerical problems	• Testing cognitive areas	Useful for testing the application of a principle or theory. Useful for both formative and summative assessment. It is generally both a reliable and valid assessment tool	Some pupils appear to have difficulty in transferring the skills learned in mathematics lessons to their science lessons. Simple errors in mathematics can cause the pupil to get the problem wrong even though they understand the scientific principles
Assessing a written report	• Testing cognitive areas • Assessing practical work	Useful for both formative and summative assessment. Written plans and reports are the main form of assessing practical skills. This is the main method of assessment used for investigative work in the NC and for practical work in post-16 courses	Pupils may need to be guided as to what to write otherwise they may tend to ramble. Pupils may omit key points or observations from their reports because they regard them to be insignificant. A rigorous set of criteria needs to be used to assess the report fairly. It is not always easy to see if a pupil has met a criterion statement. Where pupils work together in investigative or practical work, teachers need to separate out work that is done collaboratively from that which is done by an individual
Using an observation schedule or checklist	• Assessing practical work • Assessing a pupil presentation to a group or class discussion	Useful for both formative and summative assessment. Can provide immediate feedback to the pupil, if appropriate	Removes some of the freedom of the teacher to teach during lesson time as s/he is tied up in assessing duties. The pupils may feel threatened if the teacher chooses to walk around the room with a clipboard

You are faced with the dilemma that on the one hand it is very time consuming to correct pupils' work but on the other hand if you do not correct it they may learn something that is incorrect. Inaccuracies must be corrected and if a brief statement in the pupils' book is insufficient then you must either refer the pupil to a source of correct information or ask him/her to come and see you.

- How are you going to get pupils to carry out corrections or completion of unfinished work?

  It is a good idea to set pupils a deadline for getting their work up to standard. You will need to have a note in your mark book to remind you that the work requires checking.

- Are you going to correct spelling and grammar?

  Five per cent of the total marks in GCSE science examinations are allocated for the use of accurate spelling, punctuation and grammar. It is, therefore, worth while encouraging pupils to write correctly in their science lessons.

- How are you going to motivate pupils and make them work harder?

  While you will need to point out errors in pupils' work you should also look for ways that you can praise positive achievement and give suggestions and encouragement for improvements.

- When are you going to mark books?

  Most of your marking is likely to be done in the staff room or at home but you should not rule out the possibility of occasionally marking the books in the presence of the pupils. If the pupils are engaged in a task that gives you the opportunity to circulate around the room you can check through a pupil's book and give some immediate feedback on the standard of work.

One final point before leaving this section. It is worth while bearing in mind that parents, and sometimes headteachers and inspectors, look at pupils' books and, rightly or wrongly, they judge the quality of the teaching by the degree to which the book has been marked.

Using a written test

Written tests are one of the few ways that teachers can determine what each individual in the class knows and can do with a fair degree of accuracy. With many other aspects of school work there is the possibility that pupils may work on a collaborative basis where it is difficult to identify the contribution made by each individual. It can be said that written tests introduce a certain amount of rigour into a course with clear cut-off times for achieving specific goals and no one would argue against the fact that pupils need to practise answering questions in a formal situation in preparation for external examinations.

In planning an end-of-topic test you might first look at questions that have been set by other people, such as fellow teachers, end-of-KS3 statutory tests and examination papers set by the examination boards. In addition you will find it useful to look through published sets of questions such as the question banks for GASP.[8]

Things to do

Look through past copies of externally set tests for the course that you are teaching. You may need to bear in mind that syllabuses change from time to time and questions from old past papers may not be relevant to the present work. What do you notice about:

· the layout of the questions?
· the style of presentation (e.g. do they require one-word answers or labelling of a diagram, or are they multiple-choice questions)?
· the length of the questions? and
· the type of language used?

Take a sample of the questions and work through them yourself. What type of demand are the questions making on the pupil? Do they require the pupil to recall information or are they asking for higher intellectual skills?

The next step in setting an end of topic test might be to check back through your SoW and lesson plans noting the content of the work covered and the lesson objectives. A decision must then be made as to whether you are going to attempt to test every aspect of the work or whether you are going to sample. At the end-of-topic stage it is unlikely that you will be able to test everything that has been taught and, therefore, you will need to highlight a cross-section of the work that you think symbolises the key points.

There is one further consideration to bear in mind before you start the question writing, i.e. the ability range of the pupils for whom the test is designed. We have all, at some time or another, felt the despondency when confronted with a test that we cannot do. Success in a test leads to greater motivation and better work from that pupil in the future. It is therefore important that you consider ways of ensuring that all pupils have some degree of achievement. This can be done by either having different tests for different ability bands, such as the KS3 statutory tests and GCSE examinations, or by having a paper that starts off with easy questions and gradually moves to more difficult ones. If tests have been devised for differing ability bands within the science department then it is worth while involving the pupil in making the decision as to which test tier s/he should take, easy, medium or hard.

Obviously, the easiest way of writing a test is to use questions from question banks. You need to exercise caution when selecting your questions and look out for those that bring in areas of work that you have not covered in your lessons. The questions may have been written for pupils who have completed the whole course and involve bringing together several aspects of the syllabus in the one question. Writing your own questions can be time consuming but gratifying in the knowledge that it is your own piece of work.

Things to do

Write a test on a topic that you have just taught. Evaluate the test by asking yourself the following questions. You should talk to the pupils to obtain some feedback from them as to how the test went.

- What is the overall spread of marks for the group or groups within the class? Are you satisfied that everyone achieved some success?
- Which questions were answered well by the majority of pupils?
- What are the reasons for pupils underachievement? (Is the problem to do with the test or the fact that the pupils have no interest and are not prepared to revise for the work?)
- What questions were answered poorly by the majority of pupils?
- What do the results of this test tell me about my teaching? In what way should I modify my approach to teaching and assessing this topic next time?

Methods of assessing practical work

Prior to the introduction of the GCSE examination in 1988 (GCSE courses started in September 1986) there was very little emphasis on practical assessment in pre-16 courses. At A-level, practical work was generally assessed by practical examinations set by the examination boards. These were administered by the teachers in the schools and the written reports were sent to the examination boards for marking. Some A-level boards continue with this practice but the majority require teachers to assess pupils' practical skills over the period of their course. The main mode of assessment of practical work at all levels is that of teacher assessment with outside agencies (examination boards) moderating the marking of the work. There are many reasons why we have moved away from external practical examinations such as those listed below but the overriding factor must be the fact that teachers are in a much better position to fairly assess practical abilities than a remote examiner marking a report of a practical experience.

Some of the advantages and disadvantages of teacher assessment of practical work are:

Advantages	*Disadvantages*
• practical work is best carried out in a non-stressful environment	• it can give rise to suspicions in the minds of the users about the validity and reliability of results
• pupils can be assessed over many practicals thus eliminating the problem of a chance failure or success	• it is difficult to moderate
• it is easy to test a wide variety of practical skills	• it can take a lot of time and effort to set the experiment up

Having placed the assessment of practical work firmly in the hands of the teachers, the thorny question then arises as to how do we do it. One approach would be to have a series of mini practical examinations, mimicking the method used by the examination boards in the past. This has the advantage that the testing can be carried out under examination conditions with no collaboration between individuals. As such the outcomes would be seen as valid and could be justifiably used as marks to submit for course work to the examination boards. Many teachers have initially taken this approach because they feel secure in using a tried and tested method and one that can be seen to be fair to all individuals. SEAC and the examination boards,[9] however, encourage teachers to assess pupils' practical abilities during their normal practical sessions. Such practice has two major advantages: (a) it avoids putting pupils through the stress of an examination situation where they may not be able to perform to their normal standards; (b) it can save laboratory time as no special occasion needs to be set aside. There are drawbacks that need to be considered such as:

- the problem of maintaining standards over different lessons
- the problem of the differing level of difficulty between practical tasks, and
- the problem of how to measure an individual's contribution if pupils are working in groups

However, these are not insurmountable problems and the overriding decision must be based on what method gives the best picture of a pupil's practical ability: monitoring the day-to-day practical tasks or using a practical examination?

The rest of this section takes the standpoint that practical work should be assessed on a day-to-day basis and examines ways of over-coming the problems of this approach. The first step to consider is whether we assess the work by observing pupils carrying out their practical procedures or whether we mark the product of their work, the practical report. There is evidence to show that the practical report alone cannot give a clear indication as to the overall accomplishment of a pupil in practical work.[10] For example, it will say nothing about how safely the pupil has worked, there may be little true indication as to how accurately measurements were taken and we may fail to give credit to pupils for their ability to manipulate scientific equipment. Although it may be difficult to assess pupils' practical skills while they are performing the experiment it is vital that teachers take some note of what the pupils are doing. Kempa[11] reminds us that there may be a lack of close relationship between the quality of the outcome achieved in practical work and the quality of procedure used. To obtain an overall picture of a pupil's ability to carry out practical work we must look at both the process and the product of the activity.

One way of monitoring pupils while they are carrying out a practical task is to use a checklist of points appertaining to the abilities you would expect to be demonstrated while the pupils were working. This helps to focus the teacher's attention on to key parts of the practical rather than try to make judgements on the activity as a whole. For example, within the context of Sc1 the teacher can focus on particular observational and measurement skills (level 3b) that are relevant to the practical work being carried out. With this method there is no need to assess all the pupils in a class on any one occasion, indeed it would probably be impossible to do so because of other demands made on the teacher during lesson time. The procedure can be repeated on other occasions using the same basic criteria but applying them to the different practical situation. This approach to assessment should be administered as informally as possible and there is no intention that the teacher should walk around the class with a clipboard, ticking off points each time a pupil fills a measuring cylinder correctly. It is more a case of the teacher making brief notes from time to time in as unobtrusive a way as possible.

The written account is generally the only tangible piece of evidence that the practical activity has taken place and is usually the principal factor in assessment. It is also the case that while pupils may work together in groups on a task, they write it up as individuals each giving his/her own interpretation to the experiment. If, however, a teacher chooses to reduce the assessment strategies to simply marking the written report, s/he could be unfairly penalising those pupils who are poor at expressing themselves in writing. On the other hand, if the teacher is not busy with the assessment process during a practical session s/he is free to offer advice and help when it is required.

Pupils will need guidance as to how to write up their practical work, such as how to present the results and how to draw valid conclusions. Guidance sheets as illustrated in Figures 5.5 and 5.7 can be used to direct the pupil towards fulfilling the criteria that you are using to assess the piece of work.

Assessing investigative work

At present the assessment of investigative work is the area where teachers have the least experience. However, it is not entirely new and writers such as Gott et al.[12] and Bryce et al.[13] have led the way in providing resource materials for teachers. The basic principles of practical assessment such as using a combination of observational, oral and written techniques are just as appropriate for assessing investigative work. The practice for awarding marks in investigative work is somewhat different to that previously used at GCSE level and still used at A-level.

The fine detail of the NC strands are given in the PoS and the criteria listed in the SoAs, for example comments on safety, recording of results and taking cognizance of errors may be found in the PoS for KS3 and KS4. A common criticism given by teachers is that the criteria descriptors for Sc1 are not entirely clear and are open to different interpretation by different individuals. In order to clarify the situation, SEAC have produced guidance and exemplar material showing examples of marked pupils' work with comments on how the levels were ascribed to each pupil.[14]

In addition sample material is available from each of the examination boards[15] to help teachers assess work for KS4. A useful way of working so that there is reasonable agreement between all the members of the science department is to rewrite the SoAs in terms of the particular investigation being carried out. This provides the teacher with much clearer criteria for allocating levels for each of the strands. An example of this approach is given in Figure 9.3 for an investigation on heats of reaction. While the statements do not always fit exactly to those of Sc1, there is reasonable agreement throughout and a steady progression of difficulty as you move to the higher levels.

There is a major difference in the way in which an investigation is carried out in contrast to the methods used for a traditional practical exercise. The traditional route involves pupils following instructions supplied by the teacher, but with the investigative approach the pupils are following their own plans. Because pupils will not be following tried and tested routines in their investigations there is a greater likelihood of their requiring support from the teacher. This may mean that the teacher will have to consider how s/he is going to allocate his/her time during the lesson. The APU has considered this problem and has provided useful guidance based on its research findings. They have shown[16] that if pupils are successful in the planning part of the process then they will be successful in the implementation of the plan and, therefore, may not need much help. Other pupils, who may not plan their work so well, may still carry out the investigation well but will need observing carefully so that due credit can be given to them or they may need support so that they achieve something.

Topic: Investigating heats of reaction. Neutralisation of an acid with a base	KS: 4 Year: 10

NC reference (PoS): Sc3 strand iii	NC reference (SoA): Sc3/10b
Pupils should study chemical reactions in which there is energy transfer to and from the surroundings. At a later stage that the energy transfer is associated with the making and re-forming of chemical bonds and can be determined quantitatively by experiment and by the use of data	Understand chemical reactions in terms of the energy transfers associated with making and breaking chemical bonds

Setting the scene:	Previous work on the reactions of acids and bases. The ionic equation for neutralisation. Experience of measuring heats of reaction experiments, for example using zinc and copper(II) sulphate solution. Knowledge of molar amounts. The investigation could be set in the context of, 'What determines the amount of heat evolved in a neutralisation reaction?'

Possible independent variables: Categoric	Possible dependent variables:
• the type of acid (e.g. hydrocholoric, sulphuric, nitric, ethanoic) • the type of base (e.g. potassium hydroxide, sodium hydroxide, sodium carbonate, ammonia solution) • the type of reaction vessel **Discrete** • the number of stirs of the reaction mixture **Continuous** • the volumes of acid and alkali used • the concentrations of the acid and alkalis used	Temperature

Scientific ideas: Equimolar amounts of strong acids and strong bases react together, releasing the same amount of heat energy. $\Delta H = ms\,(\theta_2 - \theta_1)$. Assumption that specific gravity of the solution = specific gravity of water, 1 g cm^{-3}. Assumption that specific heat of solution = 4.2 J g^{-1}°C^{-1} $H^+(aq) + OH^-(aq) \rightarrow H_2O(l)$: $\Delta H = -56.7$ kJ mol^{-1} 1 mol of H_2SO_4 gives 2 mol $H^+(aq)$. Weak acids are not fully ionised in aqueous solution	Textbook reference:

Teacher's notes: There are many approaches to this investigation. For example: (1) Pupils may wish to investigate the effect of changing the volume of acid added to a fixed volume of alkali and note which volume of acid gives the largest temperature rise. (2) Pupils may wish to measure the molar enthalpy of reaction for different acid–base combinations. The experiment could be monitored using a temperature probe interfaced with a computer

Figure 9.3 **An example of a teacher planning sheet for investigative work with criteria for assessment guidance**

	Strand i	Strand ii	Strand iii
4	Predict that heat will be evolved when an acid reacts with a base. Also that different amounts of heat will be evolved depending on the nature of the acid and base (strong or weak) or the amounts of acid and base	Carry out a fair test comparing, for example, heat evolved in reacting HCl (aq, 1 mol dm^{-3}) + NaOH (aq, 1 mol dm^{-3}) with CH_3COOH (aq, 1 mol dm^{-3}) + NaOH (aq, 1 mol dm^{-3})	Links results with original prediction (e.g. strong acids release more heat energy than weak acids when they react with bases)
5	Suggest that the amount of heat liberated is proportional to the (molar) amount of ions in the solution	Choose a range of concentrations or volumes of acids and bases to give a reasonable set of results	Criticises own results. An awareness of the fact that the results can only be fairly compared in terms of heat evolved and not just increase in temperature. Is able to discuss heat loss from the calorimeter (plastic cup), etc.
6	As above plus a prediction that equimolar amounts of strong acid and strong base will release the maximum heat of any strong acid–base mixture	Carry out the investigation with different combinations of acid and base in a controlled manner. Do everything possible to prevent heat loss during the experiment and make accurate measurements	As above plus plotting of graphs of heat liberated for various acid–base mixtures. Explanation of results in terms of the breaking and forming of bonds
7	As above plus a prediction that a weak acid will react with a strong base releasing a different amount of heat	As above but also investigate weak acid – strong base reactions	As above plus comment on the difference between strong acid–base mixtures and weak acid–base mixtures. Comment on the consistency of the results
8	Strong acids and strong bases are completely ionised in water. Therefore the same quantity of heat is evolved when equimolar amounts of any strong acid and strong base are reacted together. A weak acid has to ionise first before it reacts with the base	As above but with further refinements such as an appreciation of the errors involved in making the measurements or monitoring the experiment using a temperature probe and interface to a computer	Shows a thorough understanding of the principles involved in calculating the enthalpy of reaction. Is able to discuss the assumptions used and the errors in making the measurements

Figure 9.3 continued **Performance required for attainment in each Sc1 strand. Levels are given in the left-hand column**

Things to do

Review the methods you use to assess pupils' practical work in both
pre-16 and post-16 courses. Consider:

- What do you do to ensure that the same standard of marking is applied
  over the period of assessment?
- Is the feedback that you give to pupils sufficient for them to see clearly
  where they have gone wrong?
- What do you do to ensure that pupils improve their practical and
  investigative techniques?

9.3 ASSESSMENT AND THE NATIONAL CURRICULUM

This short section cannot hope to completely cover all the intricacies
of NC assessment in science and will, therefore, restrict itself to the
broad principles. It is likely that the detail will change from year to
year and it is important that you keep up to date by referring to the
most recent publications from SEAC.

Assessment at KS3

Teachers are required to assess pupils in all four science ATs. In
addition to the guidance material for the assessment of Sc1 previously
mentioned, SEAC have published similar exemplars for Sc2–4.[17] At
the end of the KS (at the end of May for year 9 pupils) teachers must
be able to state what level each pupil is performing at in each of the
ATs. This type of assessment will be carried out over the three-year
period of the KS and gradually the teacher will be able to build up a
picture of a pupil's achievements within every strand of each AT. It is
important that teachers retain some evidence to support the levels
ascribed to pupils.[18] This evidence may be written work carried out by
the pupil, test papers or notes that you have made of discussions with
the pupil. You should keep a record of why you have selected these
items of evidence, such as, 'This is the type of work produced by a
pupil working at Sc2/5'. This evidence can be used to support your
arguments for assigning a level to a pupil when you have to report to
other individuals such as parents, governors and the audit agency. In
addition it is useful to have such information when carrying out
internal standardisation of ascribing levels within the science
department. No statutory use is made of the teacher assessment unless
the pupil is absent from the statutory tests with good reason. In that
case the teacher assessment will be substituted for the test level. If,
however, a pupil is ill *during* the tests then the teacher assessment
cannot be used to replace the test level.[19]

In June, statutory tests (previously called Standard Assessment Tests, SATs) covering Sc2–4 are set by external agencies (examination boards). Teachers guide pupils to sit papers in one of four different bands; papers covering levels 1–4, 3–6, 5–8 and 7–10. In each of the four bands there are three papers. Not all strands of the ATs are tested and pupils do not know in advance which ones will be used. They only know that at least half the strands will be covered. All pupils throughout the country sit the tests at the same time. Teachers are provided with a mark scheme from the external agency and are given a set time in which to complete their marking. A sample of the test papers are moderated by a process known as the 'Quality Audit', which is managed by the examination boards. The intentions of the audit are to:

- provide a check on the quality of teachers' judgements about pupils' attainment levels
- ensure that these judgements are consistent both within the school and in relation to other schools
- help schools reflect upon, and, if necessary, revise their assessment procedures
- give parents and the public at large confidence in the school's assessment arrangements

Assessment of Sc1 is by teacher assessment only. The teacher will examine the levels reached by each pupil in each of the three strands of Sc1 and will look for the highest level that has been consistently attained. It is inappropriate to take the average of the levels in the three strands and therefore SEAC have suggested that teachers use their professional judgement to decide upon an overall level for Sc1.[20] Schools also need to submit a sample of Sc1 work to the Quality Audit agency. This will consist of a number of individual pieces of work from pupils in different teaching groups across year 9. The whole package will be composed of a minimum of twelve pieces of work, to include two pieces of work from each year 9 teaching group. In order to assign an overall level for science, the levels from the four attainment targets are averaged.

Assessment at KS4

Assessment at KS4 is by means of the GCSE examination with Sc1 being assessed by teachers. Practical investigative work need not be the only item of course work assessment. Examination boards can allow teachers to introduce other course work up to a maximum of 30%. Every science course must have a terminal examination and in the case of non-modular courses this will account for at least 70% of the final mark. Modular courses must have a terminal examination, which must be at least 50% of the final mark, with the other percentage being made up from the mark for Sc1 and end-of-module tests taken throughout the course, and contributing no more than 25% to the final mark. There are three possible routes which all satisfy NC requirements: single science, double science and the separate sciences. There are many syllabuses and types of courses from which to choose (see Table 1.1). In addition to the changes in the examination syllabuses there have been a number of changes in the grading system. Table 9.3 compares the old GCE, CSE and GCSE grades with the new NC levels. Level 10 requires a very high level of performance and is pitched above the old GCSE grade A. The first cohort to take the National Curriculum GCSE science examination in 1994 will be graded on the old A–G scale, however, there will be a starred A grade for those pupils who achieve at a level more demanding than the current grade A. The GCSE will only provide certification for pupils who achieve level 4 or above. The boards are investigating alternative certification for those pupils whose achievements lie in the levels 1–3, which will probably involve larger amounts of coursework assessment.

Table 9.3   **The relationship between previous methods of allocating awards at 16 and the National Curriculum levels**

CSE grades (up to 1987)		1		2	3	4	5	
GCE O-level grades (up to 1987)	A	B	C	D	E			
GCSE grades up to and including 1994	A	B	C	D	E	F	G	U
Levels from 1995 onwards	10,9	8		7,6		5	4	3,2,1

NOTES AND REFERENCES

In order to reduce confusion with the many SEAC KS3 documents, which all look very similar, their reference numbers have been given in addition to the normal information.

1. See the chapter on 'Equal opportunities and bias in assessment', in Gipps, C., 1991, *Assessment: A Teachers' Guide to the Issues*, Hodder & Stoughton, London.

2. Bloom, B.S. (ed.), 1956, *Taxonomy of Educational Objectives: Cognitive Domain*, McKay, New York.

3. Guidance on pupil involvement in assessment can be found in references 9 and 22 and the following publication: Schools Examinations and Assessment Council, 1991, *KS3 Teacher Assessment at Key Stage 3: An In-service Resource*, SEAC, London (Ref: A/002/B/91).

4. Dobson, K., 1987, *Co-ordinated Science, The Suffolk Development*, Collins, London.

5. Parkinson, J., 1991, *Advanced Level Practical Work in Chemistry, A Students' Guide*, Blackwell, Oxford.

6. Rowntree, D., 1987, *Assessing Students: How Shall We Know Them?*, Kogan Page, London.

7. Schools Examinations and Assessment Council, 1993, *School Assessment Folder: Assessing SC1*, SEAC, London (Ref: A/057/B/92).

8. Banks of questions suitable for assessing the science National Curriculum are available from Stanley Thornes Publishers. There are three groups of questions: easy (levels 1–4), medium (levels 4–7) and hard (levels 7–10).

9. For example, see: Schools Examinations and Assessment Council, 1991, *Teacher Assessment in Practice*, SEAC, London (p. 8) (Ref: A/019/B/91).

10. Buckley, J.G., 1970, 'Investigation into assessment of practical abilities in sixth-form chemistry courses', M.Sc. thesis, University of East Anglia.

11. Kempa, R., 1986, *Assessment in Science*, Cambridge University Press, Cambridge.

12. Gott, R., Welford, G. & Foulds, K., 1988, *The Assessment of Practical Work in Science*, Blackwell, Oxford.

13. Bryce, T.G.K., McCall, J., MacGregor, J., Robinson, I.J. & Weston, R.A.J., 1991, *How to Assess Open-ended Practical Investigations in Biology, Chemistry and Physics*, Heinemann, Oxford.

14. The two SEAC publications helping with the assessment of Sc1 are given in references 7 and 22.

15. Examples of syllabus support materials for Sc1 are: Southern Examining Group, 1992, *GCSE National Curriculum Science, Syllabus Support Material, Including Practical Investigations*, SEG, Guildford. Midland Examining Group, *GCSE National Curriculum Co-ordinated Science Teacher Support Material (including assessment of Sc1)*, MEG. University of London Examinations and Assessment Council, 1993, *GASP Teachers' Handbook*, ULEAC, London.

16. Strang, J., Daniels, S. & Bell, J., 1991, *Assessment Matters: No. 6, Planning and Carrying Out Investigations*, SEAC, London (Ref: D/012/B/91).

17. Schools Examinations and Assessment Council, 1992, *Pupils' Work Assessed, Science,* SEAC, London (Ref: A/027/B/92).

18. Schools Examinations and Assessment Council, 1993, *KS3 School Assessment Folder 1993 Audit of Teacher Assessment in En1, En4/5, Ma1, Sc1, Te5 and The Assessment of Statutory Tasks in D & T, Welsh, Welsh Second Language*, SEAC, London (Ref: A/055/B/92).

19. Schools Examinations and Assessment Council, 1993, *KS3 School Assessment Folder, End of Key Stage Assessment Arrangements for English, Mathematics, Science, Technology, Welsh, Welsh Second Language*, SEAC, London (Ref: A/041/B/92).

20. Schools Examinations and Assessment Council, 1993, *KS3 Pupils' Work Assessed: Science (Four pupils' folders)*, SEAC, London (Ref: A/065/B/93).

CHAPTER 10

Beyond the laboratory

Teaching science is a very demanding occupation, requiring you to be competent in many different areas of the subject and to have a multitude of teaching skills. How can a new science teacher possibly find the time to devote to other issues in the school outside teaching in the laboratory? On entering the profession you might initially react by posing the question, 'What's in it for me? I have enough to cope with understanding the National Curriculum'. There are many reasons why science teachers should be involved in all aspects of school life, for example:

- Isolation in the science department can give rise to a very one-sided view of a pupil's school experience.
- You can benefit enormously by talking to other teachers about the teaching methods used in their subject areas.
- You can investigate areas of overlap between subjects and consider ways that you may collaborate.
- Introducing aspects of other subject areas into science can enrich the presentation and promote interest.
- The school is required to ensure that pupils have access to certain themes and skills which go across curriculum boundaries.
- Science GCSE syllabuses encourage science teachers to work with teachers in other disciplines. The extract below is taken from a syllabus for the separate sciences:[1]

The approach used in constructing these syllabuses, particularly the use of common themes and clear assessment criteria, lends itself to the establishment of links with other areas of study.

10.1 WHOLE SCHOOL ISSUES

There are aspects of school life that affect all school teachers, such as attendance of pupils, behaviour, maintaining the general ethos of the school, whole school activities (plays, sport, etc.) and the place of the school within the local community. Becoming involved with these types of activities is all part of being a teacher and doing your share of the teamwork that goes to make the school an effective and enjoyable place to learn. There are many jobs to do and it is no use always thinking that Mr Smith should do it because he gets paid far more than you do. A good school is one where teachers work together to give the pupils an all-round education. Involving yourself in activities such as games, clubs, concerts and displays helps you to get to know pupils in a different light and can help to develop your relationship with them.

A very important part of your job as a teacher is to look after a form or tutor group. This should not just involve keeping accurate records of attendance, important though this is, but should comprise sessions concerned with your pupils' welfare and general well being. The school will probably have organised a programme for your tutorial periods based around the Personal and Social Education (PSE) policy for each year. These can be exciting and valuable sessions bringing together different aspects of school life and helping to prepare these young adults for life after school.

The place of science within the whole curriculum

In Chapter 2 mention was made of the overlap between science and other curriculum subjects when looking at the teaching of science in its social, economic and environmental contexts. In addition science has always had strong links with the mathematics and technology departments within a school. Science has now become so broad a subject, touching all aspects of our lives, that there is not one subject on the curriculum that does not have some connection with science. There will be times when you want to introduce a European slant to your lessons and you will find it useful to talk to the modern linguists in the school. You will almost certainly get involved in teaching aspects of science that may run contrary to certain religious beliefs and will find it helpful to consult colleagues from the RE department. Sports science is a topic that can excite even the less well-motivated pupils and linking up with the PE department to carry out activities in measuring heart rate, work done and optimum performance can prove to be a most worthwhile venture.

The links can be either be casual so that they fulfil a need when it arises or they can be built into the schemes of work of the departments concerned. The links can help pupils to make connections between the different disciplines and they can learn from being immersed in the vocabulary of the topic. One approach is for departments to work together to ensure that there is not too much repetition of material and thereby save valuable teaching time. There are very close connections between aspects of the geography NC and the science NC[2] and it would be foolish for these two departments not to work in harmony (see Table 10.1). Another approach is to have a theme for a week or fortnight for a number of departments. This means has been used with great success in primary schools for a number of years but has generally been neglected in the secondary sector because of the problem of co-ordinating the large number of teachers who see any one class. An example of the thematic approach for the topic of weather is given in Figure 10.1.

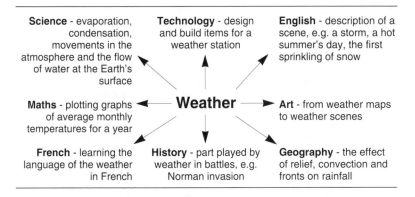

Science - evaporation, condensation, movements in the atmosphere and the flow of water at the Earth's surface

Technology - design and build items for a weather station

English - description of a scene, e.g. a storm, a hot summer's day, the first sprinkling of snow

Maths - plotting graphs of average monthly temperatures for a year

Weather

Art - from weather maps to weather scenes

French - learning the language of the weather in French

History - part played by weather in battles, e.g. Norman invasion

Geography - the effect of relief, convection and fronts on rainfall

Figure 10.1 **Possible interdepartmental links based around the topic of weather for KS3 pupils**

Schools are required to make provision for elements of education that are not restricted by the traditional bounds of curriculum subjects. These are described by the NCC[3] and the CCW[4] as: themes, competencies or skills and dimensions. Introducing these cross-curricular aspects helps to ensure that all pupils receive a broad and balanced education with equal opportunities and equal access to education regardless of sex, social, cultural or linguistic background or physical disadvantage.

The cross-curricular themes are:

- careers education and guidance
- community understanding (Wales) education for citizenship (England)
- economic and industrial understanding
- environmental education
- health education

A full list of the curriculum guides is given in Chapter 2.[5]

The competencies or skills are:

- communication (including literacy and oracy)
- the use of information technology
- numeracy
- problem solving
- studying
- personal and social

Table 10.1   **Links between the science NC and the geography NC for KS3***

Abbreviated extract from the science NC PoS	Abbreviated extract from the geography NC PoS
Weather Sc3 (iv) – know the factors that influence weather, including how different airstreams give different conditions; – be acquainted with meteorological symbols; – appreciate the effects of weather on buildings and on rocks, and examine soil-forming processes	Gg3 strand (iii) – the main components of the hydrological cycle; the difference between weather and climate; – the effects of relief, convection and fronts on rainfall...; – the effects of frost action, chemical and biological weathering and the distinction between weathering and erosion
Environment Sc2 (iii) – study the effects of human activity, including food production and the exploitation of raw materials, on the purity of air and water and on the Earth's surface; – appreciate that beneficial products and services need to be balanced against the harmful effects on the environment	Gg5 – how the extraction of natural resources affects the environments; – the differences between manufactured goods and natural resources; – the differences between renewable and non-renewable resources; – the effects of developments in technology on the exploitation of natural resources and the management of environments
Energy Sc4 (ii) – survey national and global sources of energy; – consider energy from the Sun, nuclear energy, the origin and accumulation of fossil fuels and the use of biomass as a fuel	Gg5 – the effect on the environment of the development of at least two energy sources
Rocks Sc3 (iv) – investigate, by observation, experiment and fieldwork, the properties and formation of igneous, metamorphic and sedimentary rocks, and link these to major features and changes on the Earth's surface; – be aware of the time-scales involved in the operation of geological processes and be able to evaluate earlier ideas about the age of the Earth	Gg3 – the nature and effects of earthquakes and volcanic eruptions, and how the latter produce craters, cones and lava flows; and to investigate the global distribution of earthquakes and volcanoes and how this relates to crustal plates
EIU Sc3 (iii) – study the energy requirements and the social, economic, environmental and health and safety factors associated with the manufacture of materials	Gg2 – how sources of energy have influenced the location and development of manufacturing industry Gg4 – why economic activities develop in particular locations; the advantages and disadvantages of locating similar economic activities in the same places, and to analyse the distribution of farming manufacturing industry and retail industry and the effects of changes in these distributions

*The attainment targets for geography are: Gg1: Geographical skills, Gg2: knowledge and understanding of places, Gg3: physical geography, Gg4: human geography, Gg5: environmental geography.

The dimensions are:

- the fostering of sympathetic awareness and understanding of the *cultural diversity of society*
- provision of *equal opportunities* for all pupils, irrespective of gender, ability or cultural and ethnic background
- catering for the *special needs* of pupils in ways which make the curriculum accessible to all pupils

And, in addition, for schools in Wales:

- demonstration of the cultural relevance of the curriculum to its Welsh setting

The SATIS[6] units from the ASE provide excellent resource materials for teaching the cross-curricular themes through activities such as role play, debates and reading exercises. Since many of these issues are topical, with articles frequently appearing in the press and on the television, pupils should be encouraged to take note of the media coverage and report on it in class. It is a good idea to video programmes that are likely to be of use and to keep a selection of newspaper cuttings that deal with relevant situations. Pupils can be asked to analyse the articles in terms of correct science and bias from the reporter. Wellington[7] describes how such cuttings can be used for a variety of activities including: an initiator for discussion; a starter activity for a new topic; and part of a poster-making activity.

Health education

We often read in the newspapers about people who die from smoking-related diseases, from taking drugs or alcohol, and from heart problems brought on as a result of a poor diet. Yet we still see or hear about large numbers of young people who smoke, drink, take drugs or eat the wrong types of food. The heath education programmes introduced into schools have made a major impact on improving people's attitude towards these issues but there is still a long way to go. Nowadays you will generally find that there is not a single subject in the school that does not consider some aspect of health education at some time in its programme. Indeed there is a danger that there may be considerable overlap and repetition of topics between subjects, if proper co-ordination is not carried out. There should be a teacher in the school who has been given the job of ensuring that there is not undue repetition and that a distinct programme that meets pupils' needs as they grow older is implemented. It would be unfortunate if we were constantly confronted with remarks like, 'Please, Miss, not sex again. We've just done it in RE. Can we do the operational amplifier instead'.

The school will have a policy for sex education that has been approved by the governors and you must ensure that you do not breach its guidelines. The NCC[8] have given direction as to how health education could be taught across the different curriculum subjects and PSE through the four key stages. They have divided the main issues into nine component parts:

- substance use and misuse
- sex education
- safety
- food and nutrition
- personal hygiene
- environmental aspects
- psychological aspects

To a greater or lesser extent all these components can be found in various parts of Sc2 at both KS3 and KS4. Running alongside the knowledge and understanding that pupils need to know to pass their examinations will be the issues that probably concern them most because they are directly related to their everyday experiences. Discussion about the personal side of these concerns can arise quite naturally out of the biology being taught rather than the more artificial, *'We're doing drugs today'* approach.

Before you start teaching them you should be quite clear in your own mind as to what you are trying to do. It may be that, for very good reasons, you have very fixed opinions on some issues and may wish to press your case very hard. While this may prove possible, there is a danger that your over-fervent presentation will have the opposite effect to the one you desired. Shock tactics or trying to frighten pupils into adopting a healthy lifestyle can also prove to be unproductive in terms of developing positive attitudes in the long term. You should not support any practice that is illegal such as under-age drinking, taking drugs and sexual intercourse with a minor. In addition, clause 28 of the Local Government Act 1986 expressly forbids the presenting of homosexual or lesbian partnerships as normal.[9]

Much of this work can prove to be very emotive and spirits can run high with eagerness and ebullience. You need to be prepared for the fact that language may revert from the biologically sound to the terms used in the street. Fortunately there is a wealth of materials available to support the teaching of this topic from such bodies as the Health Education Authority[10] and the Family Planning Association Education Unit.[11] There are written materials and videos available that not only give information but prompt pupils to think and ask questions. Much of the teaching of these topics will be through sensitive delivery of information followed by activities that involve pupils talking about the subject and raising their own concerns. You must take great care to ensure that any discussion does not become personal. Although you would wish to set a good example to the pupils, you are not expected to be a saint. You should stop any conversation that attempts to delve into your private life and you should not try to find out about pupils' private affairs. You should also quickly put the dampers on conversations about other teachers and their smoking, drinking or sexual habits. Some pupils are very keen to gossip and want to know what the latest information is on other teachers but your professional conduct must prevent you from talking about colleagues in front of pupils.

Economic and industrial understanding

Science teachers have always had very strong links with industry with many schools having close ties with local manufacturers and/or multinational organisations. The petrochemical industries, Shell, Esso and BP, all produce useful resource materials for schools as do many other large-scale chemical companies. British Gas, British Telecom and the electricity companies have also led the way in supporting teachers in a variety of ways. There is a plethora of information available, from videos to business games and computer software to help teachers show the relevance of school science to the world of manufacturing industry. In fact, the problem for science teachers may not be in terms of where can I get information, but which information is most useful for my purposes. This is where documents such as *The Good Resource Guide*[12] are invaluable. The Royal Society of Chemistry promotes industrial understanding through its activities, in particular the Society organises short residential Industry Study Tours[13] at locations throughout the country where teachers can spend time on an industrial site learning about the manufacturing process and the structure and organisation of the company. The Chemical Industry Education Centre provides many useful publications for teachers such as *The Essential Chemical Industry* and the *Making Use of Science and Technology (MUST)*[14] series. School links have been established through bodies such as the School Curriculum Industry Partnership (SCIP) and some teachers have spent time in industry through the Teacher Placement Service of Understanding British Industry (UBI).

Economic and industrial understanding (EIU) and environmental education are inextricably linked through the manufacturing processes and the effect that they can have on the environment and, as such, there will be times when the two issues will run side by side in a lesson. The knowledge and understanding, skills and attitudes relating to EIU have been set out in the curriculum guidance materials.[15] Teaching aspects of EIU may involve liaising with people from local industries, perhaps inviting them into the school to talk to the pupils or maybe arranging for the class to visit a manufacturing plant. Pupils could also be asked to write away for information, use *Which?* reports or other data, or even collect their own information by carrying out a small-scale survey. You may find it useful to seek help from the teacher responsible for the business and industrial practices aspects of the technology NC. Examples of the types of exercises that could be carried out with KS3 pupils are given in Table 10.2.

Table 10.2   *Examples of introducing aspects of EIU into science at KS3*

NC reference	Possible areas of study
Sc2 strand (i) – uses of enzymes and microbes in the baking, brewing and dairy industries	Source and cost of the raw materials, the relationship between production cost and retail cost, speed of delivery and shelf life of the product, adding preservatives, consumer survey of a dairy product, e.g. brands of yoghurt
Sc3 strand (iii) – illustrate ways in which chemical reactions lead to the formation of new materials and relate to everyday processes such as corrosion and food oxidation	Industrial corrosion problems, protecting buried pipe work from corrosion, consumer survey of rust-removing products, cost of manufacturing goods from materials that do not corrode, the problems associated with such materials
Sc4 strand (ii) – survey national and global sources of energy	Cost effectiveness of the various types of home insulation, comparison of the methods of producing electricity, a study of different energy sources used in countries throughout the world

You may have heard some teachers say that teaching about the economic aspects is not really important and that you only need to mention it briefly. Others may argue that it is the manufacturing industries of this country that produce the wealth to keep our education system going and who, indirectly, pay teachers' salaries, therefore perhaps they deserve a little more than a passing reference.

Environmental education

Naturally enough young people are very concerned about our environment and are usually well versed in the topics of pollution and recycling before they come to the secondary school. As teachers, we need to build on this enthusiasm for the subject and use it as a gateway to as many aspects of science as we can but, being careful, not to 'do it to death'. Confusion about environmental issues can easily arise, partly due to advertisers using phrases such as 'environmentally friendly' as one of the key selling points of products when the friendliness may be nothing more than a packaging gimmick. Environmental terms have become part of our everyday vocabulary and you will hear people talking about things such as the 'greenhouse effect' and 'the hole in the ozone layer' without really knowing what they mean. Our role as science teachers is to help pupils to have an understanding of environmental issues and to present them with a balanced viewpoint of our environmental problems. Pupils should understand that we all contribute to our environmental problems and we all must recycle products and reduce pollution. These issues need to be discussed against the background of our consumerist society with an understanding that goods have to be manufactured from raw materials to meet the demands made by the public.

Support materials for teaching environmental education as a cross curricular theme has been prepared by the curriculum councils.[16] In planning for the incorporation of environmental education within science, the NCC suggests that teachers should consider three aspects:

- education *about* the environment (i.e. knowledge), e.g. about materials, resources, energy, plants and animals
- education *for* the environment (i.e. values, attitudes, positive action), e.g. solving environmental problems
- education *in* or *through* the environment (i.e. as a resource), e.g. field work

The curriculum guidance provides teachers with four principles on which to base their teaching of environmental education:

- the environment as a common heritage of mankind
- the common duty of maintaining, protecting and improving the quality of the environment
- the need for a prudent and rational utilisation of resources
- the way in which each individual can, by his/her own behaviour, particularly as a consumer, contribute to the protection of the environment

As with EIU there is plenty of information available to help you to plan interesting and exciting lessons on this topic. The Council for Environmental Education[17] provides news sheets, resource sheets, INSET packs and many other items that give suggestions for teaching. Organisations such as Friends of the Earth[18] and the Royal Society for the Protection of Birds[19] have packs of materials that can be used to support your teaching. The topic does give plenty of opportunities for different teaching approaches, such as:

- Practical activities. For example, pupils could investigate the effect of pH on the amount of aluminium ions leached from soil. They could monitor acid rain.[20]

- Role play. For example, The Limestone Enquiry (SATIS unit 602).
- Field work. For example, pupils could investigate a local environment and the impact humans have had on it. They could examine the lichen growth in different environments as a monitor of the level of pollution.
- Pupil surveys. For example, how many families recycle bottles, newspapers, plastics, etc.?
- Manipulating data. For example, how long will our natural resources last?
- Class discussion. Should we reduce our consumption of resources such as oil so that future generations will be able to use it? Are we exploiting the resources of the less-developed nations?

Table 10.3 shows further examples of teaching ideas that come directly from the PoS for KS3.

Environmental issues are a mixture of complex and, sometimes, controversies involving social, cultural, political, economic and other factors. They need to be handled sensitively by teachers, bearing in mind the pupils' level of maturity. There is a danger that teachers with very strong opinions will tend to promote their own convictions rather than allow pupils to make up their own minds by examining the issues from all points of view.

Table 10.3 **Examples of environmental topics in science at KS3**

NC reference	Possible areas of study
Sc2 strand iv – classification of waste products of human activities as biodegradable or non-biodegradable, and investigate ways of improving the local environment	Categorise items into biodegradable and non-biodegradable. Carrying out an environmental audit of various parts of the school.* How long do things need to degrade? What causes them to degrade?
Sc3 strand ii – introduced to radioactivity and radioactive substances	Is the background radiation different in different parts of the school? What are the problems of using radioactive materials in different industries and medicine? (Are they all bad or are some worse than others?)
Sc4 strand iv – effects of loud sounds on the ear and the control of noise and sound levels in the environment	Do ear defenders cut out all sound or only certain frequencies? (A possible investigation involves looking at such things as ear plugs, cotton wool and commercial ear defenders). What is an acceptable level of loudness? (A pupil survey)

*See Box 7 A, page 27 of the CCW Curriculum Guidance[15] for an example of a school environmental audit.

Things to do

Working with other colleagues from the science department, if possible, consider what you might do in the following situations:

1. You have asked pupils to come to school prepared to go on a field trip by bringing clothes suitable for wet conditions. One girl refuses to bring wellingtons (they are not fashionable) and as a result gets very wet. Her mother complains saying that it is up to the school to provide all the necessary equipment.

2. You have just completed a series of lessons looking at the pollution of land, water and air. A father complains that his son has become very depressed, believing that the world is heading for disaster. He will no longer eat meat and only eats vegetables that have been grown organically.

Links with the mathematics and technology departments

Science and mathematics have always had close interdepartmental links through the mathematics skills required by pupils studying science and the science examples used in mathematics problems. Data handling is an essential part of both subjects with pupils being taught how to represent data graphically and how to use computers to manipulate data sets. Measurement is another area of shared interest with quantities such as distance, volume, time and weight being taught in both subjects. The introduction of the NC brought with it new areas of overlap associated with helping pupils to develop the skills of planning and carrying out a task on their own. In mathematics this work is part of Ma1: Using and Applying Mathematics, which states that:

Pupils should choose and make use of knowledge, skills and understanding outlined in the programme of study in practical tasks, in real life problems and within mathematics itself. Pupils would be expected to use with confidence the appropriate mathematical content specified in the programmes of study relating to the other attainment targets.

The three strands of Ma1 are:

1. Application/strategy: choosing the mathematics and approach to problem solving, posing questions, reviewing progress.
2. Mathematical communication: discussing, interpreting, recording and presenting findings.
3. Reasoning, logic and proof: deducing conclusions, making and testing generalisations, defining, hypothesising, justifying and proving.

Scientific and mathematical investigations have many similarities: making and testing predictions; formulating hypotheses; detailed planning; selecting materials and methods; systematic recording and interpreting results. Mathematics and science teachers would find it beneficial to work together in helping pupils to develop the skills that are common to both Sc1 and Ma1 activities. Practical investigations, similar to those carried out in science, are currently being used in mathematics lessons. Tanner and Jones[21] have developed a series of practical activities for mathematics lessons, many of which are closely linked to work in science.

Technology also has traditional areas of common interest such as matching the properties of materials to their use in constructing artefacts, using measuring instruments and nutrition. In NC technology[22] pupils are involved in designing and making articles to fit a particular use. The general requirements are:

Pupils should be able to design and make products safely by applying knowledge and skills from the programmes of study for technology and where appropriate from other subjects, particularly art, mathematics and science.

The design and technology experience has much in common with the way of carrying out investigations. In technology, pupils have the opportunity to be inventive and develop new ideas or modify existing ones. They will have to make decisions about what plan to carry out and will evaluate what they make and draw conclusions from their experience. Pupils will be working with a variety of materials and equipment that are common to science and technology and activities in one subject area could very well lead to related work in the other area. For example, KS3 pupils will carry out work in science on logic gates together with input and output devices and in technology they may design and make a control device that would warn of potential hazards in the home. While there are considerable overlaps in these two subjects, it is important to appreciate that there are differences. Whereas the goal of science is enquiry and the acquisition of new knowledge and understanding, in technology the aim is often the successful production of an artefact or system that will have practical effects on people and/or control some aspect of their environment.

10.2 COMMUNICATING WITH PARENTS

The topic of parental involvement in education continues to be an issue of national and local interest, with league tables of examination results being published and parents having the right to choose which school will be the best for their child. Whether we like it or not, schools are in the business of marketing themselves and developing the corporate image of the school. Parents are not just customers, some play a very active role in the running of the school or by helping to raise much needed funds. Developing home–school relationships is a large and complex job requiring not just action on a local basis but also support from the education service as a whole. It is an area of education that is receiving a great deal of attention at present and there are many school-based initiatives[23] examining ways to improve their links with the home but it will inevitably be the teacher who will form the focal point of communication between the parent and the school. It will always be the class teacher who knows the pupil best and is able to comment on the pupil's capabilities, attitude towards work, behaviour and interest in the subject. It would be wrong, however, for you to directly initiate communications with the parents of any pupil in your care as you could quickly find yourself in a difficult situation that may have undesired consequences. You should first consult with the person in the school who is responsible for this aspect of school life or, if there is no one who is clearly identifiable then you should see the headteacher.

Your pupils spend far more time at home than at school and, arguably, it could be said that parents have a greater influence on their child's education than schools. As teachers we would like parents to support our work both in terms of gaining new knowledge and of developing positive attitudes towards learning. Parents can, and should, be partners in the teaching and learning process, strengthening your position in school. There are various ways that you might consider on how you can best involve parents, for example:

- Make sure that there is an attractive and informative section on science in the school brochure.

Ask pupils to make contributions and get them to proof-read it to ensure that you have avoided educational jargon.

- Ask pupils to write a letter to their parents, summarising what they have been doing in science recently.

- Ask pupils to prepare a termly newsletter on their science activities.

You could add an editorial indicating how parents might help with the next topic, e.g. keeping food labels for a lesson on different food types, helping with a survey of the power requirements for different electrical appliances in the home, allowing pupils to test various household liquids with indicator paper. Not only will it give the parents a sense of feeling more involved but it will also ensure that they have time to get organised and not have to rush round at the last minute getting things together for their daughter or son.

- Use homework diaries or checklists.

Ask parents to check that homework has been done by countersigning the entry in the homework diary or the list in the back of the pupil's exercise book. You could also ask parents to comment on homework under headings such as frequency, nature of tasks, pupil's ability to do it, time spent on task.

- Make a presentation at parents' or open evenings about the nature of the course you are teaching.
- Make the most out of parents' evenings.

Parents' evenings

You will meet parents at various functions throughout the year, such as open evenings, sports days, social events and, of course, parents' evenings. It is at parents' evenings where you are given the almost impossible task of summarising the progress of the pupil, making suggestions as to where s/he can improve and listening and reacting to remarks from the parents. This might be possible if you had several hours to spend on each individual, but usually you have only a few minutes to complete the process because of the large numbers of parents you have to meet. In order to get the maximum benefit out of parents' evenings it is worth while spending some time planning things out. The following list gives some suggestions for maximising the efficiency of parents' evenings.

- Know what you are going to say about each pupil whose parents are coming to see you. Write down brief notes on the pupils under specific headings, e.g. attitude to work, ability to recall information, social skills, behaviour. Always have something positive to say about the pupil but highlight areas of weakness and make suggestions as to how s/he can improve. Put forward some suggestions as to how the parents might help the pupil, e.g. making sure the pupil has somewhere quiet to work at home, advice about the town library. Within reason, offer help to the pupil so that s/he can make maximum progress. (Be careful that you do not commit yourself to long hours of unpaid tuition after school. Remember what you do for one you should be able to do for all.)
- Organise a display of pupils' work around the laboratory or class-room. This helps to give parents some idea of the kind of work you are doing with the class. They will be looking for things like: level of difficulty; how interesting is the work; how relevant is it.
- Have examples of pupils' work available. Parents can browse through their son's or daughter's science book while they are waiting to see you. They can read your comments and get a feeling for the standard of work their child is achieving.
- Have a copy of the SoW and/or workbooks available. Parents can then see what has been done and what needs to be done. You might use this to show parents why pupils need to work hard to get through the large volume of work still to do.
- Make a few notes during or immediately after each consultation. These will be things that you want to follow up on afterwards. It also shows the parents that you take their comments seriously and intend to act upon them.

- Involve the pupils in the consultation process as much as possible. There should be no reason why the conversations between the teacher and the parents should be kept secret. You need to avoid the 'I'm going to tell your Mum about you' scenario.

Things to do

Find out about the home–school links in your school. Who is responsible for liaising with parents? What methods of communication are used? How can you use the established system?

Consider ways in which you might improve your communications with parents and how you can increase their involvement in helping their child to learn. Start by considering the following suggestions made by Bastiani[24] for improving your performance at parents' evenings:

- tape record yourself at the next parents' evening and examine what takes place
- analyse your next consultation evening, perhaps by asking parents to complete a questionnaire about the sort of information they want to know
- ask a colleague to watch your approach and comment on it
- visit other schools' parents' evenings by appointment.

There is much to be gained from the development of home–school relations not just in terms of the immediate people involved but also the benefits that such a system can bring to the community at large.

10.3 CREATING LINKS WITH LOCAL PRIMARY SCHOOLS

You will always find teachers who say, 'Oh yes, primary–secondary liaison, that's not my problem The deputy head always sorts that out'. Teachers in both sectors of education are extremely busy people and it is all too easy to dismiss the links and get on with trying to solve 'our own' problems. Some secondary science teachers have been guilty in the past of completely ignoring the work carried out in the primary schools and have built their secondary curriculum on the basis that the pupils are empty vessels when they enter the science laboratory for the first time. The introduction of NC science into schools has led to a clearer picture of the work that children do in primary and secondary schools. But, it is only a rough guide to what actually takes place in classrooms and does not reduce the need for liaison. So, why is it important that you get involved in primary–secondary liaison and not leave it all up to the deputy head? One very good reason for being involved is that you cannot expect the deputy head, no matter how good the person is, to give you a clear picture of what is going on in science in each of your partner primary schools.

The problem

Pupils face a whole range of changes as they move from one school to another. For example, in year 6 they will have been the 'top dogs' of the primary school with perhaps special privileges and responsibilities but in year 7 they are the 'new boys and girls' in a strange environment. In addition, pupils have to face getting to know new people, making new friends, and the fear of being left out of the social group and possibly becoming a loner. There are also many changes to do with the way the school day is organised and the lessons delivered. Table 10.5 lists some of the major discontinuities that pupils have to endure. In secondary schools it is generally in the PSE lessons where new pupils are introduced to the secondary environment but all teachers need to contemplate how they are going to introduce them to their new working situation. Judgements will need to be made about how firm are you going to be with the class when you see them for the first time. How are you going to introduce secondary science to them, get them to write out the laboratory rules or get them to do something interesting and exciting? Science teachers need to plan for a curriculum that has continuity over the two phases and allows the pupils to make suitable progress. Secondary science should build on the knowledge and skills that pupils have developed in their primary schools. As teachers, you need to be sensitive to the differences in approach used in the secondary sector (see Table 10.4) and should make an effort to gently introduce new pupils into the secondary system.

Table 10.4   **The major differences in methods of teaching science between primary and secondary schools**

Primary education	Secondary education
Science is mainly taught in the classroom	Science is usually taught in purpose-built laboratories
Science is taught as part of a theme or topic and is linked to other areas of the curriculum	Science is generally taught in isolation from other curricular subjects
The 'science lesson' is not constrained by the school bell ringing every 30 minutes or so	The science has to be 'delivered' in packets corresponding to the length of a school lesson (perhaps 2 x 35 minutes or every 60 minutes)
Science and technology are often inextricably linked	Laboratory work is mostly pure science rather than applied although pupils use simulations to study the industrial aspects of the work

---

Things to do

It is said that pupils are ready for a change of teaching and school environment at the age of 11. Which of the changes given in Table 10.5 do you think will benefit the pupils as they transfer from the primary to the secondary phase?

Table 10.5 **Discontinuities experienced by pupils as they change from primary to secondary education**

Status change	Pupils move from a position of prestige in the primary school to a lowly position in the secondary school
Change of friendship group	Secondary schools have many partner primaries and pupils are generally mixed in their new comprehensive classes. Pupils are then faced with the sometimes difficult task of making new friends and becoming part of a new social community
Loyalty change	Pupils have to change their allegiance and fidelity from one establishment to another
Change in the nature and size of school	Many primary schools are small establishments where all the staff know all the pupils. Secondary schools are often a direct contrast to this. Primary schools are often close to the child's home whereas secondary schools may be some considerable distance away involving the pupil in a long bus journey
Change in the method of curriculum delivery	A thematic approach is often employed in the primary school. In secondary schools the separate subjects are often taught in isolation from one another
Organisational changes	In primary schools one teacher takes one class for most of its lessons whereas in secondary schools pupils experience a large number of teachers in any one day
Pedagogic changes	Primary work is generally delivered through small group work. Whole class teaching is still common in secondary schools
Changes in parental involvement	Parents are frequently involved in day-to-day activities in the primary school. There is little parental involvement of this nature in secondary schools

Methods of achieving effective liaison

Liaison is at its worst when the secondary science teacher tells the primary science co-ordinator, 'This is what the pupils need to know before they come up to us, please make sure that it's done'. Fortunately this is rarely the case as most schools nowadays make a great deal of effort to work together and liaison takes place on a regular basis. The new teacher needs to be actively involved in liaison projects as s/he is likely to have a high percentage of younger children to teach. The more that can be done to get to know the children before they come to the comprehensive school or learn about the teaching styles used in the primary sector the better equipped the teacher will be.

1.   Setting up of discussion groups.

Representative teachers from all the partner primary schools and the secondary school could arrange to meet on a regular basis such as every half-term. The venue for the meeting could change each time and the chair and secretary could also be rotated on a regular basis.

2.   Visits by groups of pupils.

Primary pupils could visit the secondary school to familiarise themselves with the new environment and to experience some teaching. The lesson could be jointly planned and delivered by teachers from both sectors. Secondary pupils could also visit primary schools to talk to pupils about their experience of moving to the 'big school'.

3.   Visits by teachers.

Secondary teachers could spend a period of time, perhaps half a day, teaching in a primary school to experience the type of work carried out. Primary teachers may find it difficult to do the reverse of this if they possess little expertise in science, however, they could be involved in a team-teaching situation in the secondary school.

4.   Workshops for teachers at both schools.

Teachers could get together to produce a curriculum whose emphasis is the progression from KS2 to KS3.

5.   Parental involvement.

It is important that parents become familiar with the 'new' way of working in a secondary school. Many parents feel isolated from the secondary environment whereas they generally find primary schools more welcoming. One way of introducing both parent and child to the new school is to invite both to visit for a short period of time looking at the work of year 7 pupils.

6.   Joint display of science activities.

Year 6 and year 7 pupils could work on a joint topic, perhaps carrying out separate investigations in their own schools. This could lead to joint displays of their work.

7.   Extracurricular clubs open to all pupils.

Science clubs in the secondary school could be open to partner primary schools.

8.   Equipment loan.

Primary schools rarely have a great deal of science equipment but could borrow it from their local secondary school.

9.   Joint INSET sessions.

There are many common problems facing teachers in both sectors and teachers would benefit from joint in-service training work.

Things to do

Although this section has dealt with the continuity of education from primary to secondary it is not to say that other transitions in education are devoid of problems. At the transition to further or higher education we tend to think that students are mature enough to cope with the situation. This is often not the case and many pupils are unable to survive in their new learning environment. Write down the problems you think will confront a pupil as s/he moves from an 11–16 school to a tertiary college. What types of links should be established between schools and tertiary or sixth-form colleges?

10.4 LIFE BEYOND SCHOOL

Teachers are always talking about teaching, from the staff room to the pub they will be found talking shop. It is an absorbing job to work in and, if you are not careful, it can take over your whole life and you may find that those friends you had a few years ago have now found that the local accountant is more exciting to talk to than you. It is perhaps the intense nature of the job that makes teachers this way, they are constantly interacting with other people. One minute they may be explaining something to a class, the next they have to adopt an authoritarian stance to discipline pupils and moments later they may have to talk to parents. It is the sheer variety of the job that makes it so interesting, which I feel sure is not matched by any other profession. People outside teaching cannot possibly understand the different demands that are made on a teacher in any one day. There is no doubt about it, teachers have to have the wisdom of Solomon and the patience of Job as well as being thick skinned and having unlimited amounts of energy. All the pressures that face teachers are bound to lead to some sort of stress. It is something that all teachers suffer from, although you need to bear in mind that it is a symptom of many other professions as well and may well be a feature of living in the late-twentieth century. In addition to personal causes such as ill health, family problems or financial problems there are many school-based factors that can give rise to stress. New teachers have to adapt to new situations and get to know large numbers of people. In addition, they have to cope with the time-consuming task of preparing many lessons from scratch and all the other pressures faced by the science teacher (see Figure 10.2). Stress can manifest itself in many different forms, Dunham[25] has classified four main types of stress reactions:

- *Behavioural*: characterised in behaviour such as heavy smoking and/or drinking, driving too fast and an inability to sit still and relax.
- *Emotional*: characterised in emotions such as a general feeling that the work-load is so heavy that it is impossible to cope.
- *Mental reactions*: the teacher requires constant self-control to establish priorities and carry them out, attempting to please everybody, guilt, becoming 'uptight', lack of confidence.
- *Physical symptoms*: characterised by constant headaches, inability to sleep properly especially on Sunday nights, irritability.

Figure 10.2 **Some of the factors that can lead to stress for science teachers**

People respond to stress in different ways. A common reaction is to go out and get drunk, but this is only a very short-term solution and may have long-term consequences. Kyriacou[26] lists the following ten actions most frequently quoted by teachers for dealing with stress:

- try to keep things in perspective
- try to avoid confrontations
- try to relax after work
- try to take some immediate action on the basis of your present understanding of the situation
- think objectively about the situation and keep your feelings under control
- stand back and rationalise the situation
- try to nip potential sources of stress in the bud
- try to reassure yourself everything is going to work out all right
- don't let the problem go until you have solved it or reconciled it satisfactorily
- make sure that people are aware that you are doing your best

You will find it very helpful if you have someone you can talk to and share your problems with. Colleagues can often help to share your burden, even the process of talking to someone can help to relieve the stress, making you believe that things are not as bad as you first thought. We all have classes that we are not keen to teach or duties that we would prefer to avoid. Rather than worry about these events, plan out what you are going to do and then think beyond the unpleasantness to some enjoyable event. This way you will carry out the tasks with less stress and consequently perform better. You must set aside a period of time every day for relaxation where you forget about work completely. Sport, in particular, helps to reduce stress by releasing stored up aggression and restoring your physical and mental equilibrium.

Things to do

This activity is best carried out with a group of teachers. Write down five factors that have caused you stress in the last week. Discuss them within the group and then ask the chairperson to try to categorise them. There are bound to be some similarities. Why are teachers reluctant to discuss their problems with others when there is so much commonality? If you wish to take this activity further you will find it useful to use the INSET pack prepared by Naylor and McMurdo.[27]

10.4 AND FINALLY

There has been a great deal of change in science education over the last ten years and there is likely to be just as much, if not more, change in the next ten years. As science teachers we need to be constantly updating ourselves both in terms of knowledge of our subject and teaching methods. It is important that teachers constantly review and reflect on their teaching practices and look for ways that they might improve. INSET courses, ASE local and annual meetings and higher degree courses (M.Ed., Ed.D., etc.) all have a place in the further professional development of the science teacher.

You should try to learn about your strengths and weaknesses in teaching by carrying out regular self-appraisal exercises by using an evaluation schedule such as the one shown in Figure 10.3.[28] You will also find it useful to ask another teacher to watch you teach, and evaluate your practice. Once you have identified areas that need attention you can set yourself clear targets to aim for in the future. A good teacher always reflects on his/her current practice and considers how s/he can improve.

Lesson planning and preparation

Plan each lesson thoroughly with clear objectives	
Use a variety of activities, matching them to age, ability and needs	
Arrange for resources to be available at the appropriate time	
Having confident knowledge of syllabus requirements and subject matter	
Consider class management implications of planned lessons	
Take account of evaluation of previous lessons	

Managing pupils' learning

Understand how pupils learn	
Use a variety of teaching strategies and styles	
Use methods suitable for: whole classes, groups, individuals	
Carry out planned activities effectively	
Respond to differences in age and ability	
Modify your approach in response to pupils' difficulties	

Classroom skills

Begin lessons effectively	
Speak clearly and vary the tone, volume and pace of speaking	
Give clear instructions and explanations	
Effectively question individuals and class	
Organise and manage class discussions	
Use the blackboard and ohp neatly and effectively	
Use IT as part of teaching and learning	
Use other visual aids competently	
Communicate enthusiasm for your subject	
Provide pupils with oral and written feedback	
Mark and record pupils' work using the school's procedures	
Adjust your teaching in the light of work assessed	
End lessons appropriately	

Class management and control

Achieve ordered pupil entry and exit from classroom	
Manage the start, transitions and end of lessons	
Achieve acceptable levels of talk, movement ,etc.	
Gain pupils' attention when required	
Awareness of what is going on	
Effectively discipline pupils when necessary	
Effectively praise and encourage pupils as appropriate	
Project a sense of authority and control	

Wider professional role

Establish good working relationship with colleagues in the school	
Take part in pastoral/form tutor roles	
Involve yourself in other school activities, including extra-curricular	
Update teaching skills and knowledge of science education through INSET and/or other courses	

Awareness of cross-curricular and whole school aspects	
Evaluate your own teaching effectiveness	
Update personal knowledge of all aspects of science	
Develop professional habits of punctuality and reliability	

Figure 10.3 **A Personal evaluation sheet**

NOTES AND REFERENCES

1. Welsh Joint Education Committee, 1993, *GCSE Syllabus for 1995 in Science:Biology, Science:Chemistry and Science:Physics*, WJEC, Cardiff.

2. Further examples of interdepartmental links can be found in: Curriculum Council for Wales, 1992, *Non-statutory Guidance for Science in the National Curriculum (1991 Order)*, CCW, Cardiff.

3. National Curriculum Council, 1990, *The Whole Curriculum: Curriculum Guidance No. 3*, HMSO, London.

4. Curriculum Council for Wales, 1991, *The Whole Curriculum: 5–16 in Wales*, CCW, Cardiff.

5. See Chapter 2, reference 6.

6. Science and Technology in Society (SATIS), a series of twelve books plus SATIS update 1991. Each book contains ten units. Published by ASE.

7. Wellington, J., 'Using newspapers in science education', *School Science Review*, 1992, **74** (266), 47–52.

8. National Curriculum Council, 1990, *Curriculum Guidance 5: Health Education*, NCC, York.

9. Harris, N., Pearce, P. & Johnstone, S., 1992, *The Legal Context of Teaching* (in The Effective Teacher Series), Longman, London.

10. Information from: Health Education Authority, Hamilton House, Mabledon Place, London, WC1H 9TX.

11. Family Planning Association Education Unit, 27–35 Mortimer Street, London, W1N 7RJ.

12. *The Good Resource Guide* is available from the Chemical Industry Education Centre, Department of Chemistry, University of York, Heslington, York, YO1 5DD.

13. Details of the RSC Industry Study Tours can be obtained from the Education Department, Royal Society of Chemistry, Burlington House, Piccadilly, London W1V 0BN.

14. See reference 12 for the address where these publications can be obtained from.

15. Curriculum Council for Wales, 1990, *Economic and Industrial Understanding: CCW Advisory Paper 7*, CCW, Cardiff. National Curriculum Council, 1990, *Education for Economic and Industrial Understanding*, NCC, York.

16. National Curriculum Council, 1990, *Environmental Education*, NCC, York. Curriculum Council for Wales, 1992, *Environmental Education*, CCW, Cardiff.

17. Information can be obtained from: Council for Environmental Education, University of Reading, London Road, Reading, RG1 5AQ.

18. Information can be obtained from: Friends of the Earth, 26–28 Underwood Street, London, N1 7JQ.

19. Information can be obtained from: RSPB, The Lodge, Sandy, Bedfordshire, ST19 2DL.

20. Dillon, J., Watson, R. & Tosunoglu, C., 1993, *Chemistry and the Environment*, Royal Society of Chemistry, London.

21. Tanner, H. & Jones, S., 1993, *Hands on Maths*, University College of Swansea, Swansea.

22. Department for Education and The Welsh Office, 1992, *Technology for Ages 5 to 16 (1992)* (Proposals of the Secretary of State for Education and the Secretary of State for Wales), HMSO, London.

23. See the *Directory of Home–School Initiatives in the UK*, available from RSA, 8 John Adams Street, London, WC2N 6EZ.

24. Bastiani, J., 1989, *Working with Parents: A Whole School Approach*, NFER, Nelson.

25. Dunham, J., 1992, *Stress in Teaching* (2nd edition), Routledge, London.

26. Kyriacou, C., 1992, *Effective Teaching in Schools*, Simon & Schuster, Hemel Hempstead.

27. Naylor, S. & McMurdo, A., 1990, *Supporting Science in Schools: Ideas, Activities and Resources for Professional Development*, Breakthrough Educational Publications, Manchester.

28. Adapted from self-evaluation forms used by the University of Oxford and University College of Swansea Education Departments.

GLOSSARY OF TERMS AND ACRONYMS

Affective objectives objectives that are concerned with attitudes and feelings.

Aggregation combining a learner's assessed scores, obtained over a variety of tasks, to give a single score for recording and reporting purposes.

Aims are general statements of educational intent.

APU The Assessment of Performance Unit has monitored pupils' progress in a number of curriculum subjects, including science. They have prepared substantial reports on pupils' performance in science at 11, 13 and 15. Summary booklets are available from APU.

Attainment targets (ATs) represent the knowledge, skills and understanding that pupils of different abilities and maturities are expected to have by the end of each key stage.

BTEC Business and Technician Education Council.

CLIS(P) Children's Learning in Science Project.

Cognitive objectives objectives concerned with thinking and intellectual processes.

Concept is a general notion or idea.

COSHH Regulations Control of Substances Hazardous to Health Regulations. The principal requirement of these regulations is that an assessment should be made of the use at work of substances that are hazardous to health, and that steps should be taken to prevent or, where this is not reasonably practicable, adequately to control exposure to these substances.

CPVE Certificate of Pre-vocational Education.

Criterion-referencing a system where pupils' achievements are judged in relation to objectives irrespective of other pupils' performances.

DART(S) Directed Activities Related to Texts.

DATA Design and technology association (a subject teachers' organisation equivalent to the ASE for science teachers).

DES Department of Education and Science (the government department that looks after matters relating to education. The Secretary of State for Education is the head of the department).

Diagnostic assessment type of assessment aimed at identifying particular learning difficulties or strengths in order that appropriate action can be taken.

DFE Department for Education (replaced the DES in 1992).

EATE Economic Awareness in Teacher Education.

EMU Evaluation and Monitoring Unit, a section within SEAC responsible for monitoring and evaluating the National Curriculum Assessment arrangements and reviewing the effectiveness of all aspects of examinations and assessment.

ERA Education Reform Act (1988).

Explorations see investigations.

FEU Further Education Curriculum Review and Development Unit.

Formative assessment assessment that provides information on individual achievement so as to inform and guide the next stage in the teaching and learning process.

Hypothesis an idea used to explain certain facts.

INSET in-service training.

Investigations alternatively called explorations. A type of practical work involving pupils in observing, thinking about and raising questions about objects, events and situations. A **closed** investigation is one where there is only one way of approaching the task. An **open** investigation is one where there are either multiple solutions or there is one solution but many ways of approaching the task.

LEA Local Education Authority.

Moderation the process of achieving comparability of different teachers' judgements through training, agreement trials, classroom support and cross-checking.

NCC National Curriculum Council.

Norm-referencing a system in which pupils are placed in rank order. It implies that levels are assigned by comparison to other pupils' performances, rather than any absolute quality of the performance.

NVQ National Vocational Qualifications.

Objective questions questions that are constructed so that the score of a respondent to the test or question is independent of the marker. Such objectivity is attained most easily by providing a small number of fixed responses to each question, of which only one (the key), is correct, the remaining incorrect responses being known as distracters. Examples of objective questions are: multiple choice; multiple completion; matching pairs (classification); assertion–reason; true–false; completion items.

Objectives are specific goals of educational intent.

OFSTED Office for Standards in Education (the office that oversees school inspections).

Programme of study the programmes of study (PoS) outline, in general terms, the content, skills and processes that are to be taught to pupils of different abilities and maturities during each key stage.

Psychomotor objectives refer to objectives concerned with skills, e.g. the ability to use a measuring cylinder correctly.

SATIS Science and Technology in Society.

SATRO Science and Technology Regional Organisation.

SCAA Schools Curriculum and Assessment Authority (this one body replaced NCC and SEAC in 1992).

SCIP School Curriculum Industry Partnership.

SEAC Schools Examinations and Assessment Council

SSCR The Secondary Science Curriculum Review. This project was active from 1981 to August 1989. Its main aim was to encourage schools to provide a broad-based science curriculum for all youngsters to the age of 16.

Summative assessment assessment that provides a summary of the achievements of pupils.

TAPS Techniques for the Assessment of Practical Skills.

TGAT The National Curriculum Task Group on Assessment and Testing. Its main report was published in January 1988, and three supplementary reports in April 1988.

TVEI Technical and Vocational Education Initiative

Variables

A **categoric variable** is a non-numerical quality; e.g. shape, texture, pattern, colour.

Confounded variables occur when two or more variables are changed together so the effect of neither can be judged separately.

A **continuous variable** can have any numeric value; e.g. volume, mass, temperature.

A **control variable** is the factor that the investigator must hold constant, otherwise the results of an investigation would not be valid.

A **dependent variable** is one that is measured or judged in an investigation; e.g. the volume of gas liberated in a fixed time, the distance a trolly moves before it stops.

A **derived variable** is one that must be calculated from more than one measurement; e.g. heat, speed, density.

A **discrete variable** is a quantity that can only have certain integer values; e.g. the number of layers of insulation on a pipe.

An **independent variable** is one that the investigator chooses to change systematically; e.g. the volume of hydrochloric acid (2 mol dm^{-3}) added to each sample of solid, the texture of the runway for the trolly.

Index